Advance Acclaim for *The Merciful Scar*

"We shouldn't be too surprised to discover that a singer-songwriter as gifted and sensitive as Rebecca St. James has produced an amazingly moving novel—one that young women will find both relevant and deeply satisfying. Beautifully crafted with co-author Nancy Rue, *The Merciful Scar* will not only touch your heart, it might just help heal it."

—KARI JOBE, DOVE AWARD-WINNING
ARTIST AND SPEAKER ON THE REVOLVE TOUR

"My brother Joel and I speak after shows to teens and young adults across the country. Because of this, we know that the message of this book is relevant and timely! The mix of humor, insight, and drama in *The Merciful Scar* helps to powerfully convey needed truth. Congrats to our sister Rebecca and Nancy on a great book!"

—LUKE SMALLBONE, FOR
KING AND COUNTRY

"*The Merciful Scar* is a tender, beautiful, and insightful book about a difficult subject. Nancy Rue and Rebecca St. James have crafted a heart-touching story that feels more real than imaginary. While reading, you might need to remind yourself that these characters are fiction. The plot-lines, twists, turns, and heart-wrenching situations will wrap around your heart in such a way that you can't help but be affected."

—LORI TWICHELL,
FICTION ADDICT

The Merciful Scar

Also by Rebecca St. James

What Is He Thinking??
Pure
Wait for Me
Sister Freaks
She
Loved
40 Days with God

Also by Nancy Rue

The Reluctant Prophet series
The Reluctant Prophet
Unexpected Dismounts
Too Far to Say Enough

The Sullivan Crisp series
Healing Stones
Healing Waters
Healing Sands

Tristan's Gap
Antonia's Choice
Pascal's Wager

The Merciful Scar

A NOVEL

REBECCA ST. JAMES AND NANCY RUE

THOMAS NELSON
Since 1798

NASHVILLE DALLAS MEXICO CITY RIO DE JANEIRO

Published in Nashville, Tennessee, by Thomas Nelson. Thomas Nelson is a registered trademark of Thomas Nelson, Inc.

Authors are represented by the literary agency of Alive Communications, Inc., 7680 Goddard Street, Suite 200, Colorado Springs, CO 80920, www.alivecommunications.com.

Thomas Nelson, Inc., titles may be purchased in bulk for educational, business, fund-raising, or sales promotional use. For information, please e-mail SpecialMarkets@ThomasNelson.com.

Library of Congress Cataloging-in-Publication Data

Rue, Nancy N.
  The merciful scar : a novel / Nancy Rue and Rebecca St. James.
     pages cm
  ISBN 978-1-4016-8922-3 (trade paper)
  I. Title.
  PS3568.U3595M47 2013
  813'.54--dc23

                          2013010269

Printed in the United States of America
13 14 15 16 17 18 RRD 6 5 4 3 2 1

For the brave women who shared their stories so that others may find their voices . . . and God's.

For he is our God,
and we are the people of his pasture,
and the sheep of his hand.

O that today you would listen to his voice!

PSALM 95:7

A Note from Rebecca and Nancy

Hi to our readers! We wanted to share with you about a unique ministry tool that this book provides. At the end of every chapter is a quote that we've selected as a potential ministry tool for you. We know how crazy busy all of our lives are and that it's hard to think of social media content that can provide God-honoring encouragement for our family/friends. So we have included these quotes for those of you who might want to use them as "ministry content" in your twitter/Facebook feed. Though the Internet can be used negatively, as believers we can be a light shining in the darkness, online and everywhere!

Shine on, friends . . .
Rebecca and Nancy

Part
ONE

He . . . went a day's journey into the wilderness, and came and sat down under a solitary broom tree. He asked that he might die.

1 KINGS 19:4

Chapter ONE

It was the only real fight Wes and I had ever had. Actually it was the only fight I'd ever had with anyone. That's probably why I wasn't very good at it.

Now *discussions* . . . we'd had those, and that's how it started out that night. Another conversation about Wes moving in with me.

I should have known that was where we were headed when he tugged at the back of my shirt and pulled me against his lean self and said, "You know what I love about your couch?"

"That you never have to get off of it from the minute you walk in the door?" I said.

He let his blue eyes droop at the corners until they teased at his cheekbones. That was Wes pretending to be hurt. "Are you saying I'm a couch potato?"

"I'm saying I wait on you like you're the couch prince." I leaned forward and picked up the all-but-licked-clean plate from my IKEA coffee table. "More quesadillas, your highness?"

Wes scooped me into him, plate and all. "It wouldn't be that way if I wasn't a guest, Kirsty."

Yeah, there it was. Again.

"First of all," I said, "you know I hate it when you call me that. It makes me feel like I'm on a Jenny Craig commercial."

"Huh?"

"Kirstie Alley. She was their poster girl before Valerie Bertinelli—"

"You're getting off topic."

"What topic?"

Wes scooted himself sideways so he could face me without letting go. He knew as well as I did that I was about to wriggle away and go do . . . something. Anything to not have this discussion for the ninety-sixth time.

"Come on, babe, you know what I'm talking about. It doesn't make any sense for me to get an apartment for the summer when you've got room here."

"I have one bedroom." Which, may I just add, was incredibly difficult to say with his long-fingered hands holding my face and his nose headed for mine for that irresistible pre-kiss thing he did. "And I need my other room for my studio—"

"I know."

"And you also know where I am on this."

"I do. You've been there for three years, six months, two weeks, four days, and . . ." He glanced at his watch. "Twenty-seven minutes."

He let his lips bounce off my nose and onto my mouth but I talked right through the kiss.

"It's going to be another however long," I said, "so get over it."

This was the part where he was supposed to say, *You're killin' me, Kirsten. Killin' me.* And then I would let him kiss me one time and then I'd get up and make another batch of quesadillas. That was how this déjà vu conversation was supposed to go.

But Wes stiffened all six foot two of himself and took me by both shoulders and set me away from him like he was stacking a folding chair. I watched him step over the coffee table and shove his hands into the pockets of his cargo shorts and pace to the back window where he stopped, rod-necked and tight-lipped, his blondness standing stiff on his head. It wasn't a pose I'd ever seen him take. That's when my skin started to burn.

"What does 'however long' mean, Kirsten?" he said.

Until we're married. That was the answer, stuck in my throat where it had been for three years, six months, two weeks, four days, and twenty-seven minutes. I just closed my eyes and crossed my arms so I could rub both shoulders. The burning kept on.

Wes faced me now, muscles working in his square jaw. "Do you know how hard it is to love you and not be able to . . . love you?"

I attempted a wry look. "Uh, yeah, I do."

"Then what the—" He crossed to the coffee table and sat on it. "Look, I think I've been way more patient than any other guy would be."

"Good thing I don't want any other guy," I said.

"Stop it, okay? Just stop it."

"Stop wh—"

"The cute remarks and the little dance you always do. I want to talk about this. Now."

I pressed myself into the couch. "We've talked about it a thousand times, Wes. We've worn it out."

"So you just want to keep on dating forever?"

I swallowed, hard. "Way back when we first started dating, we both agreed that neither one of us wanted to have sex outside of marriage."

Wes let his mouth soften and took both my hands. "How old were we then, babe? Eighteen? Nineteen? I think we were pretty naïve."

We'd never gotten this far into the discussion. If we had, I might have come up with a retort to get us out of it. Something along the lines of *No, naïve is when you think you can lose ten pounds before Christmas.* But here we were, and my determination that I wasn't going to be the first one to say it seethed under my skin.

"I thought we were being true to the faith that, if you'll recall, *you* introduced me to," I said.

"I'm not buying it," Wes said. "We haven't been to Faith House since you started grad school. What's that, nine months? When was the last time we went to church, either one of us?"

"That doesn't mean I don't still believe—"

"Nuh-uh." Wes let go of my hands and waved his palm like he was erasing my words. "That's not what this is about. You want me to marry you, don't you?"

My throat closed in on itself. At least once a day during those three years and twenty-seven minutes or whatever it was, I had imagined Wes broaching the subject of marriage. The images went from Wes on one knee amid glimmering candlelight to a proposal tucked into a Big Mac. But none of them had included an accusation in those blue eyes or all my anxiety mobilizing under my flesh.

"That's it, isn't it?" he said. "Why didn't you just come out and say it?"

"Because I wanted you to say it first!"

The words sliced their way out of me before I could stop them, and they seemed to want to keep on slicing all on their own.

"I don't want us to be like everybody else—just having sex and living together and then someday deciding we might as well get married. Look at Caleb and Tess. They're like a pair of reclining chairs. I'm not doing that, Wes. I'm not."

He was staring at me as if I was a stranger suddenly intruding on the conversation that had long since stopped *being* a conversation.

"Y'know," he said, "I've been practically begging you for, like, forever to open up with me and tell me what's on your mind."

"I wanted it to be on yours." My words had lost their edge. Others spun in my head. *Clever, Kirsten, very clever. You picked a fine time to, I don't know,* grow a backbone.

Wes sagged onto the couch beside me. "Look, babe, I'm not in a good place for this. I didn't graduate—I have to make up the class this summer—I don't know what I'm gonna do after that."

"I know all that—"

"But you—you're set. You always are. That's why you're my rock. I just need you to be here for me just a little while longer. Can you do that?"

What does that even mean? I wanted to scream. But I'd done all the slicing I could do for one night. It was more slicing than I'd done my whole life. At least, that kind.

"Okay, look, I'm gonna go," Wes said.

"Now?"

Nice touch. Pathetic is always good.

"Now." Wes gave me half of his usual who-loves-ya-baby smile. "Before I get you drunk and take advantage of you."

My reply was automatic. "Like either one of *those* things is gonna happen."

Again, that was his cue to say, *You're killin' me, babe.* But what he said was, "Yeah." Just yeah.

He pulled me up from the couch and walked ahead of me to the door. Hand on the knob, he turned only slightly toward me. "A bunch of people from my class are hiking the M tomorrow."

I groaned silently. Hiking the M was a Montana State graduation tradition that entailed making one's way up a steep trail and a long ridgeline in the brutal Montana sun to get to a huge M made from white rocks, and then partying and turning around and coming back in the now even more brutal Montana sun to party some more. I'd skipped that when I graduated the year before; I would actually rather poke a fork in my eye than have that kind of fun. Since Wes had missed graduating by one class, he hadn't gotten to have that kind of fun either.

"I'm sorry," I said.

"No, they want me to go with. What's three credits? To them I'm there. I just didn't have to sit through a bunch of speeches in a bathrobe with a board on my head."

"I don't even know what to do with that," I said. "So what time?"

"We're leaving Caleb and Tess's at seven." Wes lifted a sandy eyebrow. "If I can get them out of their reclining chairs."

Ouch. Bet that gotcha right in the heart.

"You want me to pack a picnic?" I said.

Wes's gaze shifted away and he ran a hand over his flattened blond spikes.

"Or we can grab something at the store in the morning," I said.

"Here's the deal . . . I think I just need to go single. Most of these people I'll never see again, which is weirder for me because I'm staying here. I don't know, it's just a thing."

Right in the heart fell far short. I was stung to the bone. I didn't want to go. I just wanted him to want me to go.

Beyond pathetic. We've moved into pitiful. I mean, way in.

"Okay, so . . . okay," I said.

"I knew you'd get it." Wes kissed my neck. "You always do."

The Nudnik voice didn't wait until Wes was out the door before she started in. I always thought of it as the Nudnik, which was what my kindergarten teacher used to call us kids when we pestered her to the brink. *Nicely done,* the Nudnik said now. *Ya made everything all right when it* clearly *isn't. Another layer of unadulterated bad stuff, right under your skin.*

Forget it. I'm not doing it. I haven't done it for—I don't know—a long time.

Not since Valentine's Day when yet again our sweet Wesley didn't come through with a ring. Or was it Easter? Yeah, you did it on Easter. But then, who's keeping track?

You are! I wanted to say out loud. But I always stopped short of audibly answering the Nudnik. If I did that, I really would have to admit I was crazy.

But she was right. I'd been holding back for six weeks, since the beginning of April. I promised myself that was the last time, because I was so sure Wes would propose when he graduated. And then he didn't. He'd spent last Saturday hiding out here playing Scrabble with me instead of walking with his class to receive his diploma. It wasn't a good time for a proposal. Clearly there never was a good time.

The Nudnik was quiet now, although she couldn't have been heard over the screaming of my skin anyway. It needed my attention more.

I made sure Wes's Mini Cooper, the one I loved to watch him fold his lanky self into, was gone before I slipped into my bedroom and closed the door. Even alone in my tiny cottage, I always ensured my privacy. This was one thing that was all mine.

The instruments were in a polished African mahogany box under my bed, but I didn't take it out yet. I sat on the rug and pulled off my turquoise top that Wes always said made my eyes look like blue topaz. How could someone so certifiably romantic be the cause of so many scars?

But as I ran my fingers over the fine remnants of delicate incisions on the tops of my shoulders, I stared down at the less precise ones on my belly. Those didn't come from man trouble. I could, in fact, name every one of them.

The wobbly ones that traced the lines of my ribs were drawings of freshman year panic, when I suddenly found myself alone here in Bozeman with four years of expectations stretching out before me like an endless road up a mountain.

The staccato dashes below my belly button were the beat of the summer before my sophomore year, when I went back home to Missouri for the last time.

And the long clean cuts on my sides, those were the hopeless trails of the first week of that sophomore year, when I was running out of both hope and places to relieve the pressure where no one could see.

All of those happened before I met Wes. Those and the ones I didn't look at now—the faded but still harsh scars on my thighs. And the one on the inner left that I'd promised the night I made it that I would never look at again. They were as old as the pain itself. Only the ones on the tops of my shoulders belonged to Wes.

Yeah, blame poor Wes, whose crime is wanting to get you in bed. What is wrong with that red-blooded American boy, anyway?

I didn't *blame* Wes. I actually didn't blame anybody except myself. Really, what did I have in my life that was so bad it raced under my skin until I couldn't stand it anymore and I had to give it a place to come out? I didn't know. At moments like this, when my flesh cried out for relief, I didn't have to know. I just needed to make it stop.

I lifted the pleated bed skirt and pulled out the wooden box. Inside, the instruments were lined up on a folded snowy-white pillowcase, still sterile and gleaming from Easter night.

Let the surgery begin. Nurse, scalpel, please.

But it wasn't like that, not really. It was nothing so clinical. This was release, and the longer I lingered over the silver straight razor and the pewter letter opener and the pen with its so-very-fine tip, the more my skin pleaded for help. I selected the calligraphy pen, a graduation gift from Wes that I'd never used for anything but this. I was on my way to the bathroom with it, silently assuring myself that soon it would be all right, when my phone jangled out blues piano.

Wes's ring. Pen still in hand, I ran for the kitchen counter where I'd left my cell and answered with a breathless hello.

"Babe?" he said.

His voice rattled as if something in him had been jarred loose. I pressed my hand to my throat. "Wes, what's wrong?"

"I can't—I don't want to talk about it over the phone."

"Do you want to come over? It's okay—you can come over."

"No, not now. I just want to say—I love you, Kirsten. You know that, right?"

"Yea-ah. Baby, what *is* it?"

"Just say you know it."

"I know it."

My free palm left a sweaty imprint on the granite countertop.

"Okay. Okay, just don't ever stop loving me, you got that?" he said.

"Why would I?"

"Because of the way I acted tonight. I'm sorry, babe, believe me."

He didn't give me a chance to say whether I did or not. My throat was closing anyway. "Here's what I want to do," he said. "Tomorrow I'm going to clear my head, okay?"

"Okay."

"And then I want to come over—maybe have a nice dinner together. I'll help you . . ."

I couldn't even remind him that he didn't so much as know how to operate the microwave. I just kept saying, "Okay."

"And then I want to talk to you. Seriously. I'm ready to talk about the future."

That called for more than an *okay*. "What happened since you left here?"

"It just hit me how much I love you. We have to talk. Tomorrow. I'll be there at six."

"Six," I said.

"Say you love me."

"I love you."

"Thank you, God," he said.

I didn't realize until he hung up that I still had the calligraphy pen in my hand. I opened my palm and let it roll to the counter, where it landed next to the pottery cookie jar that Wes could never stay out of.

Wait, let me get this straight: you're about to implode with your little neurosis and then Mr. Wonderful calls and you're magically healed. In what universe does that happen?

In the universe where you held out for what was right and the man you thought was wonderful really turned out to *be* wonderful. In the universe that had suddenly stopped spinning so fast I couldn't hold on.

I returned the pen to the box and slid the whole collection back under the bed. Tomorrow I'd get rid of all of it.

Before I went to bed, knowing I wasn't going to sleep much anyway, I wanted to tell Isabel. My best friend. All right, let's face it, my only friend, the one girl I trusted not to dis me on Facebook. We'd been close since junior year when Wes and I met her at Faith House after she transferred in from a community college, and we'd become more so since we were both accepted into the M. Architecture program. She was the only person in the world who knew the agony I'd been in over Wes. She called it Wes Angst.

I texted her: *Xpect good news soon!*

Her reply would be instantaneous. She lived with her thumbs on her phone. I had actually seen her move them in a dead sleep like she was texting her dreams.

When I didn't get an answer after two minutes, I texted her again: *R u trapped under something heavy?*

I snickered to myself. The only time Isabel didn't text me back within a nanosecond was when she was with a guy. At twenty-three she was convinced she was going to be, as she described it, "a spinster with seven cats and hemorrhoids" if she didn't snag one soon. I was never sure how the hemorrhoids fit in, but her social life was like a buffet of potential candidates for the husband position. Curly-haired and tiny and pert—my exact opposite in looks—she was adorable enough to have been married multiple times, except that she was beyond picky about the groom.

Obviously she was busy interviewing somebody right now, but I had to tell her. I opened my laptop and got on e-mail. As I typed I could hear her saying, *Why are you telling me what I've been telling you about him all along? Can we please be done with the Wes Angst and get back to my problems?*

Izzy,

I know you're going to find fifteen ways to say I told you so, and I am totally okay with that! I'm not going to go into all the details—much as you're dying to hear them, they are SO none of your business—but tonight Wes said he wants to talk seriously about the future. HE wants to. It's a little bit surreal still. I mean, I've waited for so long—rehearsed every possible scenario in my head. And in yours, actually. Now that it's finally happening, it's like it must be happening to somebody else. Am I completely neurotic? I am, aren't I? I should be in a Woody Allen movie. I think I AM Woody Allen. Okay, I stopped making sense about five sentences ago. That's what happens when you aren't here to talk me out of the crazy tree. So CALL ME as soon as you decide whoever you're with isn't going to make the cut. I'll be up late.

Love you, sister,

Kirsten

I stared at my name for a few seconds before I hit Send. The Kirsten who wrote that e-mail and had lattes with her best friend at Wild Joe's and commiserated with her over the misogynistic travesties that took place at the School of Architecture wasn't the same Kirsten who a half hour before had been about to add another scar to the gallery on her skin. Nor was she the same Kirsten who was constantly poked by an imaginary voice with a taunting tongue. Those Kirstens were real, but the Kirsten I was with Isabel was just as real, like every piece in the pie is real. That Kirsten was the easiest one to be. I hit Send and let that Kirsten declare her good news to her best friend.

———

When I woke up the next morning, there was still no text from Izzy, which could mean things I didn't even want to think about. Sometimes her "interviews" went into the third round.

Besides, I had things to do. Actually laughing out loud at the idea of Wes helping with dinner, I composed a shopping list while I had my coffee and was out of the house on a mission by nine a.m.

My neighborhood was in an old part of Bozeman, cloistered from the rest of the bright naked college town by trees and Victorian two-stories. Most of my fellow students lived closer to campus, out in the Montana openness, but when my father went house-hunting with me just before my undergrad years were over, he insisted on something more "Kirsten." Like he knew who that was somehow. His view of me had cozied me into my quaint two-bedroom bungalow with my nearby landlady's gardens fluffing their way from her big house to mine and the Colorado spruces shielding me from whatever encroachments my father thought were afoot. Seeing how the one-on-one time we'd spent in my life could be described in a one-paragraph summary, he'd been uncannily right about where I should live. I liked the feeling of being cocooned.

But as I drove my Beemer—okay, it was an old used one my dad got a good deal on—into the sunny openness, it was okay. The mountain ranges on every side were enough protection today.

I avoided the Nineteenth Street corridor with its endless chain of big box stores and headed straight for the Gallatin County Farmer's Market. This was the first weekend it was open so there wouldn't be a wide selection of produce, but the meat sellers would be there and I wanted some fresh Black Angus steaks to cook to perfection. When I got out of the car, before I wove my way through the already thick crowd of so-ready-for-summer Montanans, I shaded my eyes with my hand and looked up at the giant white-stoned M. Wes was at least an hour into his climb right now, and I imagined his head getting clearer with every step. I didn't question how he was going to do that with Caleb *et al* jacking their jaws all over the place. I just trusted the voice I'd heard on the phone last night.

Between the farmer's market and the self-consciously trendy shops on Main Street, it didn't take me long to drop two bills. I never really spent much out of the account my dad kept for me. I probably inherited my frugality from my pinch-fisted Missouri . . . well, my mother. Today I had no guilt pangs as I tucked the bags full of tender new lettuce and finely marbled rib eyes and crusty artisan bread into my car with more bags that held the new outfit and the scented candles and the hand-blown glasses Wes and I would be toasting with. My father loved Wes from the Christmas we'd spent with him in Big Sky. He'd be fine with this shopping spree.

I made one more stop on my way back to the house. Two little kids, a towheaded boy and his even more towheaded sister, were just settling into their lopsided lemonade stand as I drove past them just around the corner. The boy, about a head taller than his more demure business partner, held up a beer-sized plastic cup of their product and sloshed it in my direction, shouting like the best of ballpark hawkers, "Lemonade! Get your ice-cold lemonade!"

The scene was so Little Wes and Little Kirsten I had to pull over onto the gravel shoulder and walk back with my wallet in my hand. We were going to have kids. Towheaded kids like us. Both skinny and lanky and blue-eyed because we were. I had to have a taste of the future.

Because it was impossible for me to get through a day without being Nudniked, she started in on me as I was setting the table four hours before Wes was scheduled to arrive.

Kids, huh? You do know you're going to have to sleep with the man to get said kids, right?

Well, no kidding. Wes might think I was naïve, but it hadn't been any easier for me to resist falling into bed together than it had been for him. We'd gone far enough for me to know what passion was.

Lovely. Surely it will be so passionate that he will never notice what you've done to your body for the last, what is it now, seven years?

I sank into the chair I'd just draped and tied with muslin. There was no denying that at least part of my refusal to sleep with Wes was my fear of what he would say about the scars. I'd always been careful to cut where the general public couldn't see them. When I'd run out of room and started on my shoulders, the simple solution was to always wear at least short sleeves, which most of the time wasn't a problem in Montana weather. But there was going to be no hiding them from Wes. I'd have to find a way to explain.

Ya think? Of course, you could always put him off a little longer and opt for plastic surgery. Oh, wait, Daddy probably isn't going to pay for that, is he? After all, Daddy doesn't know!

I launched myself into the kitchen and got out the scissors and did a full-out attack on the stems of the roses I'd bought. Get these babies down to vase length. Make them perfect for the table. Or maybe the bedroom.

No, I wasn't going to put Wes off a little longer. Maybe I wasn't even going to put him off tonight. With the future finally unrolled before us like a white aisle runner, what did it matter if we crept between clean sheets—I had a set I'd never used in the back of the linen closet—and spent tonight in each other's arms?

With the lights out, no doubt.

After I told Wes everything. I rehearsed as I chopped walnuts.

Baby, I know at first it's going to look to you like I had a close encounter with a pack of porcupines . . .

No, too flippant.

Baby, a long time ago I was going through a really bad time and I—

Uh, no. Not even the truth.

I know it was beyond absurd, but you know me—

Definitely too cavalier.

What about: Sometimes the stress and the old stuff I still wrestle with teems under my skin and I have to let it out. But I won't need to do it ever again. I promise you that.

I closed my eyes and saw Wes's blue eyes glisten with understanding tears.

Don't forget the violins.

No, what I was going to forget was Miss Nudnik. Other voices were going to outsing hers now.

I successfully shut her out as I marinated the steaks and tossed a salad Rachael Ray would salivate over and took a luscious bubble bath. When I'd slithered into the silk tunic that clung and yet teasingly didn't cling, I unbuttoned the top two buttons. Then the next two. Chortling, yes, chortling at myself, I clipped my bangs so that a straight blond panel dipped over one blue eye. Oh *yeah,* baby.

———

With summer approaching Montana, dusk didn't happen until after seven. When very little sunlight was making its silvery way through the spruce trees, Wes still wasn't there. Pushing back visions of grizzlies, landslides, and marauding bands of banditos at the M, I texted him with a gentle *Where are u?*

Though not as thumb-ready as Isabel, Wes always answered within five minutes. After six I texted him again. After ten I called but his phone went straight to voice mail. Then I started to pace, and every time a magpie squawked or the wind hissed through the spruces I ran to the window to look for the Mini Cooper.

When I hadn't heard from him by eight, I texted Isabel and then called her. No response there either, even after I sent *URGENT!!!* My throat was so tight I could feel its pull all the way up to my jaw. Fingers shaking, I texted Caleb. He was definitely more Wes's friend than mine—maybe they all were, come to think of it—but surely he'd answer, right? If he didn't I would know Wes had fallen off the side of the mountain and he and Tess and Isabel were trying to figure out a way to tell me. There could be no other explanation.

When my phone signaled a text I almost jumped out of my now

on-fire skin. It was from Caleb: *I haven't seen Wes all day. He didn't do the hike.*

I couldn't put that anywhere. I'm not sure what I would have done if I hadn't heard a car pull into my driveway. Why I looked out the window first instead of opening the door, I don't know. Maybe it was because the engine didn't sound like Wes's. The Mini Cooper didn't purr. In fact, nobody's engine did except the one in Isabel's Miata.

I pulled aside the curtain on the window in the door and peered into what was now almost complete darkness except for the porch light that created only a pool of yellow on the steps. It was enough for me to make out Wes's long body, leaning into the driver's side window of the black sports car. I still didn't open the door, which was perhaps the only good decision I made that night, because as I stared between the muslin panels into the yellowed darkness, I saw Wes push his head through the open car window and give the driver a long, tender kiss. The driver. My best friend, Isabel.

Before Wes could extricate himself from the window, I snapped the curtains closed and flew around the room with my silky tunic flailing out behind me. With one trembling hand I snatched up the flowers from the table, with the other I doused the candles without bothering to wet my fingers. I dumped it all into the kitchen trash can and was on my way back to pick up the tablecloth—china, crystal, and all—when the front door opened. I abandoned that idea and, with my back to Wes, buttoned my tunic all the way to my chin.

"I am so sorry I'm late," he said.

I whirled to face him, and he knew. I knew he knew by the panic that flickered through his eyes. A panic that had nothing on what was racing up my throat.

"Kirsten, it isn't what it looks like," he said.

I gave my head a wild shake and smacked away the hair that was no longer seductive. "Why do they always say that?" some other Kirsten's voice said.

"Who, babe?"

"Men who get caught with their girlfriend's best friend. Why do they always say it's not what it looks like when it is *exactly* what it looks like?"

"It isn't. I swear to you it isn't."

Wes came toward me and I put up my hands to ward him off. He grabbed them anyway and towed me to the couch and held me there until I stopped struggling. He had a hold on me unlike any he'd ever tried.

"Let me explain," he said.

Only because he spoke in the same voice he'd used on the phone the night before did I nod. I couldn't speak, and for once neither could the Nudnik. All my mind could do was spin.

"I didn't go on the hike today."

"You lied to me."

"No. Listen, please." He was just short of shaking me. "I intended to, but when I left here last night, Isabel called me freaking out. She needed my help today and I had to go with her."

"This isn't making any sense. Why didn't you tell me that last night when you called me?"

"I couldn't. She made me promise."

"I don't understand. If she was in that much trouble, why didn't she call *me*?"

I watched him swallow. "She didn't want you to know."

"Know *what?*"

I tried to pull away but he tightened his grip. "I can't tell you. But it doesn't matter now. It's taken care of."

"Really?" I said. "Was kissing her like that in *my* driveway taking care of it?"

"Yes. It was. It was a good-bye kiss."

Everything that coursed through my flesh erupted in one burst of strength. I wrenched myself from Wes and retreated to the other side of the room. As I bumped against the table I'd set with so much hope, a crystal goblet tipped into its neighboring plate and smashed politely into splinters.

"Good-bye after what, Wes?"

"It just happened, babe."

"How long?"

Wes stood up but I stuck out a warning palm. This time he heeded it. For a crazy moment I thought he was going to put up both hands in surrender.

"It just started out with us talking. I couldn't get you to talk to me so I went to her—"

"I changed my mind. Stop."

"Babe, come on, let me finish."

"No," I said—in spite of the pleading in his voice and the desperation in his arms and the glistening tears that weren't the ones I'd hoped to see tonight. I couldn't let him tell me the rest. Not until I got a handle on myself.

"I need you to go," I said.

"I'm not leaving until you hear me out."

"Then stay," I said, and somehow made my way into the bathroom.

A moment after I slammed the door, I heard my front door slam as well. I wasn't sure which one shook the house—or was it me it shook? I was undoubtedly headed into a panic so strong I had to stop it before it quaked me over an edge I wouldn't be able to come back from.

I did something I had never done before, not in the seven years since

I'd first dug a fingernail into my flesh. I acted without ritual, without a plan, without the certainty that all that was bad in me was about to seep from my bloodstream. I just snatched up the scissors I'd used in another life to make myself sexy and held them against the inside of my forearm. What did it matter now if I cut where everyone could see?

I did take a breath, a long one that settled the wildest of the thoughts spinning in my head. With practiced pressure I let the tip of the scissors ease its way in until the first bead of blood escaped. Leaning against the safe bathroom door, I started the gentle pull in a fragile straight line—until the doorknob jiggled and Wes's voice cut through.

"Kirsten! Open the door, please! We have to talk!"

I couldn't answer. When I'd startled, the scissor blade had dug in deeper than I'd intended. The blood was coming out too fast. This wasn't right.

"Kirsten! What are you doing? What's going on?"

Wes banged on the door and it lurched open, slamming me against the sink. I felt the scissors stab into my arm—deep, and then deeper when Wes yanked me to face him. I stared in horror at the blade still embedded beyond the surface skin it was intended for. But my own horror couldn't match the terror in Wes's eyes. Before I could stop him he jerked the scissors free—and released a fountain of blood. Not the blessed blood of relief. Blood that was trying to drain my life from me.

Share this chapter with your friends!
You made everything all right when it clearly isn't. #TheMercifulScar

Chapter TWO

The night became a montage of blood and sirens and patches of blackness that sometimes gave way to figures from Edvard Munch paintings. Its soundtrack was chaotic—too many wails and shouts and the Munch figures asking, "Kristen, can you hear me?" I knew I should tell them that wasn't my name, but it didn't seem to matter as I sank away again.

Then came the lights. Glaring, awful eyes that stared at me from a stainless steel face. All around me were words I didn't understand. *Severed the radial . . . losing the pulse . . . whole blood.* But one phrase made its way to a clear spot in my mind.

"Failed suicide attempt," someone said.

"No!" I said. And then again, "No!" Because it was all my tongue could manage.

One of the painted faces came close to mine and I could see it was real.

"Kristen, we're going to save your life whether you want us to or not."

I didn't care now what they called me, but I had to make them see they were wrong. Why didn't Wes tell them? Where was Wes?

I tried to call for him, but all that came out was, "No!" over and over until I once again went someplace dark.

———

When I emerged from the cave of no-thought, I still couldn't quite put anything together. An eerie calm had settled over me when I wasn't looking. It was several minutes before I knew I was in a hospital with an IV in my arm, and several more before I figured out that the white-coated person standing over me wasn't happy to be there.

"Do you know where you are?" he said. Or perhaps it was his long, continuous eyebrow that said it. I couldn't tell.

"Hospital."

"Do you know your name?"

"Kirsten Petersen. Kirsten, not Kristen."

I had the strange sensation that I was somehow talking like a caterpillar. How did caterpillars talk? Did they?

"Hey, stay with me."

I forced my eyes open to look at Unibrow.

"Do you remember what happened?"

I let my eyes close.

"Hey."

"It was just an accident," I said into my eyelids.

"You slit your wrist."

"No. No—I was only . . . ask Wes. He'll tell you."

"That the guy who called 911?"

"My boyfriend. Wes." I struggled for his last name. "Rordan."

I heard computer keys. Then Unibrow was back.

"Open your eyes, Kirsten."

When I looked, the hairy line had folded almost over his eye sockets, scolding me. Why was he scolding me?

"You with me?" he said.

No, I was with Wes. But where was he?

"Kirsten—"

"Yes."

"I'm Dr. Giacomo. I'm a resident here in the ER."

"Okay."

"Here's what happened. You slit your wrist with a pair of scissors and you would have bled out if your boyfriend hadn't found you and called 911. The paramedics brought you here in an ambulance—"

I shook my head, which was a mistake. The room went into a sickening spin. Dr. Unibrow was quick with the pan and all but rolled his eyes as I threw up into it. I didn't even do that proficiently, a result of not having eaten anything for what now seemed like days.

He set the pan aside and leaned on my table. "Look, we can see you're a cutter," he said.

I cringed.

"And evidently it wasn't working anymore."

"It would have. Wes banged on the door and the scissors slipped. I didn't mean to hurt myself this bad."

I thought we agreed pathetic isn't effective.

Nudnik's voice was vague. Even she was having trouble getting through and for once I wanted her to.

"Well, you did hurt yourself this bad." The doctor lifted my arm, apparently so I could see the bandage that mummified my wrist. "You almost died. How old are you, Kirsten?"

Why should you tell him? He hasn't believed anything else you've said so far.

"Twenty-two," I said.

"Were you ever sexually abused?"

"I'm sorry, what? No!"

"You're sure."

"Yes!"

"Physically abused growing up? Bad childhood?"

"No. I don't understand—"

"Have a history of depression?"

Who doesn't?

"Could you please tell me why you're asking me all this?"

He folded his arms across his coat, covering the name I couldn't remember anyway. "I'm trying to find out why an attractive twenty-two-year-old with her whole life ahead of her would want to do this to herself."

"I didn't want to die. Really, it was an accident."

"Even if it was, it wouldn't have happened if you hadn't had a pair of scissors pressed against your radial artery."

The door opened, and the room was invaded by the sound of someone crying out in pain. It was muffled as the door closed again.

"Did you hear that, Kirsten?" the doctor said. "That's somebody who didn't ask for the suffering she's going through right now—"

"Okay, I think this conversation is over."

It was a female voice, and I didn't care who it belonged to; I loved her.

"Are we stable?" she said.

"Physically," was the answer. "The artery clotted so we didn't have to do surgery except to stitch her up."

"Then I guess your job is done."

She was close enough for me to see her now—a strawberry blonde with a thick braid who was tall enough to tower over Dr. Unibrow. I loved that about her too. Her face remained impassive until the door closed behind him. I saw her eyes go into green slits before she turned to me with a professional smile.

"Hey, Kirsten," she said. "I'm Dr. Oliphant. And, yes, I got teased about that a lot when I was a kid."

Her tone made me grope for my sense of humor. "I was going to ask," I said.

"That's a good sign." She pulled a stool up to my table as if she and I were about to chat over café mochas. "I understand you had a bad night last night."

Understatement of the year, Doc.

"The worst," I said.

"How are you doing now? Emotionally, I mean."

Peachy.

"Right now I'm just frustrated because nobody will believe I wasn't trying to commit suicide. It was an accident."

She nodded. I couldn't tell whether that meant she believed me or not, but at least she didn't tell me I was taking up space here when other people were *really* suffering.

"They tell me you self-injure," she said.

"That doctor with one eyebrow called me a cutter," I said.

Her eyes returned briefly to slits. "We refer to what you do as SI. You'll hear people say that up on the floor, although that isn't to label you—"

"What floor?"

"The psychiatric floor, Kirsten."

"I don't understand."

I do. They're taking you where the crazy people are.

Dr. Oliphant folded her hands on my table. "When someone comes in with an injury like yours, hospital policy pretty much dictates that the patient—you—be admitted for observation for at

least seventy-two hours. Is there someone you want us to call and let
know—"

"I'm going to be on the psych ward?"

"Unless you can convince me that you had no intention of taking
your own life and that you'll be safe if I release you."

*What do you have to do to convince her? Open a vein? Oh, wait, you
already did that.*

I tried to sit up, but the room spun again. I didn't throw up this
time, probably because this doctor didn't just shove a puke pan in
my face. She eased me down and then adjusted the table so I was at a
forty-five-degree angle.

"Is that more comfortable?" she said.

"I'm sorry. I don't mean to be difficult, but I'm not going to be
comfortable until I get home."

Right. Back to the scene of the, uh, crime.

"I don't know how else to say it: yes, I was going to cut, but
that's all. Wes—my boyfriend—shoved the door open and the scissors slipped and went into my arm, and then he jerked me away from
the sink and they went in deeper and blood was just . . ." I begged her
with my eyes. "It was awful, but I didn't do it on purpose. Wes will
tell you."

Dr. Oliphant stroked her braid. "That's where we run into a snag.
Wes—that's your boyfriend?"

*Was your boyfriend. Have we forgotten that he had a little fling with
your best friend?*

I pressed my hand against my throat. I could feel my fingers
shaking on my skin.

"Yeah," I said. "Until last night."

*Ooh, bad move, Kirsten. Now she's going to think you had a reason
to slice yourself open. As always, nicely done.*

Yeah, well, I was into it now. "We broke up and I was just trying to relieve some of the pressure, but he came back, I guess to try to get me to make up, and that's when it happened."

Dr. Oliphant directed her green eyes at me. "Unfortunately that isn't the way Wes explained it to the paramedics and the ER doctor."

"What did he say?"

"He said he had to break into the bathroom because you wouldn't let him in, and when he did get in, you had already slit your wrist."

"But that's not true!" I said.

Screaming is such a great way to convince her you're sane. Go with that.

"We all see different things in a crisis situation." The doctor's voice was far too calm for the crisis I was rising to right now. "That's how Wes saw it."

"And what I told you is how *I* experienced it! I don't need to go to the psych ward. Please—just let me go home!"

Yeah, let's go home so we can confront Wes with the fact that he is a liar in the first degree.

By then things on me were shaking that had never shaken before—parts of me I hadn't even known were there. I couldn't breathe, couldn't swallow, couldn't form a thought beyond *He lied . . . he lied . . . it was all lies.*

I didn't realize I'd screamed it out loud until Dr. Oliphant put her hand on my arm and said, "All right, we're going to get you to a place where we can help you deal with that."

"I want to go home!"

"We'll give you something to calm you down and then we're going to keep you here for a little while."

I grabbed my knees and yanked them into my chest and shook and shook and shook, until someone said that ridiculous thing—"a little pinch"—and I shook slowly off into the dark again. But not before I heard the Nudnik say: *I'm thinking I don't love Dr. Elephant anymore. You?*

———

Somehow it got to be Monday. And somehow I was in a blue room where somebody had made an attempt at a serene décor that only mocked me. The staff never seemed to turn out the lights. They just left them on to expose me, but whenever I started to pull the colorless hospital sheet over my face, the Nudnik reminded me that would only make me look crazy to them. *Although, frankly,* she nattered in my head, *I think that ship has sailed.*

I didn't care now that they kept giving me medicine to maintain my calm. As deep as my hopelessness went, I wondered how I'd be acting if I weren't, as Nudnik put it, *completely loaded.*

So I slept and slept and slept, coming to only when someone came in to check my dressing or try to coax me to eat the unidentifiable things under the plastic lid. That only made me think of the rib eyes still drowning in marinade in my refrigerator, and that was one of many places I couldn't be right now. So I slept and slept and slept some more.

Until late that day—and who could tell what time it was in that endlessly blue room with no clock—when someone in pediatric-print scrubs woke me up to tell me I had a visitor.

"If it's Wes Rordan, I don't want to see him," I said.

"We haven't had a chance to get a list of approved visitors from you," she said. "So, no Wes Rordan?"

"No," I said.

Aw, come on, Kirsten. I want to see the boy squirm.

"How about your mother?"

I sat straight up in the bed. "My mother? Michelle Petersen?"

"This lady," she said, and flashed a photocopy of my mother's driver's license.

It was her all right. Thin blond bob gone almost gray. Faded blue eyes. Lips in an obligatory smile. Only the puffy places under her eyes made her look any different than she had the last time I saw her. She'd aged considerably in four years.

"I don't know," I said.

Of course you know. This is going to be a train wreck. No, actually the train wreck would be if your father were with her. Then I'm thinking more . . . Spanish Inquisition.

"She said she flew all day from Missouri to see you."

What? A flight from Kansas City is a few hours max.

"Okay," I said. Because I had a glimmer of hope. If anyone could convince these people that I didn't need to be here, it was my I-don't-believe-in-nervous-breakdowns mother. "Bring her in."

"You'll have to see her in the visitors' room," Happy Scrubs said. "There's a bathrobe hanging on the back of the door."

The idea of leaving the room and finding out how bad it really was here was almost enough to make me change my mind. That and the fact that there was no belt with the robe.

They want to make sure you don't hang yourself.

———

She was standing at one of the wide windows in the visitors' room, overlooking the inevitable mountain range. The setting sun on the other side of the sky cast a pink light on the last of the snow, but I was sure Mother wasn't making an appreciative mental note of that.

I must have still been under the influence because the moment I saw her, it occurred to me that my younger sister, Lara, and I were probably the only people in our generation who actually called their maternal parent Mother. There wasn't anything else you could call Michelle Petersen. Mom, Mommy, and Mama belonged to women who baked snickerdoodles and hung their kids' funky artwork on the refrigerator with souvenir magnets from family vacations. Lara always said Mother with an inflection reminiscent of one of Cinderella's stepsisters.

Mother didn't turn around until I'd passed three groupings of chairs. I wasn't fast enough to get my bandaged wrist behind my back before she saw it. I knew she did because her pencil-thin brows went up. Michelle didn't raise her eyebrows for just any little thing.

"Hi," I said when I reached her.

She can't argue with that.

Mother gave me an almost-there kiss on the cheek and stepped back again to look at me. For perhaps the first time in my life I was glad she wasn't a hugger. She had yet to say a word, but disbelief was etched into the bags under her eyes, which were even more pronounced in person.

Pronounced? They look like carry-on luggage.

"How did you know I was here?"

"Wesley called me."

I almost groaned out loud.

He got to her first, huh? So much for convincing her you shouldn't be on suicide watch.

"Kirsten, what on earth?"

"You want to sit down?" I didn't wait for an answer. I just led her to a pair of square, stuffed, tweedy chairs that faced each other in the corner. There was only one other knot of people in the room, but I still felt like I was about to air the clichéd dirty laundry to everyone on the ward.

Mother sat at a perfect ninety-degree angle in one chair, legs in creased gray slacks crossed at the ankles. I sat with my feet up in the other and arranged a throw pillow so I could hide my wrist under it.

Out of sight, out of mind? Good luck with that. The woman has laser vision.

"I guess you want to know what happened," I said.

"Wesley told me." Mother folded her arms so tightly I could almost hear the starched white blouse crackle. "Kirsten, what were you thinking? Or were you?"

Gee, I'm fine, Mother. Thanks for asking.

I clenched my fists under the pillow and wished I had the Nudnik's nerve. I wanted to say that very thing.

But I took a deep breath and said instead, "I'm sure Wes told you I was trying to kill myself, but he's wrong. It was an accident."

"You accidentally stuck a pair of scissors into your vein?"

I didn't answer. I just didn't have it in me to try to explain this again to yet another person who wasn't going to believe me anyway.

Mother tucked her graying bob behind her ears, and I saw that the pearl earrings were still there. Lara used to try to see whether she wore them to bed, though she never did find out. Our mother always went into and out of her bedroom fully clothed and coiffed.

The hair tuck, though, that's new. She couldn't be stressing, could she? She always says only neurotic people stress.

"Contrary to what you might believe, Kirsten," she said, "I fully understand that you were upset when Wesley broke things off."

Back the truck up!

"You were together for over three years."

Three years, six months, two weeks, four days . . .

"I've been there myself, remember?"

Yeah, what a shock when that *match made in heaven went south.*

"But you didn't see me falling apart."

I beat the Nudnik to the punch: I had never seen my mother show any emotion whatsoever.

"I had Lara to take care of. And you."

The Beloved Afterthought.

"You have other things in your life besides Wesley. Your education. Your friends. A career ahead of you."

She waited for me to nod, so I did. I was still back on Wes telling my mother that *he* had broken up with *me*. Why had I never known he could lie like that? Had everything about our relationship been one big—

Prevarication. I've always wanted to use that word.

"Not to mention your family."

Were you packed for this guilt trip?

"We do care about you. If you were that upset, you could have picked up the phone and called us.

We? Us? Who's she talking about?

She was talking about Lara, of course.

Which was why I felt myself deflate. It was still Lara, Lara, Lara, just as it had been for the last seven years. Why had I thought for a moment my mother would have my back?

You're racking up the questions here, Kirsten. That's Number Two. I'm starting a spreadsheet.

"All I'm saying is that you are not the only girl who has ever had a heartbreak. But most girls don't become suicidal over it."

"I'm not suicidal," I said. "All I want to do is go home and—"

"You can't just go home." The hair tuck again, this time so tight it made my mother's face look like a hatchet. "You have to stay here for another two or three days, and then they'll determine whether you can be released to outpatient care or have to go into a residential program which, frankly, Kirsten, I can't afford."

"Three more days?" I could barely hear my own voice.

"That's what they told me. I haven't talked to your doctor yet, but I do know this: unless you start talking to somebody about whatever it is that made you do this, three days will only be the start of it. Are you getting this, Kirsten?"

Who did she expect me to talk to?

Number Three.

"Obviously you aren't going to talk to me," Mother said.

"I don't know what else to tell you," I said.

She did her version of exasperated. Shallow sigh. Clutch bag firmly in hand. An abrupt shift to standing.

I stood, too, so at least she couldn't look down on me.

"I'm going to stay at your house if you don't mind," she said.

That's Michelle for You don't really have a choice.

"Do you have a key with you?"

Nah, I didn't have time to grab my purse when they scraped me up off the bathroom floor.

"It's a combination lock," I said. "My birth month and day."

She looked blank.

"Oh-three-oh-four."

"I know your birth date, Kirsten. All right, you get some rest and think about what I said. No more heartache for this family."

She gave me another perfunctory peck on the cheek and clicked her pumps too fast toward the double-locked door where Happy Scrubs waited.

See, first you have to have a heart before it can actually ache.

I wasn't sure I had one either anymore. I went to the window my mother had vacated and stared bleakly into the darkness. I didn't have to be able to see to know the mountains were still out there, and it came to me that that particular range was called the Crazy Mountains.

Appropriate, don't you think?

"Yeah," I whispered. "I do."

———

No one said so on Tuesday—what the Nudnik called *Day Two of Incarceration*—but it was obvious the staff had backed off on the calm-Kirsten-down drugs. I was all too wide-awake when a huge man with a white-guy Afro and dark blue scrubs that barely stretched over his muscles came into my room. They didn't have to worry that I was going to try to make an escape with this person filling up the environment. Besides, I didn't have the energy to do much of anything besides stare out the window.

Excellent plan, Kirsten. A catatonic state is definitely your ticket out of here.

Nudnik had a point. If my mother was right, my ticket out was my talking to somebody. She didn't say *what* I had to talk about.

"Hi," I said. I thought I might have forgotten how to smile but I tried anyway. "What should I call you?"

He planted his hands on the hips that formed the point of the downward triangle that was his body. "They call me a lot of things around here, most of them with a bleep-bleep-bleep in there somewhere."

I did smile at that point.

"I think you should call me by my name."

"Which is?"

"Roman."

"Of *course* it is."

He put out a hand for me to shake. Mine got lost among his fingers.

"You up for some breakfast?" he said.

"Yeah," I said, "but not here."

"I get that."

He crossed the room and opened the blinds. Montana sunshine insinuated itself into the conversation.

"Come on. I'll walk you down to the dining room." He winked a small brown eye. "You can pretend it's Denny's. They got a Grand Slam waiting for you."

"That doesn't work for me," I said as I followed him to the door. "I thought more like the Chickpea Café."

"Now you're talkin'. You had their *baba ghanoush*?"

Only every time Wes and I went there. Maybe wit wasn't going to be my exit pass but it was the only thing I had.

As the day wore on, even that wasn't enough to keep my skin from screaming at me: *I need help. Please. A butter knife. Anything.*

That wasn't happening. Roman and his colleagues had done this before, because I found nothing anywhere—dining room, visitors' room, common area, bathroom—that I could use to relieve the anxiety building under my flesh. The whys Nudnik had on her spreadsheet. The heartache I was inflicting on what was left of my family. The betrayal I couldn't look at or I would be, once more, reduced to a puddle of the shakes.

I went through all the motions of cooperating. Walking passively beside Roman everywhere I went. Telling Dr. Oliphant I had had no more suicidal urges, which was easy to do since I'd never had them in the first place. Forcing myself not to run in horror when someone even crazier than me threw a tray in the dining room. Even taking the phone call from my mother, which was right up there with eating the lima beans they served for lunch.

"All right, I don't want to hear any more about this being an accident," she said, in lieu of hello. "After I cleaned up your bathroom—which is something I hope never to have to do again—I thought I'd dust mop the rest of the house and I found the box under your bed."

Hey, is nothing sacred? Come on!

"You will never convince me that you didn't have something like this planned, Kirsten."

I didn't even try.

"I was awake all night thinking about this," she went on. "And I remember now that you were always overly sensitive, too easily moved to tears. Far more emotional than Lara."

When, I wondered, had I ever been allowed to show any emotion at all?

Number Four. Wait, we already know the answer to that one—never!

"I'll be over after dinner," Mother said. "And we *will* discuss this, Kirsten. I want the truth."

I couldn't hang up fast enough. Only lack of mechanical ability kept me from opening the phone to see if there was something, anything in there I could use to ease the pain.

Why do you think God gave you fingernails, Brain Child?

I stared down at my hands. The manicure I'd given myself for Sunday night's romantic dinner was still intact. I'd never been able to grow glamor nails, but these were significantly longer than the ones I'd used the first time I clawed at my skin. Before I learned how to cut.

I was in my room, making very little progress on my upper arm, when Roman came to tell me I had a visitor.

"I don't want to see my mother," I said. "Tell her I'm having a massage or something."

"Unless your mother is an English dude, this is somebody different."

English dude? Did I even know anybody British? Was I having a hallucination right now?

That's not even going on the spreadsheet.

"Says his name is David Dowling," Roman said, and presented me with the driver's license photocopy.

A smiling face looked back at me. Buzz cut. Glasses. Ears just a tad too big, enough to make him likable.

Oh, that David Dowling. The new chaplain at Faith House. I'd met him. Once.

"It's the *Reverend* David Dowling," I said.

Roman feigned a warning look. "We don't allow exorcisms in here, now."

"You think I need one?"

"No. But somebody praying for you can't hurt."

Praying. Now there's a concept. Long time no do, eh, Kirsten?

At least I didn't have a history with this person. If David Dowling said something that made me want to take a bite out of the inside of my cheek, it would be easier to ask him to leave.

"Take me to him," I said.

"I don't have to be afraid of lightning striking or anything, do I?" he said as he escorted me through the doors to the visitors' room.

"I don't know," I said. And really, I didn't.

When the runner-thin man stood up from the chair my mother had occupied the night before, I remembered him better. He'd taken on the job of chaplain in September, and Wes and I had gone to the welcome party. That was the last time I was at Faith House, and I was sure I hadn't made any kind of deep impression on the reverend.

If I recall correctly, you were freaking out over your next exam and you wanted to be in the library studying with Isabel—

"Reverend Dowling," I said.

Fine. Shut me down.

He greeted me with both hands out and searched my face with dark blue eyes that sparkled behind his square glasses.

"I won't even ask how you are," he said. His accent made up for the unfortunate ears.

"Thank you," I said. And I meant it.

We sat in a different set of chairs, although Reverend Dowling only used up half of his as he perched on the edge, hands on his knees.

"Can I ask why you're here?" I shook my hair, now two days past the due date for a shampoo. "I'm sorry, that sounded rude."

"Not at all. I was with Wes all day yesterday." He put up his hand as if he heard the protest in my head. "We didn't discuss you. Not ethical. But he did let it slip that you were here so I thought I'd come 'round and see if you needed anything."

Poor Wes. He was so broken up he had to seek spiritual counseling. Where is that barf bag?

"I'm fine," I said.

David didn't say anything. He didn't even raise a brow or roll his eyes. He just waited.

"Okay, I'm clearly not fine," I said, "or I wouldn't be here." I re-arranged myself in the chair. "I'm going to tell you this even though you probably won't believe it any more than anybody else has."

"Is it the truth?" he said.

"Yes."

"Then let's have a look at it."

For no less than the fourth time, I poured out what was real. Maybe I told him more about the cutting I'd done before that night than I had anyone else. In fact, I know I did. Something about the complete lack of judgment in his body language accounted for that. And the fact that at no time did he interrupt me with the kind of placating scripture references his predecessor at Faith House had been notorious for. Even Wes had said he didn't think "Be anxious for nothing" covered final exams.

When I was through I was almost too exhausted to lift my hands. They just lay limp on the arms of the chair.

"NSSI," he said.

"I'm sorry?"

"Non-Suicidal Self-Injury. You're not alone, you know. At least one young woman a week comes to see me with scars."

It was my turn to scoot to the edge of the chair. "Did you say non-suicidal?"

"I did."

"Then you believe me."

"You said it was the truth." He grinned almost impishly. "Who's not going to tell her pastor the truth?"

I felt my face color—not hard for someone to detect since my normal skin tone was like skim milk.

"I'm not sure I can claim you as my pastor," I said. "I haven't been to Faith House or church in nine months."

"Not required," he said. "I'm volunteering for the job."

My soul chose that moment to do something it hadn't done in longer ago than I could remember. It began to cry. Not a wet, weepy cry. Just hard gasps that produced nothing but more pain and more pain and more pain. Even with my hands over my face I sensed David Dowling shaking his head at a concerned Roman. And I heard him praying. Heard them both as I sobbed my dry sobs.

———

After David Dowling left, promising to come back the next day, I skipped dinner and stayed in the visitors' room. I was afraid that after all the body-wracking sobbing, parts of me would fall off if I stood up.

My mother found me there, about fifteen minutes before visiting hours were over.

Perfectly timed.

"I brought you some clothes and makeup," she said.

Does this woman not know how to say hello? Yikes, now I'm asking questions.

"They have to go through everything before you can have it. You do realize you're locked up in here, don't you, Kirsten? Is that what you want?"

Was she serious?

Have you ever known her to be anything else?

I kept my gaze on my fingernails, willing them not to go for my arms right here in front of Mother. But I looked up when I heard her sigh, because Michelle did not sigh.

"I can't wrap my mind around this," she said. "I mean, I *know* how to take care of Lara. But I have to say this situation of yours is beyond me."

I wanted to tell her it was beyond me too. Maybe I would have if she hadn't followed that up with, "Does your father know about this?"

Panic was there as if someone had kicked it right into my throat. "No!" I said. "And I don't want him to."

"So you wouldn't have told me either if Wesley hadn't."

"What good is it doing you to know? I've just upset you."

"I came to see what I could do."

Like what? Bring a new wardrobe? Let me guess: J.C. Penney.

"There's definitely nothing Dad can do," I said.

To my surprise, Mother nodded. "I have to agree with you there."

She paused—another surprise—and then her eyes went into narrow, shrewd slits.

Uh-oh. This can't be good.

"I will keep this from your father," she said, "if you will agree to accept help from someone. Talk this whole thing out. Let a professional walk you through it. I don't care who it is—you talk, and your father never has to know about this."

You know this is blackmail, don't you?

Of the worst kind. My mother went to great lengths to have nothing to do with my father. To my knowledge they'd barely spoken a word to each other since the divorce.

"Well?" Mother said.

"Can you just give me a minute?"

A minute? What's to contemplate! If the old man shows up here, you're going to go completely over the edge and you won't come back.

But I needed that minute, to picture my father's reaction if he found me here among the schizophrenics and the bipolar people and—what did he always call them?—the people who can't handle the load. I couldn't see any of the pride in his cool hazel eyes that was there when he sent me off to Montana State or arranged the finances for grad school or breezed into my rental house with a complete IKEA makeover. All I could see was contempt twitching in the lines around his eyes. The message would be as clear in him as it was in my mother.

If you can't be perfect, I cannot love you. I didn't need the Nudnik to tell me that.

My mother stood up with no disturbance to the crease in today's black slacks. "I don't know what there is to think over, but you have until tomorrow."

"I'll do it," I said. "And I know who I'll talk to."

"Who? Dr. Oliphant?"

"No. David Dowling. He's my pastor."

The arms folded. "I said a professional—"

"You said you didn't care who it was," I said.

Speak up, girl. I don't think a dog could even have heard that.

But apparently my mother did because she placed the black

leather clutch neatly under her arm and said, "All right. I'm going to go call and check on Lara. I'll see you tomorrow?"

"Sure," I said.

This time the Nudnik waited until Mother made her exit before I heard: *She wants you done so she can get back to Lara.*

I knew that. I knew it down in the dark place I tried never to go to. Ever.

Share this chapter with your friends!

My soul chose that moment to do something it hadn't done in longer ago than I could remember. It began to cry. #TheMercifulScar

Chapter
THREE

Tucked into the bag of tidy—yes—Penney's tops and lounge pants—
Who wears lounge pants?

—were my cell phone and charger. I questioned Roman about
that when he came by to escort me to lunch.

"Model patient privilege," he said.

*Yeah, but you know they went through your call history. Every juicy
text you ever sent to Wes . . .*

Roman cocked his big head at me. "You don't look too excited
about it."

I shrugged and beat Nudnik to the thought. Who am I going to
call, anyway?

*He-llo-o, vicar of Bozeman? Your mother isn't going to stand for any
procrastination on this, or you're going to have Daddy in here.*

There were times when, insulting as she was, the Nudnik kept me
on track. I did call David Dowling, who, when I told him I wanted
to talk to him some more, said, "Brilliant!" We agreed he'd come that
afternoon.

Then I spent the next two hours picking at a scab that had formed on my shoulder. I had never told anyone about the cutting until him, at least not any more than I'd had to reveal to the people here, some of whom now referred to me as parasuicidal.

Yeah, what's that about? What are you, like the paralegal—the paramedic—the paranormal of the suicide world?

I'd resisted the urge to tell them I was *anti*suicidal. They would just put that down to my being in denial. Right now the only thing I was denying was the thought of me letting David Dowling any further into my cave. I didn't even try to imagine it; I just kept picking—and thinking about my father filing me into the Loser folder and closing the drawer.

When David arrived, Roman took us to a private room where two of those square stuffed chairs faced each other over a small table with a box of Kleenex on it.

"I'll be praying for you," he whispered before he stepped out.

Right outside the door so he can tranquilize you if you flip out.

Nudnik had a point. I'd have to be careful not to go too deep. Not even with this fuzzy-headed, funny-eared man who looked at me as if he had time for no one in the world but me. My throat started to ache.

"Let's take a minute to breathe," David said.

Yoga?

"Just a nice, long, smooth inhale and an easy exhale."

He closed his eyes, which meant he wouldn't see if I didn't do it. I did it anyway. It was surprisingly hard. Took me three tries to stop feeling like I was going to hyperventilate.

"Good stuff, air." David looked around the cube of a room, eyes squinted. "Not really the most freeing place, is it?"

"No, *freeing* would not be a word I'd use to describe it."

"You'd like to get out of here then."

My next thought struck me like a slap in the face. "I'm not sure I'd be any freer out there," I said.

"Except . . ."

"Except?"

David spread his very thin hands. "I just thought I heard an *except* in there. No freer except that . . ."

"Except that out there I could cut."

You did not *just tell him that. Are you serious?*

"The pressure's building up then."

"I'm about to implode."

"Been going on a long time, has it?"

"Since—off and on since I was fifteen. Mostly off the last three years. Well, except this semester. So, yeah."

What happened to staying on the surface?

"It's sort of like lancing a boil for me," I said. "I had to have that done once when I was a kid. Who gets a boil, right? Anyway, it was so painful but after they did it, it was like the pain magically disappeared. That always stayed in my mind."

"Perfect image."

"When things got hard my sophomore year of high school, it came back to me and, I don't know how I actually put it together, but it just seemed like if I could lance *that* boil, I would feel better."

"And you did."

"Beyond better."

He's about to ask what boil there was to lance. You going to redirect or what?

"It was like I was letting everything bad escape—fast—and take the pain with it so I could stop spinning out and come back to life and feel normal."

I don't call that redirecting.

She was right. I'd gone far enough. My hands were shaking, but fortunately David was looking into my eyes and nowhere else.

I hurried on. "At first I just tried digging my fingernails into my skin, but that didn't help much. Not with stubs like mine."

"And hard on the manicure, I would suppose."

You're so witty, Pastor Dave.

I was actually grateful for the humor, and I hooked on to it.

"So then I went with toothpicks. I got pretty proficient at deep scratches with those. Until my mother went to serve hors d'oeuvres."

"Yes, those little cocktail wieners are difficult to manage without picks."

"So I raided my father's desk and made off with a box of paper clips. He wasn't going to miss those. He was never there enough to use his home office."

Careful now.

"One of those unfolded was good, but I wanted something with a point or a sharp edge. And if my mother noticed the toothpicks were gone, I didn't think she'd overlook a missing piece of her cutlery."

"Your mother spent a lot of time in the kitchen, did she?"

Look out. That's a leading question. Don't you ever watch Law and Order *anymore?*

"At that point, no . . ." Oh. This *was* leading me somewhere I didn't want to be. "Let's just say my mother always knew where her belongings were."

Except her kid.

I pressed my knees together to stop the jittering. "Things went better my senior year. My dad and I visited colleges and we decided on Montana State—his alma mater, actually—and it just seemed like the future was going to be easier. So I stopped cutting."

And do we hear an until *in there?*

"But like I said before, I started again."

"College can be demanding."

And lonely. I managed to hold that back.

"For me, the good news was I didn't have to make do with whatever was around. I could go out and buy what I needed. And I have to say that a razor blade leaves a less noticeable scar than a paper clip."

You left out the calligraphy pen. I mean, after all, it's the only part of Wes that still loves you.

I couldn't catch the gasp before it escaped. David leaned forward and his eyes softened. I wanted to cry out, *Please, please don't do kind with me. I can't handle kind.*

"And now, Kirsten?" he said.

"I want to cut. I do."

"It's become like a friend then."

"Right now my only friend. It's the only way I can deal with the pain of knowing nobody gives a rip about me."

My hands went to my mouth, but it was too late. My pain was now in David Dowling's eyes.

"How can you *not* try to find a way to lance that boil?" he said. "But, Kirsten, I do know somebody who might give a rip about you."

The shaking had spread to my arms, which I hugged around my body so they wouldn't jar themselves off.

"No offense," I said. "I mean, you're being so nice—but I hope you're not talking about God. I don't think I can wrap my mind around that right now."

"If I was talking about God, there would be no *might* about it. That's a given. Actually I'm referring to Sister Frankie McKee."

"I'm not Catholic," I said.

"Neither is she. She's a former Anglican nun. Left the order some years ago and now she works with young women who struggle the way you do."

I tried so hard to laugh. "Roman says they don't allow exorcisms here."

"I have a life-sized picture of Frankie driving out demons." David's entire face twinkled. "No, her approach is far more subtle. I think you'd like it."

"No circles where you all sit and stare at each other and the leader keeps saying, 'Tell us how you feel about that'?"

David winced. "I rather think Frankie would prefer to be shot."

"So what *does* she do?"

"She cares," David said. "She cares and she knows and she leads."

Something thick was gathering in my throat, and I was no longer shaking. Still . . .

"I'm not sure how much caring and knowing and leading she's going to be able to do here." I gave the cubicle a dubious look. "You said yourself this isn't the most freeing environment. Wherever she's going to lead me, it'll only be as far as those doors with the bars on the windows."

He smiled. "Frankie will insist on taking you out of the hospital and being responsible for your welfare."

Did you hear that? Out of the hospital. Out where relief is just a razor blade away.

Still, I sank heavily back into the chair. "My mother has already told me she can't afford private treatment for me. I don't know about my insurance."

"Frankie doesn't charge for her services. Well, actually she does after a fashion. Let's just say she has creative ways of working out payment, which I would let her explain to you."

"Can I think about it?"

"You definitely *should* think about it. For as long as you like."

Or as long as you can stand being in here.

"I'll let you know tomorrow," I said.

"Brilliant," David said.

———

A new patient was admitted to the floor in the wee hours of the morning, a patient who clearly didn't respond to the meds they'd given me on *my* arrival. This poor person screamed in such abject fear about the terrorists who were after him, I started to think maybe we *were* all about to be taken out by a suicide bomber.

You realize you're starting to sympathize with the other inmates. And it's only Day Four of your incarceration.

Yeah. I had to get out of there. And the more I thought about it, the more certain I was that Sister Frankie's program was the answer. As an outpatient I would be able to get some relief. Maybe even get back to school before the summer session started in a week. Where I was going to live—definitely not in my rental—and how I was going to avoid seeing Wes and Isabel, I hadn't figured out yet. But the more terrified our new addition became, even in Roman's giant, capable hands, the more frightened I was that I'd end up just like him.

I called David at seven a.m. and told him I wanted to sign up with Sister Frankie. He, of course, said, "Brilliant! I'll get in touch with Frankie as soon as we hang up. Do you have any questions before I do that?"

"One," I said. "Do you think she'll be able to schedule my sessions around my grad work? This is a huge semester for me."

Silence.

I don't like the sound of that.

"I'm sorry, Kirsten," David said. "I suppose I didn't make that clear. We're talking about a thirty-day residential program."

As in lockdown. I knew this was too good to be true.

"You don't understand," I said. "I'm in my last year in my master's program—"

"For?"

"Architecture. If I don't do a summer studio now, I'll have to wait an entire year, and I'd have to have special permission to do that."

I didn't add that I'd been so strung out about Wes even before the breakup I hadn't even come up with a research problem yet, so I was already behind.

Not to mention the fact that if you don't finish, Daddy will probably write you out of the will. Of course, if you don't get this craziness thing taken care of, that's a done deal anyway.

I had never wanted the Nudnik to shut up as much as I did at that moment. I was starting to spin.

"You definitely have a lot to consider," David said. "Would you like to process that together?"

"I don't know—I guess so."

Not that it's actually going to change anything . . .

"How about if you call me right after lunch? Would that work for you?"

"Okay," I said.

I forgot to add, "Brilliant."

———

Could this *be* any more complicated?

Only if your mother showed up about now.

I stopped pacing my room, fingernails pressing crescent moons into my upper arms. I hadn't thrown Mother back into the mix. How she was going to react to all this . . . I didn't even want to think about it.

I want to think about it. I love a good horror flick.

The door opened and Roman's curly head poked in. "I hate to ruin your day," he said. "But we have an issue."

Let me guess: Daddy is here.

"I can't do an issue right now," I said.

"Even if the issue's name is Wes Rordan?"

Oh, boo-*yah!*

"What?" I said.

"He's on your no-admittance list but I thought I ought to check with you before I send him packing."

"I don't want to see him," I said. "I can't see him."

"Your call," Roman said. "But just so you know, he's out there crying."

Poor baby.

"Says he thinks he can help you."

"He can't," I said. "Look at me, I'm already starting to shake."

"All righty then. He's outta here." Roman turned to the door and then turned back. His mouth twitched.

"What?" I said.

"I just hate for you to miss an opportunity for a nice cathartic showdown, that's all." He looked around the room, gaze landing significantly on the meshed windows. "Can't think of a safer place to do it. He gets out of hand and you've got me and three more my size to take care of him." He shrugged the massive shoulders. "I just thought you might want a shot at that."

I do! Yikes, I'm salivating here.

I looked down at my balled-up fists. "Will you be close by?"

"When am I not? You're my new career."

"And you'll make him leave if I tell you to?"

"You just tug on your earlobe and I'll have him out the door."

I like it. I like it a lot.

"Okay," I said. "Let's go."

Either I really was losing it or the Wes I saw leaning on the back of a chair in the visitors' room was not the same Wes I'd spent the last three and a half years with. He was a gaunt, haunted version of his former self: his square jaw had sharp corners and the too-blue eyes seemed to have sunk into their sockets. How had that happened in four days?

Um, have you looked in a mirror lately?

That actually hadn't occurred to me. I'd finally taken a shower that morning, but beyond that I hadn't done anything about my appearance. The makeup my mother had brought me was still in its plastic packaging.

Don't worry about it. At least you're an improvement over the last time he saw you.

Wes spotted me then and straightened like he was going to come toward me, and then he didn't. This place seemed to immobilize people.

Uh, no, that would be you who's paralyzing the boy. I'm kind of enjoying this myself.

It was clear I was going to have to go to him, but the closer I got the less certain I was that this was a good idea. Roman was right: Wes had been crying. The sight of his swollen bloodshot eyes wasn't what I would call cathartic for me. All I felt so far was guilt.

Guilt? Really? Really?

When I stopped a few feet from him, Wes stretched out his arms for me but I took a step back.

"They don't allow physical contact in here," I lied.

Listen, wake me up when this showdown is over, 'kay?

"Kirsten, I'm so sorry." His voice was the consistency of sandpaper. I'd never heard him sound anything but smooth.

"We should sit down," I said and headed for a chair group in the middle of the room. I glanced back to make sure Roman was at the door. He gave me a questioning "Okay?" with his fingers and I nodded.

Wes sat facing me and glanced over his shoulder at the family playing gin rummy at a table a few yards away. "Isn't there someplace we can talk alone?"

"This is as private as it gets," I said.

"Man, you gotta hate that. I know how much you like to be—"

I pressed my hands to my cheeks. "Look, I don't have much time, so maybe you ought to just . . ."

I stopped because he was staring at the bandage on my left wrist, almost as if he were surprised by it.

"Is it getting better?" he said.

"It's fine."

He nodded eagerly, as if that was exactly the answer he'd hoped for. "And how about you? Are you fine?"

"Sure," I said.

Wes ran his palms along the tops of his thighs, clad in jeans that looked like he'd been wearing them for three days. And nights. "I understand why you don't want to talk to me, but isn't that what got us here in the first place?"

Smack him! Smack him right now!

"What does that mean?" I said.

He abandoned the thighs and rubbed his hands against each other. His jeans now bore long damp strips of sweat. "Do you know how long I've been frustrated because you won't talk to me about what you're thinking? All that time you wanted me to propose to you, but you never told me. It was that kind of thing that—"

"Sent you straight into Isabel's arms?"

Atta girl, Kirsten. Again, this time with feeling.

I knew I sounded like a dial tone but it was that or start yanking on my earlobe.

"I was trying to tell you Sunday night when you threw me out," Wes said.

Wait—did I miss that?

"Isabel and I ran into each other at Joe's one night and we just started talking about stuff."

Now you're stuff? Punch him in the face!

"You mean me."

"We both love you and neither one of us could figure you out—"

"Stop, please." I was halfway out of the chair. "This was a mistake. I can't listen to this."

Shucks. Just when it was getting good.

Wes's face tightened. "I'm not leaving this time until you hear me out. I think you—I think we owe each other that."

You don't owe him jack!

"I don't see what difference it's going to make," I said.

"Maybe it doesn't make a difference to you, but it does to me, okay?"

And your point is?

I might actually have echoed the Nudnik if guilt weren't lapping at my insides. Guilt that wasn't attached to anything, but guilt nevertheless.

"Okay," I said. "I'm listening."

Wes slid closer to the edge of the chair. Even though I moved back

I could smell his breath, stale as yesterday's coffee, and the faint odor of sweat on his T-shirt. Three years together and I'd never smelled anything on him but Downy and SweeTarts.

Yeah, somebody hose this guy down. Orderly?

"Okay, so, Izzy and I started talking more and more and both of us came to the conclusion that you're just, I don't know, stable, and we're not. I thought maybe you didn't need to talk things through the way I do. The way we both did."

"You and Isabel."

"Don't say it like that. It wasn't like we planned what happened. We both needed somebody to talk to, and one thing just led to another."

He stared down at his hands.

Now *he stops giving details.*

I didn't want details. But I did want to know what happened that night—Saturday night—when Isabel's crisis brought our whole world in on itself.

"Did she give you an ultimatum?" I said.

"What?"

"Did she say you had to choose between her and me? Is that why she called you Saturday night?"

"No! Izzy would never do that. She knows I love you."

"This isn't making any sense."

Wes gripped my arms with hot, damp hands. I raised my shoulders to my ears and he let go, but he stayed close to my face, eyes digging into mine, edgy breath nearly taking mine away.

"I can't tell you why she called me. I promised her I wouldn't and I can't break that promise."

"But you could break a promise to *me*. A big promise."

"And I'll hate that I did that for the rest of my life. But this promise—it would hurt too many people if I broke it. I can't."

"So it matters more if it would hurt Isabel than—"

"It would hurt you too. You *have* to trust me on this."

And what I have to do is throw up.

"Trust you?" I said. "Really?"

"Okay, maybe I can't ask you to. But at least believe me: if you hadn't seen me kiss her good-bye, I would have come in the house and asked you to marry me and we would've worked it out somehow."

"And you and Isabel would have always had your little secret."

"It was over." Wes's voice rose and cracked. "We took care of that. We took care of everything. You never. Had. To know."

Just so we're clear: it was your *fault you saw him exchanging saliva with your best friend?*

"But I do know," I whispered. "And I'm always going to know."

That seemed like a perfectly reasonable response to me, but Wes threw himself back into the chair with his hands over his face. When he uncovered it, he was licking his lips, over and over, as if they, too, were covered in sandpaper.

"Is that what it is with you?" he said. "That you can't ever let anything go?" He lurched forward again. "See, I always thought you were a rock. But you're more like a locked-up box, aren't you?"

He was so close to the truth I almost nodded. But something besides understanding was churning in his eyes. I kept my head still.

"This," he said, nodding toward my bandaged hand. "This wasn't just about me, was it? A lot of people break up and they don't try to kill themselves over it. You didn't do this just because of me; I was just the tip of the iceberg. There's your father and your mother and your—"

"Let's get one thing straight," I said. The ice in my voice froze him for the moment I needed. "I didn't try to kill myself, and you know it, because you were there. All I wanted to do was cut myself, just a little bit, so I could relieve some of the pressure. I didn't want to die. I still don't."

Wes's face twisted. "You wanted to cut yourself? You're a cutter?"

"Yes."

"I don't—no, I don't buy that."

Oh, show him and get this over with.

Watching his face, I slid the neckline of the Penney's top down over my shoulder just enough to reveal three delicately wrought lines. The upper lip on that mouth I'd kissed a thousand times curled to his nose, and the eyes that had danced me into joy more times than that hardened into stones. It was no longer Wes I was looking at. It was the picture of revulsion.

Yeah, I'm not thinking that relationship was gonna work anyway. He's about to hurl over three scars. You'd have had to call 911 if he'd ever seen you naked.

Oddly, Wes was nodding. "See, I was right. This wasn't just about me. It wasn't my stuff that made you do that. This whole thing pre-dates me."

I didn't need the Nudnik for the poke that jabbed me in the throat. He hadn't come here for me. He had come here for him. It was all about Wes—and it always had been.

Slowly I lifted my hand and moved my fingers to my earlobe. "Did you come here to hear me say you're not responsible for me being here?" I said. "Okay, here you go: it's not your fault. Okay? You can leave here with a clean conscience." I gave my lobe a tug. "And please do."

Roman was there before Wes could even stand up. He didn't put a hand on Wes—much to the Nudnik's disappointment—but there was none of his usual charm as he said, "Time's up, dude. I think you've given her all the help she needs from you."

I stayed in the chair with my back to the door as their tennis shoes squealed across the linoleum. When I heard the locks drop into place one by one by one, I pulled out my cell phone and called David Dowling. My voice mail said: "I want to go with Sister Frankie. Can you set that up for me?"

Share this chapter with your friends!
Let everything bad escape and take the pain with it
so you can come back to life. #TheMercifulScar

Chapter
FOUR

Of course there was more to signing up with Sister Frankie than waiting out front until a cab showed up to take me to her. In addition to all the hospital red tape involved, including the removal of my stitches, David said she wanted to come down and meet and that she'd be there by two. When Roman came to get me, saying he was going to start charging me extra for escort service, I already had my meager possessions packed in the J.C. Penney shopping bag.

"Should I take this with me to the cell?" I said.

"Cell. I like it. I'm gonna start calling it that." Roman shrugged. "Bring it if you want, but you're not going to the cell. This is an outside meeting."

"Outside as in not in the building?"

"Don't get too excited. We're talkin' fenced-in patio."

Still, I should have been ecstatic. I hadn't breathed fresh air since Sunday afternoon.

Yeah, you're starting to look like the creature Gollum.

But as confining as the hospital walls were, they also separated me from everything I could do nothing about. Even my mother, who had only paid two more short—

Nanosecond goes beyond short—

—visits. When I told her I wanted to go with Sister Frankie's program, she'd pursed her lips like a drawstring bag and said, "I wish I'd never told you it didn't matter whom you talked to. These people are not professionals, Kirsten." My only response to that was to ask her again to honor her promise not to tell my father about any of this. At least her hatred of him trumped everything else.

The patio was a small area off the first floor, not far from the emergency room. Cacti in terra-cotta pots and a statue of St. Francis of Assisi made me guess it was designed for anxious relatives who felt the ER waiting room closing in on them. A blue aluminum awning was no match for the unforgiving Montana sunlight, and I stood with Roman in the doorway, blinking against its onslaught.

Yep, definitely the creature Gollum.

Apparently nobody's family members were that anxious about their condition that day because only one person occupied a round brushed-metal table: a thirty-something woman in a John Deere ball cap and cowboy boots, which she'd propped on a chair.

"I don't think she's here yet," I whispered to Roman.

"Do you know what she looks like?"

"Whatever a retired nun looks like."

"Don't look at me," Roman said. "I'm a Methodist. They said she was waiting down here."

The words were barely out of his mouth when John Deere Lady extricated her boots from the seat of the chair and stood up.

"Are you Kirsten?" she called from across the patio.

I nodded.

"They sure changed the habit since I saw *The Sound of Music*," Roman muttered out of the side of his mouth.

The woman hurried toward us, revealing with her smile a row of big, square, bright teeth that could have belonged to a third grader. As she got closer, though, I could see her face was sun-worked in early-leathered lines that fanned out from her eyes. Despite the trim figure in blue jeans and a crisp striped blouse, she had to be forty-five at least, but not the iron-haired, religious-looking spinster I'd expected.

I couldn't have predicted her voice either. The words, "I'm Frankie McKee," came out soft and warm. Like fleece. Not so much with her hands. They were strong and slightly hard as she grasped one of mine between her palms. She directed large oak-brown eyes at Roman. "What are the chances of this being a private conversation?"

"Good if you have some ID," Roman said.

Yeah, I want to see some, because—what nun wears a cell phone clipped to her belt?

Frankie dug into her back pocket and produced a driver's license. Roman scrutinized it and then her like he was an FBI agent.

"Hard to tell with the hat," he said.

She flashed him the new-teeth smile and pulled off the ball cap, uncovering a short mop of wavy auburn hair flattened to the crown of her head. Sister Frankie obviously wore that hat twenty-four-seven. As soon as Roman handed her license back she snuggled the hat onto her head again, and the tendrils at the nape of her neck curled up around it.

"I'll be over by the door," Roman said to me.

Before he turned away, he tugged at his earlobe.

Don't you start tugging yet. I want to see what this character is all about. Am I smelling horse poop on those boots?

As Frankie led me to the far table, closest to the low rock wall that separated us from the parking lot, I noticed that she was about a head shorter than me and more anchored to the ground. I felt too tall and klutzy, especially when I caught my foot on a chair leg and almost did a face-plant right there on the piazza. Frankie was either blind or she ignored it.

"You want anything?" she said when we reached the table. "Latte? Tea?"

I'll take a large caramel macchiato.

"I'm good," I said.

"You sure? I bet you haven't had a decent cup of coffee since you've been here."

"I haven't had a decent anything since I've been here," I said. "Except Roman. He's decent."

She slid neatly into a chair. "Does he refer to you as an SI?"

I shook my head.

"Then he's pretty decent. I have a problem with psychiatric labels. They limit us to our pathology."

Us. This woman couldn't possibly have a pathology. She was as together as any person I'd ever met. I could feel it all over my untogether self.

She adjusted her cap so the bill didn't cover half her face, and I could see the eyes that, now that I thought about it, almost matched what hair I could see.

"Tell me why you'd like to come and stay with me at Bellwether Ranch," she said.

"I don't," I said. "I just don't have any other choice."

Tell me you did not just say that.

I couldn't believe it myself as I clapped my hand over my mouth. I could feel my face simmering to red. "I'm so sorry," I said into my palm.

"Please don't be," she said. "I like your honesty."

Yeah, well, don't get used to it. It's not her typical MO.

"To tell you the truth, I usually am a young woman's only choice."

That didn't make me feel any better. My hands were oozing sweat.

She smiled without the teeth. "I get the feeling that kind of honesty is a new thing for you."

She's been wiretapping your brain.

"I don't lie," I said.

"It's okay if you don't really want to come. But can you tell me what you *do* want?"

"No," I said. Truthfully. "But I can tell you what I *don't* want. I don't want to die."

I see where you're going with this. But do you seriously believe she's going to buy that any more than anybody else you've tried to sell it to? Except the vicar, but he—

"And how do you want to live?" Frankie said.

"I don't even know."

"Then that's the perfect place to start."

The Nudnik's response was *Huh?* But there was something about this lady with her fleecy voice and her unapologetic hat head that made me want to be honest. Or at least commit no lies of omission.

"Aren't you going to tell me I have to stop cutting?" I said.

"No. It seems to be serving a purpose for the moment."

What?

"But this is going to be an environment where there'll be nothing I can use to cut myself, right?" I said.

"Is that what you want?"

"Well. No."

Frankie shrugged one shoulder. "Then no. Finding something to use would become your whole focus, wouldn't it?"

I nodded.

"You're an adult. Treating yourself better is your responsibility. But let me ask you this: do you *want* to stop hurting yourself?"

Let's see what you do with this one.

I looked at Frankie's sun-lined face and I couldn't tell it anything but what I knew.

"If I gave up cutting," I said, "I think I'd be giving up the only thing that's keeping me sane."

She didn't even blink the brown eyes. "All right then. But I will ask you to do one thing."

Here it comes.

"Try to replace the word *cutting* with *hurting*. Can we agree to that?"

Not exactly a deal-breaker.

"Okay," I said.

"And instead of calling yourself a cutter, try to think of yourself as someone who is involved in self-injury." She smiled, and for the first time I saw dimples that had just begun to stretch into lines. "Among all the other things you are."

Where do I start?

I pushed that one aside. There was something I didn't understand.

"If you're not going to try to get me to stop cutting—um, hurting—myself . . . no offense, but what is the point in my going with you?"

To get Mother off your back!

Frankie closed her eyes and opened them again before she answered. "I'm going to try to help you get to the place where you don't *need* to hurt yourself anymore."

My throat tightened. "And if I don't get there?"

"Then you'll be no worse off than you are right now, will you?" Her voice was soft.

Why are we even talking, then? What a lovely place to wind up. Right back here!

But *something* had to happen in thirty days, right? I could figure some things out and maybe even make up time in the studio when I got back. Still finish my degree on schedule?

Oh yes, we want to get on with that career you chose for yourself. Oh, wait . . .

I could do anything for thirty days. Especially if I was allowed to cut—hurt—myself when I needed to.

Ouch. Doesn't quite have the same ring to it, does it?

Then I could come back and—

Yeah, and?

"Okay," I said. "I'll come. When do I start?"

Frankie looked unsurprised, as if I'd just processed the whole thing out loud.

"We can leave here as soon as your psychiatrist releases you into my care and we get some instructions on how to take care of that wrist. I started the paperwork just in case, so it shouldn't take more than an hour. That will give you time to get your things together."

For the first time since we'd sat down, I smiled. Sheepishly. "I'm already packed."

"Then we both knew, didn't we?" she said.

Could we slow down a little? I'm having trouble keeping up.

"It's a four-hour drive to the ranch, so the sooner we get started the better."

Um, has it even occurred to you to inquire—

I tried to laugh and came out with a semi-croak. "I guess I should ask you what kind of ranch it is."

"David didn't tell you? It's a working sheep and cattle ranch up near Conrad."

No, David hadn't told me. Otherwise, all bets would've been off.

"He did tell you that I won't charge for the inner work I'll be guiding you through."

I gave the slowest *yeah* in the history of I-don't-want-to-hear-this.

"Your living expenses will be paid for by the outer work you do."

"With cattle?" I said.

"No, with the sheep and me. Is there anything else you need to grab before we go?"

I shook my head. "I might need to go by my house and get some, I don't know, jeans maybe?"

You're going to herd sheep in skinny jeans and leggings? This oughta be good.

"If you want to grab undies and pj's," Frankie said, "we can definitely make a stop. But I have everything else you'll need."

How about a straitjacket?

Was it really worth going back to the place where my heart had broken and poured its contents all over the bathroom floor? Even though my mother had said she'd cleaned it up, no amount of scrubbing could've scoured away the pain.

And Mother. She was already skeptical about me going off with a former nun. When she found out I was going to be shoveling manure, she would probably try to have me *and* Sister Frankie committed. Still, I had to tell her something.

How about adios?

"While you're doing the paperwork," I said, "I'll call my mother and ask her to pack a bag for me and we can just . . . pick it up."

"Whatever works for you," Frankie said.

It's not gonna work for Mother. Just sayin' . . .

I couldn't leave town without at least saying good-bye. And making sure that since I was keeping up my end of the deal, Mother was going to keep up hers. No Dad. Period.

After I said a tearful farewell to Roman, it took me as long to convince my mother that I was not being kidnapped into a cult as it did for Frankie to officially get me out of the hospital. The Louisiana Purchase couldn't have taken that long.

"I'll pack some things for you," Mother said on the phone. "But I think you're being too dramatic about this. There has to be some other program."

"Not for free," I said.

"Nothing is for free. Kirsten, you're too trusting."

So far we have too sensitive. Too easily moved to tears. Too emotional. Too dramatic. And now too trusting. Gee, Kirsten, looks like you're too everything.

While Mother, on the other hand, was never too anything. Never too flashy. Too intellectual. Too happy. Too affectionate. Too silly.

Everything except too nutso about Lara.

"I can't stop you from doing this," she said now. "But if you don't show improvement in thirty days, I will intervene."

No pressure or anything.

"I'll see you when we get there," I said. Although I was already planning to ask Frankie to go up to the door and get my bag for me.

You realize, don't you, that right this very minute your mother is going through your lingerie?

I didn't care. Suddenly all I wanted to do was get out of town.

———

By the time we reached my place in Frankie's somewhat-the-worse-for-wear Suburban, it was almost four o'clock and blazing hot. I wished for some dusky darkness so I didn't have to see the flattened flowers in the front yard where paramedics had tromped through with a stretcher, and the driveway where Wes had leaned into Isabel's window and betrayed me with a kiss.

I'm thinking he betrayed you with a lot more than that.

What I didn't see was a rental car parked there. My zebra-striped carry-on suitcase was on the bench on the porch, a white piece of paper tethered to the handle, fluttering in the ever-present wind.

Frankie swept her gaze over the scene and back to me. "You think that's your bag?"

"Would you mind?" I said, just before my throat closed.

She got wordlessly out of the car and returned with the case my father bought me when Wes and I joined him at Big Sky for Christmas. "The note is for you," she said.

My mother had apparently been through my desk, too, because the folded paper Frankie handed me was from a set of stationery she'd sent me for my nineteenth birthday and which I'd never opened.

Kirsten, she'd written flawlessly between the lacy edges.

The next flight I could get back to Kansas City leaves at 4:00, which will get me back in time to tuck Lara in. I'm sorry I couldn't wait for you. I've packed a week's worth of underwear, though I couldn't find any pajamas. I trust they'll have laundry facilities where you're going. We will want to hear from you, so please keep in touch. Remember, there is nothing you can't handle.

Yours,
Mother

The Nudnik was, of course, on it with *I love you too, Mom.*

As for me, I crumpled the note into a ball and stuffed it into the pocket of the one 100-percent cotton hoodie she'd bought me. Then I took a last look at the quaint house I'd taken such pride in fixing up. It no longer invited me in. It accused me. Of being a fool. Of being too hopeful. Of being too everything.

"I guess we can go," I said to Frankie.

"One more thing," she said.

I knew it.

"This is a four-hour drive. Plenty of time to reconsider. If at any time you want to turn back, just say the word and we'll make a U-turn."

Back to . . .

"I think I'm good to go," I said.

But when we backed out of the driveway, I said, "By going with you, am I running away?"

She looked at me, brown eyes shining. "Only you can really answer that, but I'll tell you what I think."

"Okay."

"I don't think you're running away. I think you're running for your life."

I could only hope I still had one.

> Share this chapter with your friends!
> *I don't think you're running away. I think you're running for your life.* #TheMercifulScar

Part
TWO

Now there was a great wind, so strong that it was splitting mountains and breaking rocks in pieces before the LORD, but the LORD was not in the wind.

1 KINGS 19:11

Chapter
FIVE

I lost count of how many times we crossed the Missouri River. Sister Frankie told me these were the headwaters, but with each bridge all I could think about was the fact that I was moving farther from the river's destination: the place my mother was running home to that very minute.

At least there's that.

It was my only comfort, really. The farther north we climbed in Frankie's Suburban, which smelled like wet dog—

Not to mention poop of unknown origin—

—and which even I could tell needed new shocks, the less I felt like any self I knew. In my five years at Montana State I'd never strayed far from campus and downtown, so I had no idea the seed-processing plants and funky one-casino towns we passed in our first thirty minutes out of Bozeman even existed.

You really need to get out more. Oh, wait . . . you are out. Way out.

Nudnik wasn't wrong. As we ascended into what Frankie told me was the Gates of the Mountains, I knew I was far from anywhere I had ever been. Even at dusk the walls of rock were so close I could have reached out and touched them if I hadn't been hugging my arms around my body.

"I wish there was more light so you could see the way it plays with the oranges and grays," Frankie said. "It is gasp-worthy."

Yeah, well, keep your eyes on the road, lady. If we go over the side, somebody's gonna be gasping over our mangled bodies.

Frankie went on to describe what I was missing, but most of it was in geographical terms that sailed right over my head, terrain-challenged as I was. A few familiar words came through now and then. Awe-inspiring. Majestic. Solid.

How about huge and scarier than Hades?

It was too big. Too much. I would have told Sister Frankie I wanted to go home—if I'd actually had one.

When we reached Conrad and Frankie said we were almost there, we still had several unpaved roads to traverse, each one less maintained than the one before. As we neared there, I was more disturbed by the openness than I'd been by the too-closeness of the mountains.

I thought I'd be glad to get out of the car when we finally reached the ranch and Frankie pulled to a stop behind a box of a house, but the wind lifted my hair and slapped it into my face the moment I opened the door. I had to grab the top of it with both hands; I was surprised my body didn't flap like a flag.

Frankie pulled my bag from the backseat and mashed her ball cap further down on her head. "You're getting a windy welcome," she said.

Windy? This is a cyclone! Take cover!

As if there *was* a place to take cover. Even at eight o'clock the last of the light still stuck stubbornly to the sky, and from the knoll-top we were standing on all I could see was space, dotted now and then with a dubious structure built low to the ground. Too much air. Too much openness.

Only because I was beginning to sound like my mother did I stop that roll and catch up with Frankie's pointing tour.

"That's the barn," she was saying as she gestured to the longest building in the collection. "Up the driveway and through those trees is the main house where I live and where you'll have suppers with us. Down there is the old bunkhouse."

Old *being the key word.*

"Beyond the barn, see, up on the hill? That's the sheep pen."

I followed her point with my gaze but at first I didn't see any sheep. Just a fenced-in hillside littered with low rock formations.

Yeah, well, I smell some*thing.*

It was a full twenty seconds before I realized those stones were actually wooly animals, gathered in clumps with their legs tucked under their bodies, motionless as the wind whipped around them.

Are they dead?

"You'll see them better tomorrow," Frankie said. "Let's get you settled and fed."

Bring on the trough.

Frankie led me along the side of the house down a path that was only a path because feet had made it one. Something rustled in the bushes that rose almost to the eaves, and I couldn't help jerking.

"We think a mama weasel has her nest in there," Frankie said. "I hope you get to see the babies. They're so cute."

A cute weasel. Now there's an oxymoron for ya.

We rounded the corner of the house and took several bowed-in-the-middle steps up onto a long porch that took a turn at the end and apparently went on from there. I had no desire to see where. I just wanted to get in out of the wind before it blew away what was left of my resolve.

That resolve didn't get any stronger on the inside.

Oops. Somebody forgot to call the interior decorator.

"They used to call this Crazy Trixie's House," Frankie said as she wafted a hand around the large, peeling room we stepped into, "because it was built for my great-great-aunt—my great-grandfather Maxwell's spinster sister—to stay in when she came to live with them on the ranch." She gave a husky laugh. "I guess she was a little too out-there to stay in the main house with them. When my grandparents cleaned this place out after she died at age ninety, they found the closets stuffed with every article of clothing she'd ever owned, including several corsets and about a hundred hat pins, and all these scrapbooks full of newspaper ads for everything from beauty tonics to booby traps."

Back up. What's a hat pin?

"We always called it Crazy Trixie's until the first two girls who came to us renamed it the Cloister," Frankie said. "We still kept a few of Trixie's touches, though." She pointed to a shadow box by the door that displayed what looked like a hankie, a pair of spectacles on a gold stick, and a yellowed advertisement for a three-wheeled car.

Crazy isn't even the word for it.

"When did she live here?" I said, more out of politeness than actual interest, seeing how I was now fixated on a flock of moths that circled the overhead light.

"From 1905 until 1945, and that was after she retired from thirty years as principal of the school in Conrad." Frankie's laugh was sympathetic. "Who wouldn't be a little crazy after that?"

Let's just hope the old gal had plumbing installed.

She had, as Frankie revealed on a quick walk-through. The bathroom was about the size of a linen closet with a water heater that took up half of it. I suspected the kitchen sink was the same one they installed in 1930. Everything was clean and tidy, but it still reminded me of one of those houses you see in black-and-white photos from the Great Depression.

Appropriate, don't you think?

All the rooms, except the bathroom, were huge and empty feeling, and it made me dread my first look at my bedroom. That was apparently going to be the last stop on the tour.

"You'll be sharing the house with another young woman, Emma Velasquez."

Frankie nodded at a closed door just off the second large room that backed up to the one we'd first walked into. It was like no floor plan I had ever seen in architectural school.

"She's still up at the main house but she'll be down later."

Wait a minute. Nobody said anything about a housemate.

At that point I didn't care. I just wanted to find a small place and crawl into it before I lost myself in these empty, high-ceilinged rooms.

"Yours is in the front," Frankie said and led me back through the first big area. Over her shoulder she added, "I think it's the best one in the house."

Now there's *a coveted prize.*

Frankie beamed as she set my bag on the floor of the corner room, and I didn't have it in me not to at least nod. Maybe to someone looking for a view it warranted some beaming. Two long curtained windows. Cream walls that reflected even the very last of the light. A pile of white quilts, yellowed from their life on a high, wide bed. And space. Enough space to open a cozy coffee shop. Enough space to make me as crazy as Aunt Trixie.

Frankie continued my orientation. "The closet is all yours. Lots of room here in the dresser." She dimpled. "Since they took out the corsets. I think you'll find all the ranch clothes you'll need but we'll know that better as you discover how your gifts fit ours."

I simply cannot wait. Where's Roman? I'm tugging my earlobe here!

I was still nodding as if my neck were a spring. Nodding to everything and agreeing with nothing.

"Are you hungry?" Frankie said. "Do you want to come up to the main house and have something hot? I'm sure there are leftovers."

I shook my head to both. Her whole face softened beneath the ball cap she was still wearing.

A hundred bucks says she doesn't take it off to sleep.

"This is a lot to take in," she said. "Why don't you fix yourself a snack in the kitchen and get some sleep? I'll be here for you at six—"

In the morning? Are you on crack?

"—so you'll want to be rested."

As if that was going to happen. Panic was already spinning in my head. Sleep was out of the question.

"I don't know," I said, eloquently. "I mean, what will I be doing? I'm not that coordinated—like, what do I wear?"

If Frankie thought she'd just made the first mistake of her therapeutic career by bringing me here, she didn't show it. "Definitely the hiking boots," she said. "Jeans. And a jacket at first until the chill wears off."

"Okay," I said, "but I don't know anything about . . . anything."

The husky laugh escaped again as if it came out purely by its own choice. "I doubt that," she said, "but don't worry. You'll learn as you go."

With my not entirely honest assurance to her that I had everything I needed, Frankie left and I watched her from the porch. The wind still pushed at her, but she walked as if nothing could move her from the path she was on. Two dogs—border collies from what I could tell—greeted her at the driveway and danced around, fur leaping happily with the gusts. Together the three of them disappeared through a gate and into the shelter of two fatherly cottonwoods, just as if they had stepped into another world.

And they weren't the only ones.

———

The very last of the light was sizzling out over the mountaintops when I crawled under the quilts and hid myself to sleep. When my cell alarm woke me up at five thirty, morning light was already seeping through the windows. That sealed it: there would be no getting away from the exposure up here. That was even more frightening than the prospect of going to the barn with Frankie and doing who knew what.

Doesn't actually matter what it is, you'll be a mess at it, so why are we even talking?

I wasn't. I needed coffee first and I didn't smell any, but I didn't want to go shuffling through the house to the kitchen in nothing but a too-big T-shirt when I hadn't even met my mysterious housemate yet.

So I explored the drawers and the hooks in the closet and came up with a pair of jeans that fit surprisingly well and a faded pink T-shirt that said *Agnus Dei* on the front. I wasn't sure what that meant but there wasn't too much chance it was something obscene, so I pulled it on and covered it with a brown hooded sweatshirt. Crazy Trixie had obviously not had central heating installed.

I also found a fleece-lined tan canvas jacket that had seen as many better days as Frankie's Suburban and a pair of the ugliest hiking boots I had ever seen.

And how many pairs of hiking boots have you actually laid eyes on?

One. Wes's. Right out of the L.L.Bean catalog. They made his skinny suburban self look earthy.

Suddenly it didn't matter what these camo-green and mud-brown ones looked like. I couldn't see them with the ache coloring everything.

I parked both the boots and the jacket by the front door and was about to go forage in the kitchen for coffee when I realized there was someone on the front porch. Doing push-ups.

Sheep ranch, my eye. We're talking boot camp.

So it would seem. I opened the door to find an at least partly Hispanic woman of about twenty-five pumping up and down on the porch floor, her body a perfect plank and her arm muscles toned as ropes. Although she breathed in whooshes as she counted, I didn't see even a glisten of sweat. The air was mountain-chilly, but at the rate she was going, I'd have been one large puddle of perspiration.

I started to back into the house when she jumped up and faced me, arms in C's at her sides. My back became one with the doorjamb.

"Oh," she said. "Sorry."

She stepped forward and stuck out her hand. I stared at it for an awkward moment before I realized she wanted me to shake it.

"You Kirsten?" she said.

"I am."

"I'm Velasquez. Emma."

"Petersen," I said.

"Okay," she said.

While both of us stood there groping for a conversation topic, I got a closer look at her. She had a pile of plump, dark brown curls cut to frame a small face the color of a café mocha. Her brown eyes were bright but clearly not happy, and her mouth, though full and pretty, didn't seem to know how to form a smile. She was currently chewing her bottom lip with square, Chiclet teeth.

"So the work's that hard, huh?" I said.

Emma looked at me blankly.

"Like, we have to train for it?" I said.

"No," she said.

Do I smell a duh-uh in our future?

"It's just what I do," she said.

And then she went back to doing it.

I'm not seeing you two becoming BFFs.

I couldn't disagree.

———

I made a cup of really bad instant coffee and drank it as I watched a white-bellied bird on the fence beyond the kitchen window. He was puffed up just like I was in my layers, which indicated to me that it was as cold out there as it was in here, but I wasn't about to approach the wood-burning stove in the corner, which as far as I could tell was the only source of heat in the place.

Between the chill and the caffeine, I managed to be wider awake when Frankie appeared on the porch on the dot of six. Emma had vacated so there was just me, Frankie, and two dogs with freckled noses and grinning muzzles. They pranced and jumped around me the same way they had Frankie the night before, only I didn't handle it as well as she did. As in, I backed into a rocking chair and heard myself making little oh-oh-oh sounds.

"Norwich! Undie!" Frankie said without raising her voice. "Off!"

They both dropped to a sitting position in front of me and continued to thump their tails on the porch floor as if they could barely contain the urge to bathe my face in slobber. It was more than a little unnerving. I'd never been a big fan of dogs so it didn't bother me that we never had one when I was growing up. Lara, on the other hand, wheedled for a puppy from the time she could talk until she had her personality transplant at age twelve. I had to look for a graceful way to cover my freak-out.

"Your dog's name is Undie?" I said. "Like underwear?"

Frankie chuckled. "Like Underhill. Evelyn."

Oh, that clears it up.

"And Norwich is named after Julian of Norwich. Both deeply spiritual women."

She smoothed her hand between Undie's ears. Or was it Norwich? Who could tell them apart?

Spiritual dogs. And she thought Aunt Trixie was crazy. This place gets more woo-woo by the minute, and you're only on Day One. Of thirty.

"Emma must already be up at the barn," Frankie said. "You've met her?"

Yes. Delightful girl.

"I have," I said.

Frankie picked up the two buckets she'd carried onto the porch, one metal and empty, the other a repurposed ice cream tub full of some kind of congealed greasy nastiness that made me want to lose my coffee. "She'll warm up. Emma's been through a lot."

And then without further explanation of *a lot*, she handed me a pair of heavy gloves and said, "Keep that wrist covered up until it's completely healed." Then she nodded for me to follow her.

Frankie walked softly even in boots, and yet deliberately, as if each step were intentional. Once again, beside her I felt too tall and angular and—

Face it: completely spastic.

I somehow managed to make it down the slope to the barn without falling into or stepping on anything, though when I got about six feet from the gate Frankie opened, I wished I'd at least sprained an ankle en route and was at this moment being rushed to a clinic. The smell was just about more than I could handle.

I'm thinking it's a nice mix of fresh mud, cow urine, and horse manure. I hope that empty bucket's meant for you to puke in because I don't see you getting through the next five seconds without hurling.

"Oh, for heaven's sake, Bathsheba, get down."

I followed Frankie's gaze as I passed through the gate. Above us, atop a tower of four bales of hay, sat a dog that looked—to me—just like Norwich and Underwear or whatever her name was. Actually, on closer inspection, she had a prettier face and softer eyes. Perched quietly on her tower she was preferable to the other two, who were now barking furiously on the outside of the gate. Preferable if you liked dogs, which I didn't.

"What's she doing up there?" I said.

"Being a simpleton," Frankie said. "She has fewer brains than one of these chickens."

You mean the chickens running over here to attack? Those chickens?

At least a dozen squawking, feathered beings were charging toward us, beady little eyes homed in on the bucket of grossness Frankie set on the ground.

"Last night's garbage," she said. "They love it."

So, apparently, did a gray-striped, bone-thin cat that joined the circle and took his turn at the potato peelings and bacon fat.

Yeah, good thing you didn't eat breakfast.

"They need grain too," Frankie said, "so your first job will be to feed them this."

She handed me a can that had once held coffee and was now half-filled with something brown and seedy. At least it didn't make me want to retch, but I still didn't know what to do with it.

"Spread it in a line right here," Frankie said, as if she'd read my empty mind. "I'm going to mix up formula for the bums."

What? There are homeless people up here?

"I already did it."

I looked up to see Emma, jacketless, sleeves rolled up and gloves already caked with something. I didn't ask what. She probably wouldn't have answered anyway. She didn't seem to notice I was even there.

I set about shaking seed from the container into a straight line. The chickens left the bucket to the cat and followed me in a frenzy, and it was all I could do not to drop the seed tub and escape to the top of the hay bales with Bathsheba.

I'm pretty sure Bathsheba wasn't a deeply spiritual woman. Just sayin'.

"You want me to get Hildegarde ready?" Emma said to Frankie.

"Let me get the bums fed first. Would you bring over some hay and put it in their pen?"

Okay, so bums were some kind of animal that ate hay and drank the white liquid in the I-couldn't-lift-it-on-a-bet bucket Frankie was now hauling out of the barn.

"When you're finished here, come out and see this," Frankie said to me. "This is the fun part."

There's a fun part? Really?

I took great care getting the chicken feed into a perfectly straight line, so that by the time I left the barn Emma was already coming up behind me with a bale about half the size of herself.

"Coming through," she said.

I stopped, and with an audible sigh she went around me, muttering something about me taking my half out of the middle. Feeling decidedly in the way, I hurried to the pen where Frankie was pouring the liquid into square containers on stands, each with three large red nipples sticking out of it. Below there was ceaseless movement and bleating and curly wool, all of which belonged to a crowd of lambs whose current goal was to get to those nipples.

"Where are their moms?" I said.

"Either they died or they can't feed their babies," Frankie said.

Emma grunted from the far side of the pen where she was pulling off handfuls of hay and dropping them in the corner. "That's why they're called bums."

That certainly clarifies it. What the what?

The bleating racket was replaced by eager sucking. A dozen lambs climbed on each other, all bent on nursing from the same nipple, even though there were more than enough of them for each to have its own.

"Why do they do that?" I said.

"Because they're sheep." I could hear the eye roll in Emma's voice. "One does it, they all do it."

Frankie gave her husky laugh as she hustled a few lambs to the waiting nipples. "They start acting like sheep early. I suppose we all do."

Emma grunted again.

Love this girl's vocabulary.

"You can go ahead and bring Hildegarde in," Frankie said in Emma's direction. "We'll feed the other bums."

Frankie was already headed to the barn so I followed her— because what else was I supposed to do? I wasn't going to stay out there with Emma sneering at me.

My question is, what does all this have to do with you cutting? Just asking . . .

Frankie handed me what looked like a large bag of dog food. I hugged it and fumbled to keep it from slipping down my body, though I was glad she'd given me that and not the bale of hay she placed against her hips and carried, face reddening, out of the barn and to a second gate that opened into a larger pen. I lost my grip on the dog food bag when a half dozen lambs, half again as big as the other bums, suddenly surrounded us and reared up to put their front hooves on the bag I had completely lost control of.

"You can pour that into those big metal cans," Frankie said.

She had her back turned, so I retrieved the bag without her seeing how ungracefully I did it and dragged it to the metal containers—it and three lambs who insisted on coming along for the ride.

They're like middle school kids, I thought.

Yeah, in Juvie.

While they devoured the pellets I poured for them, Frankie led me back through the gate—I thought she must spend half her time opening and closing gates that looked like large Fisher-Price toys—where something let out a long bawl that made me press against the nearest wall.

"And a lovely good morning to you, too, Hildegarde," Frankie said to a large milk-chocolate head with enormous brown eyes and pink nostrils so large I could have driven a Volkswagen through them. The cow looked like something out of a children's storybook, except for the fact that the tips of her horns appeared to have been chopped off.

She left her complaining to return to a bale of hay placed right below her. I'd have bawled, too, if I'd had to eat that way, with my head stuck between bars. We went through yet another gate so that we were beside Hildegarde, and then I realized she was in some kind of chute.

"Oh," I said.

My disapproval must have leaked through because Emma, who was perched below on a seat that seemed to have lost its tractor, looked up at me, lip curled.

"You want to try to milk her when she's not restrained," she said, "be my guest."

"No," I said lamely, "I'm good."

Frankie handed her the metal bucket. "You got this?"

Emma nodded.

"Kirsten and I will get the sheep. Just leave the milk by the pump and go meet Joseph."

Another nod.

Nice talkin' to ya, Emma.

I wanted to ask Frankie how long Emma had been there. If she was far enough along to be able to milk a cow, she must be about at the end of her thirty days. I sure hoped so.

Hands now free of buckets and bales, Frankie didn't open the gate this time but went over it. I must have climbed a fence at some point in my childhood, right? How hard could it be?

Apparently too hard for me. I got one leg over, but then neither one of them could reach the ground. I leaned to get a toe touch and suddenly I was flat on my back in what I hoped was mud.

But I'm not thinkin' so.

"You okay?" Frankie said as she put down a hand to help me up.

At least that was what I thought she said. It was tough to hear her over the hard staccato laughter coming from the direction of Hildegarde's udders.

Now *she locates her sense of humor. Nice.*

Why I expected Frankie to tell me to go get cleaned up, I have no idea. She gave my back a quick pass with her gloved hand and led me on, through the middle-school pen, where a couple of mother sheep—weren't they called ewes?—hurriedly got between me and their lambs. Some of the seventh-grade bums trotted after me, bleating for still more pellets. If they'd taken to making that disgusting sound with their armpits, I wouldn't have been surprised.

There was no end to the gates, but at least Frankie opened them instead of climbing over. Finally we were in the large pen I'd seen the night before, where the sheep had lain like statues in the wind. They were still quiet except for the occasional *baa* until Frankie called, "Avila!" and another dog bounded around the edge of the flock.

He—or was it she?—was larger than Norwich and Undie and although her white fur had been clipped into a buzz cut, I was pretty sure she was a Great Pyrenees. My father's second wife had one but I'd never spent much time around either her or the dog. Their marriage hadn't lasted long enough to get the pup housebroken.

"Avila's the guardian dog," Frankie said. "She's with the sheep twenty-four-seven. Without her, we'd lose half the herd to coyotes."

And you thought the domestic *dogs were bad.*

Avila now wove her way through the flock, and the sheep and their lambs began to stand up and stretch and pee and speak as if the white dog were giving them a wake-up call. Frankie made her way through them, too, to the top of the hill, where she stood gazing down at the milling, bleating mass. Even from the bottom of that hill, where I stood frozen with my back to the fence for fear of being trampled, I could see that she was looking for something in particular. What, I couldn't fathom. They all looked exactly alike to me. Alike and threatening, just by the sheer number of them. I didn't attempt to count, but there must have been five hundred, and now that they were stirring themselves up into the day, it was frightening.

"Kirsten!" Frankie called to me. "Come up here!"

She's as insane as old Trixie if she thinks—

But I shoved the Nudnik aside and made my way around the edge of the flock and up the hill. Most of the sheep ignored me. Those who glanced my way didn't actually seem to see me. All of them had a rather clueless look in their eyes.

"You look like I feel," I said to one of them.

I reached Frankie and felt instantly more secure standing next to her.

"I'm going down to the gate," she said. "You stand here and watch and let me know if any of them don't get to their feet. We want everybody up before I open the gate."

So much for security. But I nodded. I didn't have much choice. It was me, her, three dogs, and an endless flock. If I didn't do what she said, what *was* I going to do?

Once they were out of the pen, Frankie explained that the sheep had to be taken through the scattering of buildings, across a dry creek, and down the driveway to another gate that opened onto the public road. Once across that, they had to enter through yet another gateway and out onto their early summer pasture.

Piece of cake, right?

It was a half-mile walk. The longest half-mile I had ever taken.

I'd always thought—if I ever actually thought about sheep—that once one headed in the right direction, the rest would follow. Weren't sheep notorious followers?

It appeared that they were, but never where you wanted them to go. At least that was my take on my first herding experience. Placed at the back of the herd, my job was to make sure nobody strayed. No easy task since the entire rear flank was in roaming mode and none of them would go where I wanted them to go, and I had no clue how to change their minds.

There was definitely no point in talking to them. They were making such a racket I could hardly even hear the Nudnik. All two hundred lambs baby-*baa*ed for their mothers even when said mothers were standing right next to them. That rose to an even more deafening pitch when they got separated, at which point the little ones stood in the middle of the rushing flock and cried like Stevie Nicks until their mothers reclaimed them. As for the moms themselves, their complaints had the same voiceprints as a bunch of guys burping at a frat party. They belched—their babies cried—and everybody else served as back-up bleaters.

The dogs were no help to me. Norwich and Underwear— Underhaul—Undermine—

Whatever. Move on.

—were busy with the sides. As for Avila, she just got between me and the sheep as if to say, "Aw, let 'em have their fun."

I tried to figure out what Frankie was doing and do the same thing, but there was no rhyme or reason to it as far as I could tell. Sometimes she walked along beside them, and although I was two hundred and fifty sheep away, I could see her talking to them. Other times she broke into a run and called things to Norwich and Undie that spurred them into action but had absolutely no effect on Avila. When Frankie walked, I walked. When she ran I ran. Until my foot caught on something and I did a face-plant in the grass.

Were you planning to stay vertical at all today?

That cinched it: I had absolutely no control over my body. And this was supposed to be healing? As flailing and incompetent as I felt, I might as well go back and face Wes and Isabel and my shriveling education. Or join my mother in Missouri. Or call my father.

By the time Frankie got to me, I was on my feet, miraculously healed by lack of options.

"I forgot to tell you to watch for badger holes," she said.

"Badger holes?"

Yeah, those cute animals. Like the weasels, only meaner.

"That's what you got your foot caught in," Frankie said.

I put a speedy six feet between me and the opening, especially when she added: "We don't kill the badgers. They take care of the gophers for us."

The list of cuties gets longer by the minute.

Frankie pointed to the gate. "All right, we're looking good."

Which evidently meant the large crowd climbing over itself at the red metal gate by the road was an okay thing.

The dogs helped her move the sheep back enough for her to open the gate, and as they rushed through she opened the one on the far side of the road. I trotted aimlessly at the rear, stopping in front of the ones who had paused to graze on the grass that was right there in front of them—so why go farther, right? All I knew to do was stare at them until they turned and followed the group. Sometimes it took them as long as twenty seconds to get the message. The ones who lingered while their lambs engaged in play dates or decided they wanted to suck up some breakfast—they were harder to convince.

"Come on," I said to them, "you're going to make me look bad on my first day."

Too late.

But once the gate was closed behind the last of them and they immediately settled into quietly munching the rolling expanse of plants, Frankie smiled at me and said, "Not bad. You'll catch on."

And this is going to happen how?

———

My workday was over at noon, and the first thing I did when I got back to the Cloister was head for the bathroom to take a shower. That was when I discovered the first aid kit, a brand-new one with fresh gauze and tape and antibacterial ointment packed tidily into compartments. I could already feel relief flooding through me. First a full cleansing of the outside, then one for the inside.

Before I could do anything I had to find the vacuum cleaner and suck up the no fewer than twenty moths that had claimed the shower curtain as their home. Once I finally got the water to run hot, I hadn't even started to shave my armpits before I was standing ankle deep in gray water and Emma was banging on the door yelling, "Turn that off! You're clogging up every drain in the house!"

When I emerged from the bathroom wrapped in a towel, she was going after the kitchen sink with a plunger.

"You can't stay in there for ten hours," she said without looking at me. "The plumbing's old."

"I didn't know," I said. "Do you want me to help you?"

"Just get your stuff out of the bathroom so I can go in there and fix this."

I did get my stuff, including the first aid kit. With Emma focused on the mess I'd made, it wasn't hard at all to go into my closet, lay out the scissors and the towel and the gauze—and make a clean, shallow, beautiful incision on the inside of my upper arm.

I leaned against the closet wall, eyes closed, and let the blood go. And with it, the pain of hating myself. That was what I'd wanted to do that night: just let it go and feel the release from the burning and the spinning and the inside hurt I didn't understand.

When I opened my eyes, I focused on the fine, wet, red line, just deep enough to make me sure that I'd gone far enough, but not so much that I would die. I wasn't good enough for heaven.

As I wrapped a strip of sterile white gauze around my arm and taped it neatly into place, I decided that Frankie was wrong. I wasn't hurting myself. I was taking care of myself. Because clearly no one else was going to.

I felt better now than I had in weeks. Good enough to face the late-afternoon herding of the sheep back to their pen. And good enough to tell Frankie what I'd done as we walked out to the pasture. It seemed only fair, since she had given me the freedom to do it.

Maybe I wanted to see if she was going to chide me or comfort me, just so I'd know for sure.

My money's on chiding. Doesn't matter who it is, this stuff is a turn-off for people.

Frankie did neither. Before I even started to describe what I'd used, she held up her palm. Still walking, softly and steadily, she said, "I don't want the details, Kirsten. That is your private thing."

Didn't see that comin', did ya?

It *was* my private thing. I'd always protected it like it was something secret and sacred. But now that I'd shared it, willingly, Frankie's disinterest stung me. That and the fact that she followed up by jumping from topic to topic like a jackrabbit.

One minute she was pointing out the various kinds of grasses nodding in the wind and explaining that sheep do best in dry, arid climates but they need green grass. The next she was telling me everyone lives with some kind of paradox.

Give me Emma's grunts anytime. They're way more interesting.

One minute she was saying she had a precise plan for rotating grazing ground, and the next she was telling me everyone has a premise that guides her decisions, right or wrong.

What the—I'm getting whiplash!

One minute she was teaching me a rhyme: "Sedges have edges, rushes are round, grasses have joints all the way to the ground." The next she was saying we all need a rule to live by.

By then we'd reached the south pasture and Frankie leaned her elbow on the gate and looked at me and said, "What did you learn just now?"

That you have ADD?

I had no idea what she wanted to hear, so I just said, "That you love plants?"

Why don't you just tell *her she was boring you out of your skull?*

"Perfect." Frankie touched me lightly on the arm, right above where I had just released my shame. "Now you need to discover what *you* love."

I wanted to grab her hand and tell her I thought I did know what I loved—that it just didn't love me back.

But she had already turned to her sheep.

Getting them back to their pen was infinitely easier than herding them out of it had been. Until we got them right up to it and one group decided the grazing might be good over there between the tractor and a junked pickup truck.

"There's not even any grass there," I said to one ewe headed that way.

She stopped and looked at me, sort of, and I took a step closer to her in the hope that she would back up and we could get this done. When she didn't move I took another step, and instantly something warm was leaning against me, cutting me off from the clueless ewe. Avila was stronger than she looked. I wasn't going anywhere.

"I love it!" Frankie sang out.

You have strange taste, lady.

"Avila's telling you to give the sheep space," she said as she joined me. "We give them enough so they'll see where we want them to be and they'll follow, but we can't push them. We can only lead them."

You coulda told me that about twelve hours ago.

I had a feeling she wasn't just talking about the sheep, but I was too flustered to unpack that. I just followed Frankie on to my next task, which was locating the eggs the hens had laid in various places throughout the barn and its attached pens.

"They don't have nests?"

And then I wanted to bite my tongue off because Emma chose

that moment to appear on the scene, smelling like a horse and, of course, curling her lip.

I'm waiting for it to go up her nostrils.

"Wherever it's dark and soft, that's where they lay," Frankie said.

"Okay," I said.

"Good luck with that," Emma said.

I decided to start as far away from *her* as possible, so I went for a bale of hay that had broken open in the back corner of the barn. I hadn't taken two steps before I realized I had a companion. Bathsheba, who had been banished from the herding, brushed past me and dug her nose straight into the pile of errant straw I was headed for. I knew nothing about dogs outside of watching *Marley and Me* with Wes about six times, but I assumed the fervent wagging of a tail had to mean something.

Sure enough, when I stuck my hand in where Bathsheba was sniffing, I pulled out two brown eggs. A third one was in the dog's mouth.

"I'm just guessing here," I whispered to her, "but I don't think you're supposed to eat them."

It was too late to salvage that one, but from then on I stayed no more than a step behind her and every time she poked her nose into a hole of hay, I rescued the eggs before she could chow down on them. She never seemed to catch on.

Must be why she doesn't get to herd sheep.

I was starting to like this dog in spite of myself. We had a lot in common.

———

I planned to beg off from going to the main house for supper, but Frankie didn't offer that as an option. She just linked her arms through Emma's and mine and walked us both up the driveway and through the main house gate. Once within the shade of the two old man cottonwoods, I was at least grateful for the break from the openness. All day I'd felt exposed and vulnerable. Now I just felt vulnerable.

Well, one out of two ain't bad.

I shouldn't have been surprised by the inside of the long, low ranch house, but I was. My imagination had painted a picture of a farmhouse kitchen with a hitching post as a towel rack and a living room with a cracked leather sofa and a cowhide rug. I'd known some aggies at MSU, and their places always had that kind of décor.

Frankie was obviously no aggie.

We entered through a kitchen that seemed to be drenched in gold light, some of it absorbed by polished wood cabinets, the rest dancing on dark shiny countertops. There was no busy clutter. Only a row of pottery jars and a fat candle that burned by the sink. Yet clearly someone had cooked a meal, because the aroma that came from the spotless stove made even my mouth water. It occurred to me that I hadn't eaten for over twenty-four hours.

"Joseph made his potatoes," Emma said.

That was the second time I'd heard the name Joseph mentioned, and I still didn't know who he was. The cook maybe? If so, Emma was getting off easy working with him. Why hadn't I been offered that gig?

That theory fell apart when Frankie nodded me out of the kitchen and into a dining area. A tall, bony, sinewy man with smoke-white hair straightened from placing a crusty loaf of bread on the table and showed a weather-beaten face. Not that many chefs walked around in leather suspenders with binoculars swinging from a neck strap that had been knotted back together so many times it was basically nothing *but* knots. His face was weathered and taut across the cheekbones and I couldn't find a smile in his small blue eyes. No wonder Emma had been assigned to him.

Can't imagine a cuter couple.

"Joseph Maxwell," he said, in a voice low and crackly as a fire.

"Kirsten Petersen," I said.

"Figured as much," was his reply.

Nice to meet you too.

I pretended to be interested in the room, which was as polished and spare as the kitchen except for one of those crosses with the circle in it—Celtic maybe?—that hung on one wall and a stiff-looking painting of three primitive figures at a table on the other. I couldn't look away from it.

"It's beautiful, isn't it?" Frankie said at my elbow. "I'm not much for icons but I had to have that one." She bent her head toward an area that stretched from the dining room. "Look around if you want to. We'll be just a few minutes."

I wandered away from the once again silent Joseph, who was now lighting a pair of candles on the table, and into another room in which even the air was clean and simple save for the faint scent of incense. I suspected it had soaked into everything: the cherry shelves peopled with books and the four tweedy earth-toned chairs, each with its own generous throw. A thick round table in the middle of it all invited both propped feet and folded hands. Above the fireplace was another print, this one done in rust and brown and golden hues in a style as real as the other was abstract. A young woman sat on the edge of her bed, wrapped in an ancient robe, looking at the light pouring into her stone-floored room as if it were speaking to her. The confusion in her eyes was all too real.

Frankie materialized next to me in that way she had, an ironed and folded linen towel draped over her arm. "I see you like art too."

"I'm looking at the arches painted behind her," I lied. "I guess that's the curse of being in architecture."

"Henry Tanner had a wonderful eye for setting. You're familiar with his work?"

I shook my head.

"This one is *The Annunciation.*"

"So that's Mary," I said.

"Right."

I wish I hadn't asked. Until then I'd started to feel a connection with that girl.

"We're ready," Joseph said from the dining room.

I was expecting dinner, but when I took the seat Emma pointed me to, I learned not to have expectations in this place. None. At all.

"We would normally have our communion tomorrow night, Sunday," Frankie said, even as I gazed over the glazed pottery chalice and the matching pitcher of water and the bread and the linens. "But we thought since this is your first supper with us we'd celebrate it tonight."

"The Last Supper for your first supper," Joseph said.

I looked at him, surprised, and decided I'd just imagined that. His face showed nothing as he stared across the table at Frankie. I couldn't decide whether Emma was taking lessons from him, or she just gravitated to him because he was practically her mirror image.

"Blessed be God: our Father, His Son, the Holy Spirit," Frankie said, and began a communion like none in any church I'd been to. I hadn't read the story of the Last Supper in a while, but this was like a reenactment of it, only without Jesus.

If He shows up, you're in big trouble. 'Hey, Kirsten, haven't seen you lately.'

Despite the guilt, I took the hunk of bread Frankie passed me and dipped it into the cup I then handed to Joseph. At one point I glanced across the table at Emma. Her eyes were closed, but her mouth moved, soundlessly repeating the words Frankie was saying.

Is that the same mouth that laughed in your face earlier?

Yeah. Whatever was happening here was something sacred. But for Emma it *only* seemed to be happening here. As for me, I said the amens and helped clear away the communion things and bring on the platter of steaks and the enormous bowl of whipped potatoes and the covered dish full of roasted asparagus. I had to eat or I was in danger of passing out there on the terra-cotta-tiled floor. The first bite of meat that went into my mouth was so good it made me moan.

"You like elk, then," Joseph said.

I tried not to choke.

"A lot of people don't care for wild game," Frankie said, eyes twinkling in the candlelight.

"I guess I do," I said. "I never had it before."

I expected a guffaw from Emma, but she hadn't taken her eyes off of Joseph since we started eating. If there was anyone else at the table, she seemed unaware of it.

At least there's that.

I chowed on everything on my plate, even though I had never been a fan of asparagus, while Frankie and Joseph bantered across the table.

"Did she meet Hildegarde yet?" Joseph said.

Emma grunted.

"You get much out of her today?"

I couldn't tell which her he was talking about. It didn't seem to matter what he was saying or who he was saying it to, Joseph looked only at Frankie. Nobody, thankfully, was looking at me as I shoveled in the food.

"Not much more than a bad attitude," Emma said.

"She's nothing if not aggressively unreliable," Joseph said.

I tried not to stare.

Who'd a thought, huh?

"I'm going to have to bring Little Augie in tomorrow," Frankie said. "If you'll keep the heifer *et al* out of the way."

"*Et al*," Joseph said. "The brother to *et cetera*."

Expectations were definitely useless here. The conversation went on like that, yet just when I was getting used to the fact that this man who could pass as a cattle thief had a more sophisticated wit than most college professors, he stood up, announced he was walking Emma and me back to our place, and slung a very scary-looking rifle over his shoulder. With Frankie left behind, he said nothing all the way down the driveway and only mumbled a good night at our door before he strode down the hill. I watched from the porch as he let himself into the old bunkhouse.

"Where does he stay?"

"There," Emma said.

Charming digs. I think we got the upgrade after all.

Even though I didn't anticipate an answer, I still asked, "Who is he, anyway?"

Emma surprised me. "He's Sister Frankie's cousin. His uncle, her grandfather, owned this ranch before Frankie's parents took it over right before she was born."

"So why is he here now?" I said.

That was evidently pushing it, because Emma shrugged and disappeared into the house.

Not that it matters, Kirsten, the Nudnik said. *You're only going to be here for twenty-nine more days.*

That was suddenly the most depressing thing I could think of. I went inside and crawled under the quilts.

> Share this chapter with your friends!
> *Now you need to discover what*
> *you love. #TheMercifulScar*

Chapter
SIX

My second day on the ranch went much like my first, with one exception: Emma left before chores to ride out on horseback with Joseph.

Yes!

"What do they do all day?" I asked Frankie as the two of us and the dogs walked down to the barn.

"Joseph handles the cattle," she said. "Emma took far better to them—and to him—than she did to the sheep." She smiled faintly. "And me. Anyway, they're going out to check the steer we have grazing in a pasture we're leasing from a neighbor. We won't see them for a while."

That would have been fabulous news if not for the fact that with Emma not there, Frankie parked *me* on the detached tractor seat beneath Hildegarde's intimidating udders and tried to teach me how to milk a cow. That was one expectation that *was* met: I was a complete disaster.

From the moment Frankie showed me how to slather udder balm on Hildegarde's, well, udders, the Jersey took a disliking to me.

Dislike? Don't you think that's understating the case a bit?

"She hates me," I said to Frankie as the cow bawled and did a two-step with her back legs while I tried to grab that third, elusive hangy-down thing.

"She hates everybody." Frankie perched on a nearby hay bale and reached out to take the jar from me. "She's such an unpleasant bovine. That's why Joseph sawed off the tips of her horns."

"He *sawed* them?"

That's one guy you're gonna want to stay away from.

"Hildegarde got him one too many times."

"No wonder she yells like that."

Frankie laughed her husky laugh. "No, she just wants her calf. I have to keep them separated at night so he doesn't drink her dry before I can get to her. We may have to bring him in to get her started, but let's give it a try without him first."

You give it a try. I don't trust these steel bars to hold her.

Frankie demonstrated how she held a teat and worked her fingers to pull and stretch and squeeze, all at the same time. A thin, almost blue stream sprayed weakly into the metal bucket.

"Is that, like, the nonfat milk?" I said.

Frankie grinned. "No, she's just being stingy. But give it a go."

That was when the disaster happened. The minute I squeezed my fingers around her, Hildegarde howled like I was killing her and tried to stomp around in the chute, succeeding in knocking the bucket back far enough so she could poop right into what milk Frankie had gotten out of her.

Note to self: refuse all dairy products here . . .

"Hilda, honey, that was obnoxious," Frankie said. "Okay, Kirsten, you go clean out the bucket—there's a hose and some soap over there—and I'll get Little Augie."

Here's your chance, Kirsten. Run!

Maybe I would've if my stomach hadn't turned itself inside out while I took a hose and some disinfectant to the bucket of disgustingness. In only a little over a day I had encountered five different varieties of animal excrement—and I hadn't even been around the horses yet.

Yeah, I understand their patties are huge . . .

When I got back to Frankie and Hildegarde, a black calf had joined the party. At least, Frankie said he was a calf. I'd seen ponies smaller than he was. One look at his face and I knew why they called him Little Augie. Between the massive shoulders and the forehead that glowered rebelliously above his eyes, he was a dead ringer for a mafia hit man.

He acted like one too. While Frankie sat on one side of Hildegarde, Little Augie stood on the other side and banged his head against his mother's udder bag.

"Doesn't that hurt her?" I said.

"I don't hear her complaining," Frankie said.

Hildegarde was now giving up milk so thick I didn't see how it came out of the holes. Frankie kept two long nipples going while Little Augie sucked and slobbered and pulled at the other one. It was both fascinating and disturbing. The best part was, I wasn't involved. I sat on the hay bale and intended to keep it that way.

"Augie is getting a little big to be nursing," Frankie said, "but I don't want to wean him for at least another month. I think they both need it." She pulled out the pail and smiled up at me. "And they sure give us some great milk."

I looked down at a wisp of hay swimming at the top of the bucket. "What happens to it now?"

"I strain it and put it in the refrigerator. This will last us about a day, the way we go through it."

I swallowed. "You don't pasteurize it?"

"No, that's why I can't sell it. But you will never taste anything richer."

Uh, thanks but no thanks. I'm trying to lay off the salmonella.

"I'm sorry I was so bad at this," I said. "Emma seems like she just takes to everything."

"You'll catch on," Frankie said. "As for Emma, she mostly just takes to Joseph."

Ya gotta wonder what that's about.

Frankie joined me on the bale. "Part of the draw to Joseph, I think, is the military connection. Emma served in the armed forces, did she tell you that?"

No. You can't get that information from a grunt.

I shook my head.

"Joseph did two tours in Vietnam back in the sixties. When he got out of the army, he was only twenty and came here to help my parents run the ranch. And that was fortunate because they had no earthly idea what they were doing. They had both dropped out of Montana State to escape the Establishment, they said, but Joseph was a serious student of agriculture before he was drafted."

Frankie picked up the milk pail and led the way out of the barnyard toward the pump where she apparently always left the milk while we herded the sheep.

Reason number two not to drink that stuff.

"We were just babies when he came, so I grew up with Uncle Joe, as we called him then."

"But he was actually your cousin," I said.

"Technically, but he was always so much more than that to us. And to my parents." Her smile was wistful as she set the pail down. "They were basically hippies who had this pastoral idea about keeping sheep when they inherited the ranch from my mother's parents. If it hadn't been for Joseph, we probably would've starved to death."

"So he's been here ever since?" I said.

Frankie tilted her head, and I watched a decision being made in her brown eyes.

"In a manner of speaking, yes," she said finally. "All right, let's go get the woolies."

———

It wasn't another day of feeling totally inept that made me want to cut again that night. I did still feel like I couldn't do anything right, but I was almost getting used to that. I actually found myself being a little amused by the sheep that evening as we were herding them back from the south pasture. I could almost laugh at the way they'd head straight where they were supposed to go, but then suddenly trot off behind some teenage-looking wooly and head up a hill or come to a complete halt to graze on spiky clumps of grass when the thick, silky stuff awaited them just ahead.

At least, I *was* amused, until I watched a particularly desperate ewe take off after the one and only black sheep in the flock and suddenly saw myself in her. How much different had I been when I followed Wes around for three years, going to church and campus ministry because that was what he did? Or making his friends my friends when I had nothing in common with them?

You mean you never actually dug *online alternative rock . . . fusion food . . .*

But it was really Bathsheba who took me into I-have-to-cut territory that second day. Every time I went into the barn area, she leaped down from the tower of hay bales as if she'd been waiting there for my arrival her whole life. She never jumped around like the other dogs, but she deposited about a cup of saliva on my hands and then capered along at my side, tongue hanging out, eyes gazing up at me like . . .

Like I'd always gazed at Wes. Just like Bathsheba, I'd waited for him to show up, and I was always there with the affection and the adoration and the downright sickening devotion. That night when Frankie and the rest of us had tucked the sheep into their pen and were headed up to the main house for supper, Bathsheba stood behind the barn gate and whined as she watched me go.

"Does that dog actually do anything around here?" Emma said to Frankie.

Frankie gave me a sideways look. "I think she does now."

Oh, good. Now you're going to have that hound panting after you wherever you go.

That was the image in my mind that night when the sun finally went down around ten. Emma was in her room—I assumed she was asleep, although, "Good night, Kirsten," didn't seem to be in her repertoire—and it was dark enough that I didn't have to go into the closet with my instruments and my first aid kit. I was still stunned that Frankie had provided not only scissors but fresh disposable razors that were a snap to disassemble. But as I laid out a sharp piece on a clean towel on the dresser and opened the first aid kit, that didn't feel like trust to me.

Nah, it feels more like, You're gonna do it anyway so here's the stuff. Have at it.

That wasn't it either. I couldn't name it. But when I made the delicate cut just below the one from the day before, the perfect trickle of blood took no pain away with it. The ache I didn't understand was still in there, still in me.

Maybe it's time to go deeper. Use some elbow grease.

I tightened my fingers around the blade, but I stopped just above the skin and stared at yesterday's wound. It was still pink and tender. It hadn't even begun to scab over yet.

That one didn't last you long, did it?

I could feel bubbles of fearful sweat break out on my upper lip. Again I squeezed the blade tighter between my fingers. I might have gone deeper. I might have—if Avila hadn't barked.

I jerked my hand back and let the blade fall onto the dresser.

You think she's barking at you? You're an idiot—she can't even see you from up there!

I just hadn't heard her bark like that the nights before. Long and insistent. Urgent.

Nor had I heard the sounds that were coming through my bedroom wall, on the side it shared with Emma's room. Sharp cries cut through the wallpaper and then a scream. And another.

Pressing my hand against the blood on my inner arm, I ran through the first living room and then through the second to Emma's door.

"Are you okay in there?" My voice shook.

No answer. Just the kind of crying that made me think whatever Avila was barking at was right now attacking Emma in her bed.

"Emma!" I said, and then tried the doorknob. Locked.

Okay. Okay. Think. Go get Frankie? No, Joseph was closer.

I was headed, barefoot and still bleeding, toward the living room, when Emma's cries suddenly stopped. She moaned softly and then all was quiet. Outside, Avila was still carrying on as if an entire regiment of coyotes was descending on the sheep pen. Surely Joseph was going to go investigate—

I ran through the house and flung myself out the front door and stumbled to the end of the porch that overlooked the bunkhouse below. Joseph was just coming around the corner, long gun in hand.

"Joseph!" I called out.

He barely turned his head my way. "Get back inside."

His bark was not that different from Avila's, and I was sure the bite would be just as bad, but I leaned over the railing and screamed at him, "It's Emma! She's being attacked in her bed and I can't get in!"

He strode toward me and stopped halfway to the porch. "It's a nightmare," he said.

"I know!"

No, moron, he means an actual nightmare.

"She'll go back to sleep," Joseph said. "Now get inside."

He didn't wait for me to obey before he resumed his march toward the sheep pen and a now frenzied Avila. I crept inside and went back to Emma's door and tapped with my knuckles.

"Are you okay?" I whispered.

A sleepy moan was her reply.

I crawled into bed without wrapping my arm and listened until Avila stopped barking and all was silent again. Then I hugged the quilts and envied Emma the sweet sleep of release.

———

The next morning (*Day Three of thirty,* the Nudnik reminded me) as Emma walked with Frankie and me down to the barn, she showed no sign she'd wrestled with her demons the night before.

What are you thinking? She never shows a sign of anything.

At least not until Joseph showed up at the barn about a minute after we arrived. Then it was as if she'd just taken two shots of espresso. I let myself into the bum lamb pen to fill the pellet troughs, but I could hear the three of them in the corral that bordered it where

Joseph kept a few horses. I could also see Emma astride the top of the fence taking in his every move.

"That mother grizzly and her yearling cub killed thirty-four lambs and ewes at Cunningham's last night," Joseph said.

What *mother grizzly and her cub?*

"With the five rams they took out at McAllister's the other night, that brings the damages up to ten thousand dollars."

Joseph's voice was flat. Frankie's was not.

"Not to mention the grief and frustration," she said thickly.

I paused with one hand in the pellet-filled trough and wondered if I could feel grief for sheep. Frankly, I was having trouble feeling anything but fear right now.

Ya think? Grizzly *bears?*

Something larger than a lamb's nose nudged my hand. Joseph apparently saw at the same time I did that it was not one of the bums who was hocking back pellets as fast as he could, but Joseph's large, star-faced horse who had poked his muzzle between the rails.

"Don't let him eat that," Joseph barked at me.

How do you not *let him? That thing is a Clydesdale!*

I gave the horse's nose a timid push but he continued to chomp. Emma slid off the fence, popped him in the face with her hat, and plunked it back on her curls.

"I haven't spent much time around horses," I said.

As in none.

"Merton is not your typical horse," Frankie said.

She was the only one laughing. I didn't count the snickers Emma was covering with her hand.

"Why aren't you carrying, Frankie?" Joseph said.

I didn't have to ask what it was she was supposed to be carrying.

Joseph hitched the ever-present gun strap up on his shoulder and put his hands on his hips. He really was just bones and sinew.

"I don't think the grizzly will barge into the barn," Frankie said. "Has anybody seen my hook?"

"You're not going to take her out with a hook."

"Not the bear—the ewe I need to get back into the flock. She's getting a little lazy back there with the big bums. She's played the I-have-a-delicate-lamb card long enough."

I had no idea what either of them was talking about.

Shocking.

But it was clear what Joseph had in mind as he took his gun off his shoulder and hung it on Frankie's.

"I don't need to lug a thirty-aught-six around all day," she said.

"You need something."

"I'll get my thirty-thirty before we take the sheep out."

Joseph gave her a long, steely look that would have gone right through *me*—and nearly did when he turned it my way. I jumped and sent several bums cowering into the corner.

"You make sure she does it, you hear?" he said.

His eyes went immediately back to Frankie but I nodded anyway.

"All right," he said. "Emma, give me fifteen minutes and then you and I'll go do some real work."

"Yes, sir." Emma's dark eyes gleamed as if she were waiting for the response she knew was coming.

"What did I tell you about calling me sir?" he said. "I work for a living."

That was apparently what she thought she'd hear because Emma smiled. Big and broad and sure. It made her pretty.

"Good," Frankie said. "I need your help back here, ladies—both of you, if you will?"

I wasn't sure anybody needed my help around there but I followed Frankie to the other bum lamb pen and mentally named it Bellwether Middle School.

"So, Kirsten," Frankie was saying, "the best way to catch a sheep is by one of its back hooves."

I could feel paralysis setting in.

"And the best way to do *that* is with a hook."

Gee, what a relief. I thought we were going to have to wrestle it to the ground.

I stood, arms folded, against the ubiquitous stack of hay bales and watched as Frankie picked up a six-foot, maybe longer, metal pole with a hooklike contraption on the end, walked over to a rather plump ewe, and snapped the thing around her back hoof before the ewe even seemed to register that Frankie was after her. I guessed sometimes it was a good thing that sheep were stupid.

Great. Hooking lesson over.

But Frankie let the ewe go and handed the hook to Emma.

Uh-oh. Looks like everybody gets a turn to play Little Bo Peep.

At that point the ewe was somewhat wise to what was going on—as wise as a sheep gets—and she ran clumsily across the pen. Emma walked slowly after her and the moment one of those back feet was airborne she snapped the hook around it and the ewe went down on her side.

"Perfect!" Frankie said.

By then the ewe's equally as chubby lamb was bleating her curly head off and her mother was burping back at her as if to say, *If they take me out, run for your life!*

I was about to run for mine when Frankie unhooked the ewe yet again and walked toward me with the hook.

"I don't think so," I said.

"It's not actually that hard."

I looked, dumbfounded, at Emma. Her eyes weren't taunting and her shrug was actually a little reassuring. Only that made me take the hook from Frankie—and then look hopelessly at the ewe who was now pacing frantically up and down the pen, trying to get to the hysterical lamb Frankie had barricaded into what looked like a playpen.

"Do just what Emma did," Frankie said. "Wait until you get a clear shot at one of her back hooves and then grab it with the hook. Let the hook do the work."

I can't describe what happened next because it all went down so fast I don't even *know* what happened. After about ten tries and misses, both the ewe and I were so frustrated, I was sweating like a pig and she was peeing all over the pen.

"Give her a minute to calm down," Frankie said.

I didn't know whether she was talking to the ewe or me, but I was sure it wasn't going to happen for either one of us. I just wanted to get the whole thing over with, so I took a huge breath and moved slowly, with exaggerated strides, straight at the ewe. She was between me and the fence so there was no place for her to go. She tried to jump over another playpen, which meant a foot came up, and I lunged for it. The hook didn't catch on her hoof. The whole pole knocked the ewe completely over and left her on her back with all *four* hooves pawing the air.

"I'm sorry!" I said, and waited for the poor thing to get up. But she just kept struggling as her eyes went wild.

"Why doesn't she get up?" I sounded as hysterical as the lamb, which had gone hoarse crying for her mom.

"She can't," Frankie said. "She's cast."

Why can't these people just speak English?

"That means she's on her back," Emma said, and for a horrible moment I thought I'd blurted out the question.

"Once they land that way, they don't stop struggling so it's impossible for them to receive help." Frankie put both hands under the ewe's side and rolled her the other way. In a flurry of hooves and hay and probably poop, she scrambled to her feet and thundered across the pen to her lamb.

Only twenty-eight days to go.

I watched Frankie deftly hook the ewe again and get her and her traumatized lamb into the big pen with the rest of the flock. Something had better happen for me pretty soon or there were going to be a whole lot fewer than twenty-eight days.

"I'm glad you came."

I turned to stare at Emma, who was coming back from closing the gate behind Frankie.

"I'm sorry, what?" I said.

She shrugged her perfect square shoulders. "I'm glad you came so there's somebody to help Frankie with the sheep. That leaves me free to work with the cattle."

"You're into them, then," I said.

"Yeah. I don't have the patience for sheep."

I couldn't help laughing, although it came out more like a snort. "And I do?"

"I wouldn't have tried as many times as you did to hook that stupid ewe. I was just lucky to snag her on the first try today."

"I don't think that was luck," I said.

I felt myself warming up. Sheer loneliness will make you run to any glimmer of kindness you see. Sort of like Bathsheba.

"You must have worked on a ranch before," I said.

Emma shook her head. "I've just always liked to be outside doing stuff."

"That why you joined the military?"

Suddenly it was as if I were watching someone flash freeze. Emma's eyes went dull and her arms stiffened beside her.

Way to frost the room, Kirsten.

If Joseph hadn't called to her from the corral just then, I was sure Emma would have stopped breathing. At the sound of his voice, she visibly melted and brushed past me to go to him.

Wow, Nudnik said.

I couldn't have agreed more.

———

It was hard to get Emma out of my mind the rest of the day, unless I was thinking about the endless days I had left. They were both the same thing actually. How was being there doing either one of us any good? Emma had nightmares and turned into a pillar of salt if Joseph wasn't around. I still wanted to cut, and even that didn't have the effect it did before. I decided it was time to ask some questions that didn't have anything to do with chickens or sheep.

That night Emma stayed at the main house with Joseph after supper and Frankie walked me down to the Cloister. Being alone with her right then was the first break I'd caught since I'd been there.

Of course, once she hooked her arm through mine and we started our walk, I wanted to wimp out, so I just blurted: "Sister Frankie, no offense, but when is my therapy going to start?"

She was quiet as we continued down the driveway but I didn't get the sense that she was offended, so I waited. And waited. Until we were on the front porch. She sat in one of the creaky wooden rockers and I perched on the edge of the other. This was more like how I imagined therapy to be.

"Do you know the concept of *bat kol*?" she said.

I shook my head. "Is that a psychological term?"

"No, it's actually from the Jewish tradition. It literally means 'daughter of the voice.'"

"I don't understand."

I tried not to sound like I was gritting my teeth but I wasn't having much success. My words squeezed out like they were coming through a sieve. If Frankie sensed that—and what didn't she sense?—it didn't even flicker in her eyes. The eyes now turning the gold of the sunset beyond the porch.

"When you hear the voice of God indirectly, the Jews call it *bat kol*, the daughter of the voice," she said.

Look out, we're entering the Twilight Zone.

"It's more like an echo that comes through seemingly chance things. Like the lyrics to a song or the way a painting speaks to you or an offhand comment from a stranger. It doesn't take the place of Scripture, where God has already spoken. But it never runs counter to Scripture. It supports it, in fact."

Frankie fell silent except for the squeak of the chair as she rocked it against the porch floorboards.

O-kay. And what are you supposed to do with that?

"What am I supposed to *do* with that?"

The words were out before I could stop them, and yet I wasn't sorry, even as I heard my mother in my head saying, *Don't take that tone, Kirsten.*

Frankie stopped rocking. I held my breath.

"Kirsten, my dear," she said. "Your therapy just started."

"What?" I pressed my hands to my temples. "I'm sorry—I just don't get it."

"Evidently you do because you're starting to ask the right questions."

"What about the right answers?" I said, without prompting from the Nudnik.

Frankie leaned across her lap, hands on her knees, face alive. "Here's the first answer," she said. "Here's what to do . . ."

Wait for it . . .

"Listen for *bat kol*," she said. "Listen and you'll hear it. That's where therapy begins."

That's it?

I wondered that myself as I watched Frankie take her slow, steady walk across the grass to the waiting Norwich and Undie. She'd made it sound so simple, but I couldn't think of anything more convoluted, starting with the fact that there was no way God was speaking to me. I hadn't given him five minutes in months.

Maybe that's why He's going to do the talking through somebody else. Just sayin'.

I rubbed my thumb over the two new wounds under my arm.

"That somebody better show up soon," I whispered. "Real soon."

———

The next day, I experienced no *bat kol* or bat mitzvah or batlava—

*I think that's bak*lava *. . .*

Nor was I able to strike up another conversation with Emma or get more than the occasional bark out of Joseph. Although Frankie talked to me when we were together, it was about all the things sheep couldn't do. That included biting, kicking, scratching, spewing venom, running fast, or even looking up.

"They're basically lost without a shepherd," she'd told me. "That's why I feel like what I do is sacred work."

At least she didn't take me right to the Twenty-Third Psalm. Emma was wrong about me having patience.

Frankie and I did have one conversation I could get into. Just as

Joseph had ordered, she now carried her gun with her whenever we left the barn—hung casually over her shoulder like a Coach bag. I asked her if she would use it if we met up with a bear.

"It would depend on whether she looked like she was going to attack us," Frankie said as if we were talking about locating the cosmetics aisle at Macy's. "By law you're not allowed to shoot one unless it's going after a human."

"You couldn't shoot that grizzly if you caught her killing your sheep?"

"Nope. Our only recourse would be to call the wildlife people and they'd come and shoot her with a tranquilizer gun, basically. Then they'd take her off someplace and let her go."

Let's get back to what to do if Mama Grizzly is about to kill you.

"So if we met up with her . . . ," I said.

"Well, first of all, the best thing to do is back slowly and quietly away. They aren't usually aggressive with humans. Grizzlies are really fairly reclusive. On the other hand, a grizzly can move at thirty-five miles an hour, so you aren't going to outrun it. Just a calm, slow, backward walk is what you need."

"Why do you need a gun, then?"

Frankie's face winced. "As I said, they aren't usually aggressive . . . unless you have food, which we don't usually walk around with. The problem with this bear is that she has the cub. If she thinks you're endangering her baby, all bets are off. Were she to actually attack to protect that cub and our lives were clearly in danger, I'd have to try to take her down." Frankie tapped her gun. "With a thirty-thirty, I'd probably have to shoot until the gun was empty, and even then it would have to be in her neck or head." She stopped herself as my face went pale. I could feel it. "I'm a good enough shot that I could at least slow her down enough for us both to get away."

"And what should I do?"

Frankie grinned. "Run like your life depended on it. Because it would."

I can't believe you just had that conversation with a nun.

Nah. By that time, I could believe just about anything.

Still, my loneliness swelled. Except for Bathsheba. She greeted me every morning at the barn like I was arriving just in the nick of time with a kidney for her transplant, and no matter how hard I tried to ignore her, she followed me everywhere, including into the outhouse behind the horse corral. It was difficult to pretend she wasn't there when the thing was only three feet square. She all but fetched the toilet paper for me.

I finally gave up and let her climb into my lap when I sat on the hay bale watching Frankie milk Hildegarde, and I got permission to take her with me when we moved the sheep. She was absolutely no help, but she wasn't really in the way either. Most of the time she got bored with the whole thing and took off to chase some low-flying killdeer. Fortunately the sheep never followed her, and Norwich and Undie only looked at her with complete disdain and went back to doing their thing. When Joseph commented that Bathsheba was about as useless a dog as he'd ever seen, I decided the two of us might as well stick together. From then on, she slept on our front porch, curled up under one of the rocking chairs like a cozy ball of yarn. I was under strict orders not to let her in the house, which was fine. I was, after all, the woman who didn't like dogs.

———

Day Five dawned hazy and gray, kind of like my mood. That didn't get any better when, after we took the sheep out to the south pasture, Frankie announced I needed to learn how to buck hay.

I don't know what that is but it can't be good.

Yeah, one more thing I was going to stink at. That prophecy was fulfilled when both Bathsheba and I were standing on top of a sky-scraper of hay bales, where I was barely managing to hold one against my hips the way Frankie instructed me from the bed of the pickup truck below, and she said, "Okay, good. Now toss it to me."

Laughter exploded straight out of my gut.

"*Toss* it?" I said between snorts. "You want me to *toss* it?" I snorted again. "I can hardly lift the thing and you want me to toss it."

Funny. That's exactly what I was going to say.

Frankie said something but I couldn't hear it over my own guf-fawing. All I could do was stand there with my arms full of hay bale and howl. And try not to wet my pants.

"I'm glad somebody thinks this is fun," a male voice said.

I was surprised—okay, astonished—

I've always wanted to use that word—

—to see a dark-haired youngish guy standing beside the pickup. Make that an attractive, wavy-dark-haired guy with shoulders that looked like he'd bucked a fair amount of hay in his twenty-something years and intelligent black eyes that said he'd never done anything but disprove the Theory of Relativity. Or something.

It was in my favor that those swarthy good looks didn't fall under my type. I also benefited from the fact that I wanted nothing to do with men ever again. Otherwise I would have dropped the bale of hay the six feet between me and the ground—and possibly dropped with it.

Besides, if I was astonished by this guy's appearance on the scene, Frankie was obviously flabbergasted.

Another word I've always wanted to use.

She leaned both hands on the sides of the truck bed so that her face was level with his and she just looked at him. I could almost feel her soaking him in with her eyes.

"Andy," she said finally, in a voice I'd never heard her use. It was almost motherly, though nothing close to it had ever come out of my *own* mother.

"Do I get a hug or what?" he said. And then he grinned. I'd only seen one genuine, tooth-filled, cocoa-warm smile to match it—and that was on Frankie herself.

She gave him her replica as he held out his arms and she fell into them, right off the side of the truck. He lowered her by the waist like she was made of air and engulfed her against his chest.

Meanwhile, my arms were starting to shake as I stood there holding a hay bale that wasn't getting any lighter. I raised one thigh to try to balance it. Big mistake. Hay and I teetered sideways and headed for the ground. Fortunately the bale made it there first. Then me. Then the big handsome grin and the square, muscled hand that reached down to help me up.

I scrambled up without it and felt the spontaneous combustion on my face as I looked down at the hay that no longer qualified as a bale.

"How do you put it back together?" I said. It was the only thing that came into my mind.

The guy, whose name, apparently, was Andy, laughed. It was the same husky sound Frankie made. "Not even all the king's horses and all the king's men can put Humpty Dumpty together again."

"I thought Humpty Dumpty was an egg," I said.

You have completely lost it.

Andy dimpled. Despite the complete difference in coloring, there was no question that he was related to Frankie.

"Actually," he said, "there's nothing in the rhyme itself that indicates Humpty *was* an egg. We just assume that from the picture books. I personally have him pegged for a bale of hay."

"Kirsten," Frankie said as she nudged herself back under his arm, "this is my nephew, Andy DeLuca."

Yeah, I knew he was Italian.

"Andy, Kirsten Petersen."

My newest resident basket case.

"Hey," he said, then winced. "Bad word choice. Bad."

"Speaking of hay," Frankie said, "get yourself up there and help Kirsten. I need to get sixteen bales in before it starts to rain."

"I'm here five minutes and you put me to work," he said.

"Yes, I do." She reached in the cab of the truck and produced a pair of gloves she slapped into his hands. "And then we'll talk about what you're doing here."

Her look went sober and so did his.

Awk-*ward.*

I climbed back up on the stack and Andy climbed up behind me.

"You slide them out and I'll grab them and toss them," he said.

He could have done the whole job with one arm in a sling, but I didn't argue. Somewhere in that look he'd exchanged with Frankie, the easy charm had been sucked out. We bucked the rest of the hay without a word.

When it was all loaded in the truck, Bathsheba leaped on top of it and I followed her. The tension was so thick by then there wasn't enough air in the cab for me, Andy, and his Aunt Frankie.

"I don't know what *you're* going to do," I said to Bathsheba as Frankie ground the gears and eased the truck through the gate. "But I'm going to hold on and keep my mouth shut."

She seemed to agree.

When we arrived at the back of the barn, it was obvious from the way Andy slammed the passenger door that all had not gone well in the front seat.

"We've got this," Frankie said as I jumped down to the tailgate. "Why don't you go get cleaned up?" She gave Andy's back another long look. "And he and I will bring the sheep in tonight. Give you some free time."

Translation: You don't need to see this.

I was more than happy to leave them to it. Family conflict wasn't my area of expertise.

———

Emma, too, was apparently shooed back to the Cloister an hour later. She spent the first five minutes she was there staring out the window at Joseph as he hurried toward the main house, body leaning forward like a ladder.

"Do you know what's going on?" she said.

Since there was no one else there, I assumed she was talking to me.

"No," I said. "Frankie's nephew showed up this afternoon. I don't think she was expecting him."

Emma turned away from the window and raised an eyebrow at me. "Andy?" she said.

"Yeah." I tried not to sound too eager, but this did have the potential for an exchange of more than three words. "Do you know anything about him?"

"No. Just that he's getting his master's at MIT."

"Impressive."

"I guess. If you like the brainy type."

"I don't," I said. Too quickly. "I don't think Frankie is all that happy that he's here. I mean, she is, but I got the impression—"

"It's none of my business," Emma said. "I'm going to get washed up for supper."

Shot down again. What are we, four for four now?

A half hour later we were about to walk out the front door to go up to the main house when Joseph took the porch steps in one long-legged stride, carrying a platter covered with aluminum foil.

"You're having supper in tonight, ladies," he said. "Watch out, the bottom's hot."

I didn't even attempt to take it from him. My track record for dropping things was way too good. He handed it to Emma, who, as always, couldn't seem to take her eyes off his face.

"Is everything okay?" she said.

I thought it was none of her business.

"We just need a little family time," Joseph said, although he didn't look like this was a reunion he was going to enjoy.

He looks like he'd rather have a colonoscopy, actually.

When he was gone, Emma carried the platter into the kitchen and I followed her. The food was a good excuse.

"I'll get plates out," I said.

"I'm not hungry," Emma said.

I anticipated a stomp to her room but she dropped into one of the broad-backed kitchen chairs, made thicker by several generations of paint, and folded her arms on the table. Her head went down onto them.

Walking like the floor was covered in hen's eggs, I stepped gingerly to a chair and sat down.

"You okay?" I said.

"Does it look like I'm okay?"

I am so over this girl.

"I don't know," I said. "I can't see your face. I'm just going by your body language, which screams that you are not, in fact, okay. Excuse the heck out of me for asking, but I live here with you and I give a rip. Okay?"

Couldn't have said that better myself.

Quite frankly, it felt like the Nudnik *had* said it, using my mouth.

Emma raised her head, eyes wide. Mine were probably even bigger.

"Sorry," she said.

"I just—"

"I don't know if I'm okay or not. Not yet." She turned her head in the direction of the main house, although there were three walls between us and the nearest window. "I can't lose Joseph," she said. "I won't make it if he leaves."

"Why would he leave?"

"I don't know that either. I need to go be in my room." She got halfway up and stopped. "It's not you. I just don't know how to talk about this stuff very well."

As her footsteps faded into her room, I put my own head down on the table.

"That makes two of us," I whispered.

> Share this chapter with your friends!
> Listen for the echo of God. That's where
> therapy begins. #TheMercifulScar

Chapter
SEVEN

It's Day Six and you might just now *be getting the hang of this. Maybe.
If nobody's looking too close.*

Nobody was, at least not Frankie that next morning as we herded
the sheep out to the south pasture. Although she was as soft and
patient as always, it all seemed to be done on autopilot. She was so
preoccupied, I was sure I could have drowned in the water trough and
she wouldn't have noticed.

Norwich and Undie seemed to sense it, too, and it was as if they
knew they needed to pick up the slack. Frankie still called commands
to them, but I thought their ears perked to attention more than usual
and their curved runs were leaner, more assertive.

So maybe you oughta start acting like a dog.

Acting like the shepherd sure wasn't cutting it, so what did I have
to lose?

So I watched them. And I found myself circling the rear of the
flock, anticipating who was going to straggle and who was about to
wander off to chomp one lone hunk of yarrow and take half the flock
with her. I scampered—

Since when have you ever scampered?

Yes, I scampered to get between them and their dubious destination and stood there and stared into their vacant eyes until they *baa*ed or burped at me and turned to join the rest of the clamorous mass.

Ya gotta wonder what they're all talking about.

My guess was, *We're waaalking, we're waaalking—ooh, grass—gotta have it—uh-oh, where'd everybody go?*

You're scarin' me, Kirsten.

Scary or not, I was bordering on proud. Too bad Frankie was still too zoned in on something else to notice anything beyond the sheep basics. On the way back to the barn she told me to take the rest of the day off. I didn't think it was a reward for good behavior, but I took it anyway.

But the minute I stepped into the empty Cloister, with its cavernous rooms, the loneliness seized my skin. Yet somehow I couldn't cut there now, not with the ranch teeming just outside the walls—out there where everyone had a reason for being. It mocked me until I took the scissors from the first aid kit, tucked them into the pocket of the brown sweatshirt, and set off. I didn't know where I was going. It just couldn't be here. There was no getting out of there without Bathsheba, so it was two of us who headed west toward the Rocky Mountain front.

Listen to you sounding all geographical.

I guessed I couldn't help picking up *something* from Joseph during those after-supper dialogues between Frankie and him.

The Rockies seemed to get farther away the more we walked but there were plenty of foothills between me and them. A goal took shape: get down into a valley, away from this accusing wide-open space. Then I could find release.

To go down I first had to go up, so Bathsheba and I must have hiked at least two miles, over fences—under, in her case—and up loose-stoned paths that ended abruptly and then began themselves again yards later. I looked mostly at the ground, partly because I didn't want to fall into some hole belonging to a weasel or a gopher or a badger or a who knew what other charming animal, and partly because the endless expanse of all-seeing Montana sky above me threatened to strip me naked if I made eye contact with it.

Bathsheba fell into a rhythm of romping ahead of me, stopping to sniff the air, and prancing back to check my progress. The occasional butterfly distracted her. Make that butterfly *shadow*. As they fluttered over her head, she dashed after their dark reflections, nose to the ground, forehead wrinkled in confusion because there was nothing there to smell.

Yeah, this dog's sharing a brain with a sheep.

At one point she disappeared behind a rock formation on the slope ahead. When I looked up, eyes shaded, to wait for her to reappear, I saw a stone building.

Who puts a house up here? Some nut bar?

It wasn't actually a house. In fact, as I climbed closer to it I realized it really wasn't a building at all but a tower of flat rocks fitted together so tightly and so magically I was sure even the wind that whipped around us couldn't take it down. Tall and rectangular and tapering slightly at the top, it just stood there, atop a grassy hill, with a somewhat pointless split rail fence around it.

Yeah, what's that gonna keep out?

Certainly not Bathsheba. She wriggled under the lowest rail and trotted over to investigate. I followed her.

Way to be gutsy, Kirsten. You go.

I couldn't help being impressed by the way someone had put the stones together. The structure was sound and yet the spaces between the browns and creams and rusts allowed it to breathe. I had professors who would be profoundly impressed.

I shivered, not so much from the wind as from the distance that now gaped between me and my former life. I seemed to be doing nothing but getting farther away from everything I had ever been.

I groped in my pocket for the scissors and for an anxious moment I thought I'd lost them. When my fingers hit metal deep in the pouch I pulled them out into the light. The sky was a study in grays but still the blades took on a gleam, begging me to press them against my skin.

I sat on the rocky ground, back against the stone tower, and pushed up my sleeve. Gooseflesh spread in the chill air, forcing the hairs to attention. I turned my arm over and studied the red-yarn scar on my wrist.

Got no relief from that one, did ya?

Pain sizzled through me. That couldn't be. Something had to let the hopelessness out. It had to. And this time there would be no one to stop me.

I opened the scissors but I paused for a minute to slow things down—the pulse pounding in my temples, the breath coming out in shallow pants, the chatter in my head—

All right, go big or stay home, then, 'cause I don't see these weak little incisions doin' it for ya anymore, know what I mean?

I did. All too well.

Pressing my back into the stones and holding my breath, I carefully placed the scissors higher than the veins in my wrist so there would be no accident this time. No Wes breaking through the door. No wrestling match in front of the sink. Just the blade and me—

And Bathsheba, barking and yipping like a wild thing outside the split rail fence. My hand jerked and the scissors flew from my fingers and skidded across the tilted, stony ground. I struggled to my feet and ran after them, only to watch them tumble over a ledge of rocks, falling and glancing and falling again until I could no longer see them. Another step and I could have fallen with them.

Behind me Bathsheba was still barking, but at what, I didn't care. I stood on the precipice and gaped across the deep valley I'd been searching for. It was too big, this mass of ridges and cliffs and petrified waterfalls of rocks that seemed to move even in their stillness. Breath sucked away by wind and fear, I forced myself to look down. The towering, craggy wall of mountain beyond me cast a dauntless shadow on a gathering of toy buildings below. The Bellwether Ranch, tiny and vulnerable.

Just like me.

With no control. Not a speck of it. And in that moment I knew there *was* no control, not for me, not anywhere.

I didn't know I'd cried out until the wind snatched up my voice and carried it away to nothing.

I didn't hear an echo, did you?

No, what I heard was Frankie's voice, folding over the Nudnik's like a cloak of velvet. *Listen for* bat kol.

I did. But there was only the frantic squealing of whatever animal Bathsheba had flushed out. And the throbbing of my heart in my throat. And the wind. Always the wind.

Bathsheba joined me, tongue lolling, and emptied the usual measure of slobber into the palm of my hand. I gave it back to her in a long smooth swipe on the top of her head. Even as I petted her, Bathsheba's ears went on alert.

She's hearing bat kol? *Now* that's *scary.*

It was a helicopter she heard, *wop-wop-wop*ping its way into view to the east as if it were heading for the ranch.

Yikes. They've got Search and Rescue out looking for you.

I doubted I'd even been missed. But I shoved my hands into the pockets of my sweatshirt and followed Bathsheba back down the hill.

The first person I saw when the dog and I came around the last curve in the ranch driveway was Andy.

Aka Mr. Hottie.

He was standing next to the open door of one of the beater pickup trucks, one foot already in like he was planning to go someplace. The Suburban was missing.

The plot thickens, eh?

But evidently today I *was* the plot, because Andy marched down the driveway as if he was on a mission and the mission was me. Even though his face glowered like Little Augie's, I couldn't help noticing the way his arms pumped as he charged in my direction.

The dude's got guns, no doubt about it.

Only when he came within a few yards of me did I see the squint around his eyes. That was a what-were-you-thinking look if I'd ever seen one, and I'd seen plenty.

"Where the heck have you been?" he said. "Everybody's looking for you."

"I wasn't gone *that* long," I said. "You didn't have to call out a helicopter."

He blinked at me. Then slowly the grin spread over his face.

Nice. Very nice.

"We were about to call in the Conrad SWAT team," he said. "Except . . . there isn't one."

We both looked up at the sound of gravel spraying out from tires. The Suburban rocked to a stop next to us and Frankie leaned out of the driver's side window and scanned me from under the bill of the ever-present ball cap. To my relief, she looked relieved too.

"Okay, thank You, God," she said. "Where did you find her, Andy?"

"She found me," he said.

Nice save. Y'know, for a guy who's not your type.

I did appreciate it. But something nettled at the back of my neck.

"I just went for a walk," I said to Frankie. "You said it was free time."

She climbed out of the car and shut the door, but not before I saw the thirty-thirty on the seat next to her.

"I'm glad you did," she said. "But here's the thing: you need to check in with someone before you leave. Not so we can keep tabs on you. It's just so we'll know when to start worrying."

For some reason she cast a glance at Andy.

We are talking about some major subtext here.

"Okay," I said. "That's fair enough."

Frankie nodded and then looked past me, eyes shaded. "Here comes the cavalry," she said. She grinned the grin she shared with Andy.

Hoofbeats pounded as Joseph joined us on horseback, followed by Emma, who looked as if she were born to ride in her brown suede cowboy hat and her jeans tucked snugly into scuffed leather riding boots. But it wasn't just the outfit. She sat as if the only thing keeping her from being one with the reddish, black-maned horse was the saddle.

Joseph was wearing a Western hat, too, pulled so low over his eyes I couldn't see them. Until he put two fingers to the brim and pushed it back to reveal the glare.

This is going to be ugly.

"Kirsten," Frankie said, "You've met Merton but you haven't been introduced to Sienna."

Nor did I want to be. Standing below their immense noses made me want to find a badger hole to crawl into.

"Emma's on Sienna and—"

"Where were you?"

Joseph's eyes were drilled into me, not Frankie.

That's a first.

And, I hoped, a last.

"Up there," I said, pointing toward the Rockies. "I found a stone tower of some kind."

"I think she means the shepherd's monument," Frankie said.

"I know what she means."

Despite the wind I was starting to sweat. "I was fine. I had Bathsheba with me."

"Now there's comfort."

Frankie cleared her throat. Joseph took off his hat and wiped his forehead with the back of his hand. When he spoke again his voice was several degrees warmer. Which brought it up to freezing.

"You see the helicopter?"

"Yes."

"That was the wildlife people, looking for the grizzly and her cub. Rancher reported seeing them about two miles from where you and your guard dog were taking in the scenery."

"Oh," I said. "So—I guess I won't go up there again."

Joseph dropped his hat back over his smoky hair. "You can go anywhere you want, as long as you carry a weapon with you."

I felt my jaw drop so far I was surprised my chin didn't bang into my chest.

"You ever shot a gun before?"

"I've never even held one, and I don't—"

"Tomorrow's your first lesson, then. Right after you take the sheep out."

I couldn't even get my mouth open to protest before he turned to Emma, saddle squeaking.

"You'll join us."

Unlike mine, Emma's chin lifted. "You know I don't need lessons."

"Everybody needs a refresher from time to time."

"No!"

Even the Nudnik froze. I may have imagined it, but I thought the wind, too, held its breath.

"I'm not sure we need to settle this now," Frankie said.

I could see Emma swallowing as she looked away. I myself couldn't *stop* looking.

Yeah, this is definitely a train wreck.

And one that included Andy. I pried my gaze away from Emma to find Andy squinting so hard at Joseph his dark eyes all but disappeared. I blinked to make sure he was the same person who ten minutes before had grinned the awkward out of me.

I think there's about to be a showdown at the OK Corral.

But Joseph just scrubbed the back of his neck with his hand and then nodded at Emma. They wheeled the horses around and rode single file down the driveway. When I turned back to Andy and Frankie, Andy was already halfway to the main house.

Was it something I said?

Frankie lightly touched my shoulder. "You don't like the idea of handling a gun, do you?"

I just stared at her for a second.

We're going to be moving a little faster now. Try to keep up.

"No," I said, "I don't. As much of a klutz as I am, I'm liable to put a bullet through somebody. Falling off a fence is one thing, but . . ."

Frankie tilted her head at me. "You've been trying to convince me you're uncoordinated ever since you've been here. Keep it up and I might start to believe you."

"You've seen it!" I said.

"I've only seen you being new at everything I've asked you to try.

Nobody gets it the first time." She gave me half the grin. "Or even the first ten times."

"Emma—"

"First of all, it's time to stop comparing yourself to Emma or anybody else for that matter. And second of all . . ." She completed the grin. "It took Emma thirty minutes to hook a sheep the first time."

That would've been nice to know.

"You're doing just fine," Frankie said. "You walk two miles a day at least. You're catching on with the herding." She nodded toward Bathsheba, who was lying at my feet, head resting on the toe of my boot. "And nobody could do anything with this one until you came along."

My throat was thickening.

You're not going to cry, are you? There's no crying in sheep keeping!

"It isn't just that," I said. "The shooting, I mean."

Frankie waited.

That's one of her best skills.

"It's Joseph," I said. "I don't think he likes me, and I definitely don't feel comfortable with him. I'm just saying that if he yells at me I'll probably, I don't know, do something stupid. Like cry."

Like I said . . .

Frankie tucked her arm into mine and steered us toward the Cloister. "There's nothing stupid about crying. I weep on a regular basis. As for Joseph, I have never heard him yell and he's sixty-five years old so I don't see him starting now."

"He yells with his eyes," I said. "I feel scolded every time he looks at me."

She stopped at the bottom of the porch steps. Bathsheba vaulted to the one above us and wagged most of her body and Frankie scratched her absently behind the ears. Her attention seemed to be somewhere just over my shoulder. When her gaze came back to me, it was misty.

"Joseph's job here has always been to protect us, first and foremost," she said. "But life hasn't always protected him. So what you're seeing isn't scolding. It's fierceness."

I can see that.

"If Joseph is fierce with you, he cares enough to keep you safe."

She ushered me to one of the rocking chairs and took the other one. Bathsheba curled up under mine.

"I'm glad you found the shepherd's monument," she said. "You want a little history?"

"Sure."

"Before all this land was settled by homesteaders—most of them Scottish in this area, by the way—it was all free range. The shepherds were pretty much nomadic and they let their sheep graze a pasture for a while and then moved on. But water was like gold to them: rare but essential. When they found a water source, they built a stone tower so that when they came back that way, they could find it again." She sort of shrugged with her eyebrows. "At least that's what they say. The more cynical historians say they were just bored. Or drunk."

"I like your story better," I said. "And I can tell you, that kind of technique doesn't happen if you're plowed. It's some pretty impressive engineering."

"You would know. So tell me, do you have a passion for architecture?"

"A passion?" I watched my thumb rub across the scar on my wrist. "I'm not sure what you mean. I like it okay."

"What made you choose it?"

"Process of elimination?"

She waited. She really did do it well.

"My dad wanted me to go to MSU, and since he hadn't really been a part of my life for the two years before that, I guess I wanted to kind of keep the connection."

"Where did the eliminating come in?"

I felt my cheeks color. "I looked at the majors MSU was strong in and that was the only one I could even halfway see myself doing." I looked up at her. "Can you see me being an aggie?"

She didn't answer because at that moment Emma stormed up the steps and charged through the front door without, as my mother would have said, so much as a by-your-leave. I watched Frankie watch her. The brown eyes were so full I thought she'd go in after her. But she let her lids close for a few seconds and then stood up.

"You should probably go have some lunch," she said. "See you at six?"

I went inside, expecting Emma to have slammed into her room by now, but she had planted herself on the couch and was yanking her boots off.

When are you going to stop expecting around here?

Immediately, actually, because Emma looked up at me, eyes smoldering, and said, "What is *with* that Andy person?"

I wasn't sure why that pulled a laugh out of me.

"What?" I said. "You don't like the Italian type?"

"No, I don't like the be-rude-to-Joseph type. What is his problem?"

It sounded like a rhetorical question, so I just parked tentatively on the arm of the sofa and watched her peel off her socks.

"It's like Joseph is invisible to him," she ranted on.

"I don't think invisible is the word," I said. "More like hostile."

"You saw that too?"

Yikes, I think you're bonding.

"It doesn't make any sense," she said. "Joseph cares about him— you can totally tell that."

You can?

"And I know it hurts him, the way Andy treats him." She balled up the socks and crammed them into her boots. "I wish he'd go back to Massachusetts."

"Is that where he lives?" I said. "Oh, well, yeah, he would if he's going to MIT."

"That's where he goes to school, but this is home for him. I just don't think he belongs here anymore." Emma scratched at her curls. The rant was apparently over. "Look, I tend to go off. If you like the guy, y'know, no offense."

"It's absolutely fine. I don't know him enough to like him or not like him. And besides, I have no interest in men at all. None. Nada. So no, you didn't offend me in any way whatsoever. It is totally cool."

Emma's eyebrows pulled together. "You had me at 'It's absolutely fine.' I'm convinced, already." She stood up and retrieved her sock-stuffed boots. "I gotta go put this stuff away and get back to work."

I think you might have overdone it a little with the I-hate-men thing.

I didn't think I *could* overdo it. Andy was cute. Okay, he was hot. But he was obviously also mercurial. And I had enough family problems of my own. And I wasn't going to be an idiot over a guy ever again.

Besides, you only have twenty-four days to go here. But who's counting?

———

In spite of the familial tension that was apparently building behind the scenes, Frankie seemed more at peace the next morning, Friday. On the way back from taking the sheep out, she once more linked arms with me.

"This is your seventh day here," she said as we crunched up the ranch road. "The hardest part of the adjustment is behind you. Now I think you'll start to move forward."

I beat Nudnik to the punch with *Finally!*

"I intended to check in with you yesterday," she said, "but I'm afraid I was distracted by Andy's arrival the other day, and I hope you'll forgive me for that."

She looked at me as if she required an answer before she could continue.

"It's okay," I said.

Still she searched my eyes, probably looking for specks of dishonesty in there, and nodded.

Nodding is another one of her best skills.

"First, though, I think it's only fair to you that I explain a little bit about what's happening with Andy."

"You don't have to," I said.

Oh, come on, you're dying to know.

"Andy's story isn't mine to tell," she went on. "But I'll share my part with you. Okay?"

I nodded. It was apparently one of my best skills too.

"Andy was raised here on the Bellwether. His mother, my twin sister, brought him here before he was born, and he's never known any other home. She died when he was three years old and my parents couldn't handle raising him *and* running the ranch. They were in their forties then. So I left the order and came home to take care of him."

"So you're more like his mom than his aunt," I said.

"Right. And before I came, Joseph was like his father."

I bit my lip practically in half to keep from asking what, then, was the deal between the two of them now.

Not to mention what happened to his real father. Katie Couric you are not.

"We were so proud of Andy when he was accepted to MIT and graduated last year and got into a grad program there. But I think this year has been tough for some reason, because he's not doing his summer internship like he planned. He's come home to figure out what that's about." Frankie gave my arm a squeeze. "And now you know as much as I do."

I don't think *so.*

"He wants to sort things through on his own, and I'm going to honor that. Meanwhile, I have made a promise to you and Emma and I intend to honor that too. And I want to."

"Are you sure?" I said.

Frankie stopped just short of the narrow bridge across the creek bed. "I've been praying about it ever since Andy got here, and yes, I'm sure."

Do you always do that—pray? Do you get answers? How do you do *that?*

Those were surprising—make that shocking—questions from the Nudnik. I might have asked them out loud, but Frankie shifted gears.

"It's just about time for your shooting lesson," she said. "How are you with that today?"

"Do I have a choice?"

"You don't have a choice about doing it, unless you want to sit in the house all the time. But you do have a choice in how you approach it."

"What are my options?" I hoped it didn't come out as snarky as it felt.

Frankie counted them off on her fingers. "Resist it like a root canal. Just do it and get it over with. Or see it as an opportunity to be empowered." She patted my arm. "I think you'll do fine. He'll meet you behind the house."

I wasn't sure about fine as I continued the climb up the driveway alone. But it did strike me that Frankie was sending me off to learn how to handle a gun. A weapon. A thing that could kill somebody. Or myself.

Is it just me, or does this feel like trust to you?

Maybe *trust* was too strong a word. But she didn't think I was suicidal, that was certain. She really hadn't been placating me when she said she believed that, back at the hospital. I wasn't sure shooting a gun was going to empower me. But the could-be-trust made me lift my chin as I headed toward the house to meet Joseph.

Except it wasn't Joseph who was waiting for me there. It was Andy.

We-e-e-ll now . . .

"Um, hi," I said.

Very smooth.

"I thought Joseph was giving me the lesson . . . I mean, it's fine if you do it . . . It's just that I . . ."

Have temporarily lost my mind. It happens.

Andy, of course, grinned as he picked up a long gun from the open tailgate of one of the trucks. "It could be just me," he said, "but if I let Joseph teach you, you'd probably be even more scared spitless than you are right now."

"I don't think that's possible," I said. "You don't think we could not do this and say we did—do you?"

He just looked at me.

I'd take that as a no.

"Kidding," I said. "But just so you know, I've never even held a gun before and I have no desire to do it now."

The grin reappeared. "I picked up on that. But just so *you* know, there's nothing to be afraid of if you do everything I tell you. Besides, I've never lost a student yet."

There was something suspicious in the way his mouth twitched. I felt my eyes narrow.

"How many people have you taught to shoot?"

"Actually, none. Look, if that freaks you out I can go get Joseph—"

"Give me the gun," I said.

"Right after I show you how to keep from taking us both out."

From then on he was all business as he went through the safety rules—including don't point the thing at anybody or anything, which of course, I promptly did—and showed me how to check to make sure there were no rounds in the chamber. Pushing that lever back was harder than they made it look in those horse ranch films where the feisty rancher's daughter takes aim at every dude who hits on her.

Personally, I don't see this guy hitting on you.

I didn't either and I was okay with that. I was shaking hard enough already. Andy made me take several deep breaths with my eyes closed before he would show me how to hold the rifle. His first words: "Do *not* put your finger on the trigger until you're ready to shoot."

"Which one's the trigger?"

"Are you serious?"

"No," I said.

"Well, I am."

O-kay, moving on . . .

It took several minutes—

Define several.

—before I got the hang of how to hold the gun. Nothing about it felt natural, even though intellectually it made sense. The left hand, which held the gun, pointed at the target. The right hand, which did the shooting, took the shape of a handshake. The butt rested against the muscle on the inside of my shoulder so the "kick" wouldn't hit the bone. Feet were pointed in the same direction as the arms, hip distance apart, with the right foot back so I could naturally lean into the action.

But as I said, nothing about any of it came naturally.

"Everything looks good," Andy said when I finally got my body to do all that. "Now, take a breath and relax with it."

He's on crack.

I did try to relax and everything collapsed inward. The gun barrel wavered and I stumbled forward. It took another several minutes to get it all back together.

"Am I the worst student you've ever had?" I said.

"Oh yeah," Andy said. "But also the best. Now . . ."

He showed me how to look through the sight to line the barrel up with a target that grew smaller the longer I looked at it.

"When you're ready, you're going to firmly squeeze the trigger. And keep in mind that for every action there is an equal and opposite reacton, so it's going to kick. Don't freak out."

"Too late," I said. "I'm already freaked out."

"Okay, have you got it lined up?"

I started to say *I have no idea* but, actually, it was the only part that made sense to me. I just didn't want to say anything and mess up my form.

"When you're ready, go ahead and fire," Andy said.

I squeezed the trigger and my eyes at the same time. If I'd had them open I would have seen who punched me in the shoulder. Oh, wait—that was the gun butt. Between the recoil and the report that cracked the air, I could almost believe I myself had been shot.

"You did it," Andy said.

I turned to him, and the gun barrel went with me. He warded it off with a quick hand and a jump backward.

"Oh—sorry—I'm sorry!" I pointed the rifle at the ground and wished I could shoot a hole in it and climb in.

Not a bad idea actually.

"What did you do wrong?"

"I pointed the gun at you!"

Andy grinned. "Okay, as long as you know. So how did it feel?"

"To point a gun at you?"

"To shoot."

I puffed out air. "Like I'm glad it's over with."

Except it wasn't. We spent another endless half hour of me pulling the lever back, emptying the chamber, and shooting again with earplugs in, which were supposed to protect my hearing but definitely protected my pride. I didn't hear most of what Andy told me I was doing wrong.

By the time I'd shot twelve rounds—and, frighteningly, knew what that meant—I could almost get myself positioned right without thinking about it. And a couple of times I even hit the target.

"You done for today?" Andy said.

"Just for today?" I said.

He nodded for me to check the gun to make sure the chamber was empty. "You've got the basics," he said. "If we practice a couple of times a week—"

"I have to do this again?"

The grin appeared more slowly this time as Andy took the rifle from me. "All right, be straight with me. Is it my breath? My armpits? I bet it's my armpits—"

"I don't know anything *about* your armpits!"

No, that's not usually what you check out in a guy.

"So it's not me you want to avoid," Andy said.

Wait, is he flirting?

"No," I said. "I just thought one lesson and that would be it."

He shook his head, all seriousness again.

He's like a yo-yo, this guy.

"Right now you know just enough to be dangerous. But you'll get there with some practice—only don't do it by yourself. It doesn't have to be me who's with you—"

"I didn't mean that. You're . . . fine . . . It's just . . . I don't like this whole gun thing."

He responded with a shrug. "The whole gun thing is part of the whole living on a ranch thing. To tell you the truth, I'm not that crazy about it myself."

The guns or living on the ranch?

I didn't ask. Andy had closed the shutters on his charm.

Share this chapter with your friends!
In that moment I knew there was no control.
Are we ever in control? #TheMercifulScar

Chapter
EIGHT

I was still standing there trying to think of something to say besides *I'm sorry I offended you. Did I offend you? I think I did. I do that . . .* when Emma rode up on Sienna. Even with my mind still in Weapon World, I did see she had a rifle so she must have talked Joseph into forgoing the refresher course.

Yeah, but you have to admit it would be sort of delicious to see Andy try to give her lessons.

I smothered a grin.

Emma pulled the horse up several yards from us and Sienna snuffled and sidestepped as Bathsheba appeared and danced a figure eight among her legs.

Definitely one puppy short of a pet store, that dog.

"What's up?" Andy said.

"Joseph just spotted a ewe giving birth about a quarter mile from the flock," Emma said—to me alone. "He wanted me to tell Frankie."

"I think she's inside," Andy said. "We'll tell her."

"I'm supposed to show her where they are."

Her eyes were so obviously on me and not Andy, she was starting to remind me of Joseph.

What a surprise.

"I'll get her," I said.

But fortunately for all of us, Frankie appeared on the other side of the gate, cell phone pressed to her ear.

Yeah, you leaving the two of them alone? She's liable to take him out.

"Emma can lead us up there," Frankie said into the phone. "Yes, I know. We'll all come."

Before she even ended the call she was telling Andy and me to get in one of the pickups—one I hadn't ridden in before—and motioning for Emma to start off down the driveway.

"I'm driving," she called out to Andy. "You've been doing freeways too long. You scare me to death."

I squeezed into the cab between them and felt a spring poke me in the rear end. The header dipped like a scarf above our heads and a large section of the dashboard had been removed—or had fallen out from exhaustion—exposing wires and plugs and things I never knew were hidden behind gauges. I would be very surprised if the truck made it out of the driveway.

But the engine wheezed to life like an asthmatic old man emerging from a coma and it coughed and rattled us down the drive behind Emma, who already had the gate open. This vehicle made the Suburban feel like an airport limo.

"When are you gonna trash this thing and get a new one?" Andy said, as even he clung to the door with both hands to avoid being catapulted through the window.

Frankie grinned. "I'm just getting it broken in."

"Broken? It's about to disintegrate. Does it even have a transmission left?"

"She still has two gears. How many more do I need?" Frankie

glanced at me, eyes shining. "Kirsten, you are about to witness one of the most mysterious, beautiful things in God's world."

"What's that?" Andy said. "Us arriving with all our teeth still in our heads?"

"No. A ewe with her brand-new lamb. Or have you forgotten how glorious it is?"

Andy didn't answer.

We're starting to rack up the Awkward Moments.

Frankie continued to follow Emma east across the south pasture, leaving the flock behind us.

"I hate to drive across this good grassland," she said. "Where in the world are they?"

As if in answer, something sharp and loud and harsh echoed from the slopes to our right. If I hadn't just finished a shooting lesson, I might not have recognized the sound as gunshots—close ones that repeated like angry raps on a giant door.

"Whoa," Frankie said.

But it wasn't the shots that made her jam on the brakes and send me lurching into the nonexistent dashboard. Ahead of us, Emma and Sienna had come to a dead halt. Sienna shied and threw back her head, but Emma appeared to be paralytic on the saddle.

"That horse has heard gunshots before," Andy said. "What's going on?"

"It's not Sienna," Frankie said.

She wrenched the door open and left it hanging as she ran for Emma. Even from inside the truck I could see Emma's shoulder muscles jerking as if violent spasms had taken hold of her and wouldn't let go.

"What is going *on*?" Andy said.

One of Frankie's hands clung to Emma's shirt as she threatened to topple sideways. The other fumbled with her cell phone.

"Is she having a seizure?" I said.

"I don't know. Is she epileptic?"

"I have no idea."

The information I had on Emma would just about fill a thimble, but I had enough to know this wasn't normal for her. Something was terribly wrong, and I evidently wasn't the only one who thought so. Joseph left a tsunami of dust behind as he and Merton blew down a slope and across the pasture toward her. He was off the horse before its hooves stopped moving.

By then Emma was beyond trembling. Her feet left the stirrups and her knees bent into her chest as if her limbs were being pulled by springs. Now in a fetal position she teetered on the saddle and veered into Joseph's outstretched hands. The man I thought was nothing but bones and sinew turned into a steel crane as he lifted the curled-up mess that was Emma off the horse and into his arms.

Andy leaned across me and turned off the ignition. Without the sputter of the struggling engine, I could hear Emma screaming from the pit of her soul. Just as she'd done in her nightmare.

Joseph squatted, still holding her against him, and soothed his hands over the now hatless curls. He looked up at Frankie who was stroking Sienna's mane and whispering to her.

"Your ewe's up there just behind those rocks," he said. "Grizzly got to her. She's dead but the lamb's alive. I ran the bear off before she could get to it too." He pressed Emma's head into his chest. "I'll take care of this. You see to that—and don't waste any time. That grizzly'll be back looking for the carcass."

I heard more than felt the gasp that came out of me. It was a gasp for every level of what I'd just heard.

No one else took the time for shock. The scene through the windshield mobilized: Joseph got Emma to her feet, and Frankie hurried over to the truck.

"You two come with me," she said. "We'll go on foot."

She turned without waiting for an answer and started out across the pasture toward the rocks. I couldn't have given her one anyway. Everything on me was inert, including my mouth.

Yeah, I don't think this is going to be something beautiful and mysterious and glorious.

"Hey." Andy had the passenger door open and was holding out his hand. "Frankie needs our help."

Good. Another chance to be new at something.

The Nudnik's voice was sarcastic. But the echo of Frankie's voice was not.

I climbed from the seat and followed Andy across the pasture.

Frankie was on her knees beside what appeared to be a pile of dirty matted wool. When we got within six feet, she put up a hand, and Andy stretched out his arm to block me from taking another step.

"Stay there, Kirsten," she said. "I'm going to bring the lamb to you. Carry her back to the truck and hold her until we get back."

There was no time to even think about refusing. Frankie scooped up a white bundle and brought it to me without even completely straightening up. Her shirt and jeans were smeared with red fluid.

"Don't look at the ewe," she said as she pressed the lamb into my arms. "Just take her straight to the truck. We'll be right there."

The small being was half the size of any of the lambs in the bums' pen and her squirms to free herself were heartbreakingly feeble. But the plaintive bleating as she strained toward her lifeless mother filled the air like Emma's sobs.

"Kirsten," Frankie said. "Go."

I did, with my arms clenched around the crying lamb and my feet stumbling toward the truck. Soft clumps of wool squashed against me, but through them I could feel the little heart pattering.

It was as frightened as the mournful bleating that poured from the pink lips.

I was almost bleating myself as I pried open the door while trying to keep the lamb from escaping my hold. Though by the time I got us both into the cab and closed the door again, the squirming had stopped and the damp armful of softness was molding itself to my chest.

"It's okay," I whispered to it. And then because I could think of nothing else, I added, "It's okay."

I wondered if Joseph was saying much the same thing to Emma. They were still out there, standing between the horses, Emma leaning into Joseph with her face buried so far into his shirt I was sure her cheeks would come out plaid. She was no longer shaking. I didn't hear any crying. But like the lamb in my arms, she clung to Joseph and showed no signs of moving.

Joseph kept his eyes turned toward the rocks and the slope above, and even though I couldn't see them under the hat brim, I knew they were watching for Frankie, and probably the grizzly. Now that I thought about it, I hadn't seen Frankie carrying her gun. How had I ended up in a place where it wasn't safe unless everybody was packing?

The lamb nuzzled at my neck.

"I know, baby," I said. "Somebody will be here soon to take care of you."

Was it the right time to tell her she was now a bum lamb?

Really? Tell her anything you want. The chances of her understanding you are just about nil.

I wasn't actually sure whether I was doing it for the lamb or to keep myself from losing it, but I said, "You'll like the other bums. Okay, some of them are a little rowdy—mostly the boys. That's the thing about boys: at this age they're mostly absurd little creeps. Then they grow up and . . . they're absurd big creeps. But you'll be all right.

Sister Frankie will make sure you don't get hurt. Now, I haven't actually tasted the milk she'll give you, but from what I can gather it's pretty good. The other babies suck it right up."

I didn't add that I was a little concerned about her getting equal chances at the nipples. She was so very tiny and probably not ready to know she'd just entered a hard, competitive world. So I just whispered, "It's okay. You'll be taken care of."

Movement caught the corner of my eye: Frankie and Andy moving down the last of the slope, each holding two of the dead ewe's legs so that she swung like a bleeding hammock between them. I could see why Frankie wanted to get the lamb away from her. No one needs to see her mom like that.

The lamb stirred and I quickly buried her head in my neck so she wouldn't see them pass with the ewe. The truck rocked as they apparently slid the body into the bed, now a hearse for a beloved mother.

"You didn't even have a chance to get to know her," I whispered into the wool. "I'm really sorry."

"Go ahead and drive back with Kirsten," I heard Frankie say. "You remember what to do—put the lamb in one of the small—"

"Got it," Andy said.

Frankie rushed past and joined Joseph. I watched as together they coaxed Emma back onto Sienna and Joseph remounted Merton. There was a rope tied between the two horses, so that Emma was attached on one flank to Joseph, and on the other side to Frankie who held Sienna's reins as she walked. A memory swelled in me, a faded one kept safely folded away with the too-few others like it, of a parent on either side, holding my hands, swinging me over a curb with a *whee* worthy of the highest of Ferris wheels.

The truck door opened and Andy got in. His face was the color of cream of wheat.

"You okay?" he said.

I shook my head and burst into tears.

I heard no Nudnik reminding me that there was no crying in sheep keeping. Only Andy's voice saying, "I know, right? I never got used to it either."

I smeared at my cheek with the back of my hand and drew the lamb in closer.

"Look at that," he said. "She's asleep."

"Are you sure?" I said. "She's not—"

"Nah, I can see her breathing from here."

Andy turned the truck around and started across the pasture, driving far more slowly than Frankie had.

"You know I grew up here," he said.

"Uh-huh."

"I've seen a lot of sheep and cows and dogs die and I blubbered over every one of them." He gave me the grin. "That's why I decided to become a scientist. It's hard to grieve a dead equation."

"What field are you in?" I said.

The grin dissolved.

Oops. Isn't that why the prodigal nephew showed up here? So he could sort himself out?

"I didn't mean to get in your business," I said.

"No worries." He nodded at the sleeping lamb. "So, congratulations, Mommy."

When we got back to the barn, I continued to carry the lamb while Andy looked around and carried on a conversation with himself.

"I guess she means this pen. Probably never took it down after lambing season. Why was that ewe giving birth so late in the year? I hope there's some formula left."

"Frankie mixes it for the bums every day," I said.

Andy shook his head and motioned me into a small pen formed by four of the yellow plastic Fisher-Price gates tied together with rope so that they only looked slightly off-kilter.

"Put her in here," he said. "If you'll get some hay, I'll see if there's any newborn formula still around."

"So she's a girl?"

Andy formed the dimples without the smile. "I haven't checked. I just don't want to keep calling her It."

When I set the lamb on the floor of the pen, she looked smaller and more fragile than ever. She must have felt that way, too, because as I fumbled my way over the gate to go get hay, she stretched her wooly neck and let out a mournful, vibrating cry.

"I'll be right back," I said. "I'm going to fix you a bed."

But she cried—and stirred all the bums in their pen outside the barn into a frenzy—until I came back with an armful of hay. She didn't settle down until I had spread it on the floor and sat beside her. Andy found us there, a nippled plastic Coke bottle half-filled with something milky in his hand.

"This is almost the last of it," he said.

He joined us on the floor and peered under the lamb's leg. "It *is* a girl. Is that what you wanted?"

"I didn't even know I was expecting."

"It happens. Have you ever done this before?"

"What?"

"Fed a lamb a bottle?"

"Are you serious?" I said.

"I didn't want to insult you by starting in on a tutorial if you were already a pro."

"Wait—*I'm* going to feed her?"

"She's comfortable with you so it makes sense."

He didn't give me a chance to list the myriad reasons why the lamb would probably starve in my hands.

"So you tuck her under your arm so her feet touch the floor behind you," he said.

"Like this?"

"Yeah. Then hold the bottle in your left hand and with your right, tip her chin up."

"Is this right?"

"Little higher. Okay, now press the nipple on the side of her mouth and sort of wiggle it until she opens and then slide it in."

"Not from the front?"

"No, you have to sneak it in there at first, especially since she's never nursed."

"So—this way?"

"Don't be afraid to apply a little pressure. There you go. You're in."

The nipple was indeed in the lamb's mouth but she didn't seem to know what to do with it.

"You seriously have to teach them how to *eat*?" I said.

"From a bottle anyway. Tilt it up more. You see that hole at the base of the nipple?"

"Uh-huh."

"Keep that at the top and watch the milk. If you see bubbles you're in good shape."

"I don't see any."

"Pull out on it just a little bit and see what happens."

I gave it an infinitesimal tug. The lamb latched on and began to suck, the pink lips curled around the nipple, her eyes closed. I couldn't help holding her tighter.

"You've got this," Andy said.

"You're not leaving, are you?"

Look out now . . .

"Nah. I always liked watching them feed like this. 'Course, I would never admit that when I got past about twelve, but secretly it was one of my favorite parts of growing up here."

"You fed a lot of lambs, did you?"

"Oh yeah. And I always got to name the bums."

"Really."

"Every year I picked a theme and then mostly I—but sometimes Frankie—would give them names. Like one year it was Winnie-the-Pooh characters—that was when I was really young—then when I got older it was, like, makes of cars."

"You mean like Chevy?"

The grin appeared. "No, like Camaro, Corvette, Ferrari. One of my last themes—I guess I was in high school—was famous scientists."

I blinked at him. "I can't even think of any famous scientists."

"Sure you can. We had Hawking, for Stephen Hawking. Einstein."

"Okay, so, like Madame Curie. Louis Pasteur."

"Frankie kept getting them mixed up, couldn't remember any of the names half the time. At sixteen I thought that was wicked funny."

I checked the bottle for bubbles. The little girl lamb was still nursing away.

"Did Frankie keep up the tradition after you went off to college?"

"Don't know."

I could see the grin begin to fade again and I didn't want it to go away.

"I think you should name this lamb," I said.

"You think? Really?"

"I do."

He tilted away and took the long view of the lamb chowing in my arms.

"What's your last name again?" he said.

"Mine? Petersen."

"Perfect. I'm going to call her Petey."

"She's a girl!"

"Hello—Frankie?"

"Oh yeah, huh?"

"I like it. Petey Ketersen."

I let out a guffaw that startled the lamb and I had to sneak the nipple back into her mouth again. She sucked at it hungrily.

"That whole Pete thing really works," he said.

"How so?"

"You can be Little Bo Pete."

Hey, that was my joke! Sort of . . .

The Nudnik had been uncharacteristically silent. I would have been fine with her staying that way, but Andy pushed the right buttons to get her going again.

"I'm going to call you Bo for short," Andy said. "Can I do that?"

Flirt alert! Flirt alert!

"I guess I've been called worse," I said.

"Yeah?" Andy propped himself against the opposite side of the pen so that his feet almost touched my hips and mine his.

Boundaries, anyone?

How was I supposed to establish boundaries in a four-by-four pen? Still, I was careful to keep the space between my feet and him.

"So what have people called you?" he said.

Let's see, your mother called you Selfish. Your father's fave was Just Like Your Mother. Now, Wes, he was partial to Babe.

I refocused deliberately on the lamb.

"She's spitting it out. Is she done?"

Andy leaned forward and put his hand on Petey's bulging belly. "I think so. There's no room left in there."

"Did I feed her too much?"

"Is she puking?"

"No."

"Then she's fine."

That was apparently true, because little Petey stretched herself across my lap and soon the belly in question was rising and falling in even baby breaths.

"I was supposed to take pictures," Andy said. "But I left my phone in the truck."

"That's really okay."

I didn't add that I was sure I was a thing of beauty to behold about then. My hair was still in a ponytail from the shooting lesson, although half of it had come loose and was hanging around my face like tassels from an ear of corn, and my eyes were probably puffy-pink from my short crying stint.

"I really want a picture of this," Andy said.

He formed his index fingers and thumbs into a camera lens and looked through the hole, one eye squinted. "Okay, give me a Bo Pete pose."

"What?"

"You know, that thing you do when you cock your head and look at me like I'm insane."

"I do not!"

"You're doing it right now. That's it—that's the money shot!"

I threw my head back to laugh, and found Frankie standing just outside the pen. I couldn't put a name to the expression on her face. *How 'bout,* This isn't what I was expecting?

I was thinking more along the lines of *Now look what you've done.* But I'd done exactly what Andy told me to do. And it was Andy that Frankie was looking at. It was the closest I had ever seen her to being stern.

"Would you please go help Joseph with the body?" she said.

The skin between Andy's dark brows puckered, but he got up and vaulted easily over the gate. There seemed to be no need for words. He just looked at her and went.

Another attack of the awkwards. How ya gonna smooth this one out?

"How's Emma?" I said.

Frankie closed her eyes. When she opened them, her face was gentle again. "She's resting."

I waited for more but Frankie just let herself quietly into the pen and squatted to look at the lamb.

"Did her mom die in childbirth?" I said. "Or was it the bear?"

"I might have thought she died in childbirth. The ewe was old and probably missed a couple of fertility cycles before she bred, which was why she was so late lambing. But I'm sure it was the bear because the ewe had already licked her baby clean, and I'm sure she's the reason the bear didn't get the lamb too."

"How did she do that? I thought sheep didn't have any defenses."

Frankie smiled sadly. "They don't. But a new mother will pretend to. She'll get between her baby and whatever is threatening it and stomp her feet like she's about to attack. I have to respect these ewes for that, you know? It didn't keep the bear from attacking *her*, but she saved her baby." She rubbed a finger along the sleeping lamb's cheek. "If Joseph hadn't shot in the air and scared the bear off, this little one wouldn't have made it either. Girl or boy?"

"Girl," I said. "We named her—well, Andy named her—Petey. Petey Ketersen."

Frankie readjusted her hat.

"If that's not okay I won't mind if you change it."

She said quickly, to avoid another Awkward Moment.

"Why would I mind? I think it's perfectly lovely—and

appropriate, seeing how this is your lamb and you'll be taking care of her."

"Me?"

"It looks like she's chosen you."

"But I have no idea what I'm doing."

"You've already fed her, right?"

"Yes."

"Brought her fresh hay."

"Yes."

"That's basically all she'll need for a couple of days until she's strong enough to join the other bums in the pen. Just feed her four times a day and make sure her pen is clean. I'd say she'll be ready for another bottle right before supper, so you can come back then. Oh, and I have something for you."

Frankie stood up and pulled a small red notebook out of the back pocket of her jeans. I thought it was the one she always wrote in until she handed it to me and I saw that the cover was unmarred and shiny and the pages were crisp and white like a beginning-of-the-semester notebook. A sharpened stub of a pencil followed.

"As Petey's caretaker, you'll want to write down her date and approximate time of birth and how much she takes at each feeding." Frankie gave me a soft smile. "And anything else you want to write in there."

"Thank you," I said. "But—did you already have this on you or something? How did you know this was all going to turn out this way?"

"I didn't," she said. "I just had a God-feeling. I try to pay attention to those."

She climbed over the gate, and for the first time it occurred to me to watch how she did it, since it was one of the countless skills I had yet to master. She basically straddled it like she was sitting on a horse and then swung one leg to join the other on the rungs and hopped down.

Good to know.

"You can go have lunch," Frankie said from the other side. "Take some free time. Petey won't need you again until supper. I'll put her bottle in the fridge out here."

"I think I'll stay here for a few minutes," I said.

When she was gone I wrote Petey's information on the first page of the notebook and fluffed up the hay and inspected her for bugs and birth defects. She was perfect.

So perfect that a few minutes turned into several hours of watching her sleep and reassuring her when she woke up and rubbing the place between her ears where she seemed to like it.

I had just fetched her bottle from the fridge and was about to settle in to feed her when Joseph appeared at the pen with a long-handled metal dipper in his hand. It looked like something out of the old Clint Eastwood movies Wes used to subject me to.

"Thought you could use some communion," Joseph said.

"It isn't Sunday," I said.

"Doesn't have to be."

He lowered his eyes to the cup. When I reached out to take it from him he said, "Best communion wine you'll ever taste. Right from the pump."

His spurs clanked as he walked away, leaving me in the pen with my lamb. The water shone inside its metal chalice.

Right from the pump, huh? You think they have a filter on that thing?

Probably not. But I took a sip, and then downed all of it.

He was right. It was the best communion I'd ever had.

> Share this chapter with your friends!
> I just had a God-feeling. I try to pay
> attention to those. #TheMercifulScar

Chapter
NINE

Over the next two days, except when I was doing chores and helping herd the sheep and showing up for the obligatory suppers, I seldom left Petey's side. And Bathsheba seldom left mine.

She found an old shirt someplace and dragged it to a spot outside Petey's pen and slept there, waiting for me to climb out in the morning to run up to the Cloister for a quick shower. The dog was so delighted with the whole arrangement her body wagged from nose to tail tip almost every time I so much as looked at her.

Frankie was considerably less excited than that when she discovered I was spending my nights in the pen with Petey, and she insisted I go to my own bed so I could get some "decent sleep."

I flopped like a flounder until four a.m., imagining Petey shivering in the corner crying for me, certain I'd abandoned her. At four fifteen I couldn't stand it any longer and I slipped through the already gathering light down to the barn. She actually didn't bleat until she heard me call her name. Then she tripped across the pen, lips curved around a woeful *Where have you been?*

I recorded that in the red notebook—*Came when she heard my voice/Wednesday, June 12, 4:23 a.m.*—right below *Wormed/Tuesday, June 11, 11:00 a.m.*—and—*Docked tail/Tuesday, June 11, 3:00 p.m.*—and—*Runs after me when I try to leave the pen/every day.* I wasn't sure that was what Joseph and Frankie were writing in their ranch notebooks when they pried them from their pockets and jotted in them, but that was how I was doing it. I liked the clarity of it somehow.

While my bond with Petey and Bathsheba grew, some of my relationships with the humans foundered. At least with Andy and Emma.

Andy was quiet and stiff at suppers—which I convinced myself was because he had obvious issues with Joseph—and although he dropped by the pen now and then while I was feeding Petey, he didn't come in and sit with us in the hay again like he did that first day. His grin was just as charming and his dimples were still intact, but his eyes never seemed to rest on anything. He curled his fingers around the top plastic slat of the pen so that his arm muscles went taut and hunky-looking—

Seriously, does he have *to do that?*

And he said things like, "How's motherhood, Bo?" And "I hear you're spoiling her beyond rotten." It was just never anything I could pick up and weave into a conversation.

Personally, I think you make him nervous.

I decided on Tuesday there might actually be something to that, when his visit consisted of, "Just thought I'd bring you girls some fresh hay," and then a quick exit with the bale still in his arms.

I scrolled back through every minute I'd spent with him Sunday and couldn't find anything I'd done that might have made him now act like I was carrying the H1N1 virus.

Does it matter? You do only have twenty days to go.

Not only that, but it had also been eight days since I'd cut. I would be able to leave assuring Frankie that I'd been cured. Somehow.

Define cured . . .

But it did matter that Andy was shying away from a friendship with me, because any thread that had started to connect me with Emma had disappeared too. Granted, I wasn't at the Cloister that much, but when our paths did cross, she couldn't meet my gaze any better than Andy could. I thought she might be embarrassed about the scene on Sunday.

Yeah, that went beyond Awkward Moment for the poor kid.

I even considered assuring her that I didn't think any less of her because she . . .

What? Flipped out?

Right. Bad idea. Besides, with each passing day I was more certain that Emma didn't care whether I thought less of her or not. Weird as I felt it was, if it hadn't been for Petey and Bathsheba, I might have shriveled from loneliness.

Or taken a razor apart.

Like I said, define cured.

———

On Friday it looked like Frankie was going to take even my bond with Petey away.

When I was feeding her that morning, Frankie joined me in the pen and as always squatted and stroked Petey's cheek. "I think we need to try putting her in with the other young bums today," she said. "If we keep her separated too long she won't learn how to be a sheep." Frankie rested her warm eyes on me. "She would have learned from her mom and although you've been an amazing mother to her, you can't teach her that."

"I don't know," I said. "I feel pretty sheepish most of the time."

She chuckled. "Good one."

"No, I mean, actually like a sheep."

"And is that altogether a bad thing?"

"It hasn't worked that well for me—going where everybody told me to go, doing what the person in front of me was doing, not thinking anything out for myself."

My voice was thick, and that was a surprise even to me.

Only *to you. Look at Frankie.*

She was looking at me as if she were savoring my face. "Is that what you've discovered since you've been here?"

"It's what I just discovered ten seconds ago." I had to swallow hard. "Look, I know you've been giving me a lot of details about sheep that are obviously linked to Jesus being the Good Shepherd and all. And by the way, I appreciate you not preaching sermonettes on it."

"Doesn't sound like I needed to. You got the connection."

"But what am I supposed to do about it? I mean, you told me to listen for *bat kol* and I tried that and all I heard, frankly, was the wind. And I'm assuming from the sheep references that I'm supposed to listen for the shepherd's voice and follow that instead of all the other people who are as clueless as I am. But again, I'm not getting the message."

"Would you follow it if you did?"

"Follow what? The message?"

"Yes. If you heard Jesus say, 'Kirsten, I want you to stop going for the razor for release and come to Me instead,' would you do it?"

"If I knew how! I've been here almost two weeks and . . ." I shrugged.

"Do you want to know how?" she said.

"I guess—"

"Kirsten, don't close off. Keep going with this. Say exactly what you want to say."

Oh, she doesn't really want to hear this, trust me.

"I don't think you're going to like it," I said.

"This isn't about me. It's about you," she said.

And then she waited. The Nudnik was silent.

"Okay," I said. "What I want to know is how *you* do it."

"How I hear God?"

"Yeah. The other day you said you prayed about focusing on Emma and me with Andy here and then you knew what to do. And the whole thing with the ranch notebook. What did you say? Oh, you said you had a God-feeling that you were supposed to have it with you and you always pay attention to those." I shrugged. "I don't know how to do any of that. What is it—do you have to be a nun or you don't get to have a connection with God?"

All right, Kirsten! I didn't know you had it in you.

I wasn't sure I wanted it *out* of me, now that I'd spilled my guts all over Petey's pen.

But Frankie's face took on a glow in the always-dim light of the barn. "I don't have my connection with our Lord because I was a nun—and still am in many ways. I have it because I have immersed myself in who I was made by God to be, and that happens to be a sister. Finding that true self and embracing it is how anyone connects to God. That's how Joseph does it. That's how your David Dowling does it. That's how every girl who has lived with us has begun to learn to do it." Frankie drew her face closer to mine. "And every time, that starts with a deep longing, a hunger and a thirst, and that's where you are now. You want God."

Frankie went beyond waiting then. She became so still I would have wondered if she was still breathing if I hadn't gone into a stunned silence of my own, where even the Nudnik left me alone with Frankie's words.

I did want that. I did want the peace. I wanted to know that I would have a God-feeling to show me what to do. I wanted to be something besides a sheep who hadn't even found the flock.

"I'm tired of being lonely," I said.

Frankie put out her hand and touched me on the cheek, just as she always did Petey. "You never have to be again," she said. "The Lord be with you."

I'd heard her say that every night before we shared a meal. The response was always the same from Joseph and Emma and Andy. Now I said it too.

"And also with you."

Frankie prayed then. I couldn't remember every word even moments after her amen. But the essence of it stayed with me, like the sweet scent of the hay I slept in with Petey. I was loved, and all I had to do was talk to God in whatever way was true and right for me. I already believed in God. Now I had to accept that God believed in me.

The Nudnik didn't give it thirty seconds after Frankie left the pen before she whispered: *We'll see how that goes.*

"Just this one time," I whispered back, out loud, "I want you to shut up."

———

I didn't have time to ask God to let Petey stay in her pen with me for at least a few more days. As soon as we came back from herding the flock, we started the process of introducing my lamb to the other bums.

"As her surrogate mother, do I get to give my opinion?" I said before I deposited her tiny self into the fray.

"Of course," Frankie said.

"I think it's too soon. Look how little she is, and they're such bruisers. You can't even see her with them all over her."

That wasn't an exaggeration. The rest of the bums were on her like she was a fresh pan of pellets, all of them expressing their views on the newcomer.

"They're just checking her out," Frankie said. "Thanks to you she's strong. She'll be fine." She started back into the barn. "Let's go clean out her pen."

"That's it? We're just going to leave her here to fend for herself?"

I got the husky laugh. "You're reminding me of me the first day I put Andy on the bus for kindergarten. I cried all day. He was fine. I was a basket case."

"But they're all nudging at her. Human kids don't do that."

"Really."

I turned to see Frankie giving me a wide-open look. "I think that's one of the reasons we all end up with false selves to begin with. Petey's blessed. She has a good shepherd and she knows it."

It still took everything I had to peel myself away from the bums' pen and follow Frankie into the barn.

"I'll be back to check on you, baby," I said over my shoulder.

———

I kept that promise, especially during feeding time. At first Petey seemed clueless about the nipples on the vats that her new family all vied for like women at a 75-percent-off sale. Frankie finally let me go in there and guide her to an empty one and get her sucking on it. Of course, ten seconds later, the entire rest of the group discovered she had a nipple all to herself and they shoved her out of the way and glommed onto it, one after the greedy other.

"I'm telling you, she's going to starve," I said.

"All right," Frankie said with an exaggerated sigh. "You can give her one bottle a day, just until she gets acquainted. And she goes back in there when you're done." She grinned at me. "You're turning into a helicopter mom."

Yeah, who'd a thought, huh?

Not with the mother *I* had. I hadn't thought about Michelle much since I'd been there, and I smirked to myself thinking about what she'd be saying right now. I was in the same jeans I'd been wearing for a week, and there was so much barn goo pressed into the soles of my boots I'd stopped even trying to dig it out.

No, I was definitely a different kind of mom. Hanging around the bums' pen during my free time. Praying for Petey, since I was still self-conscious about praying for myself. And writing down my observations in the red notebook. On Saturday at noon, I recorded: *Petey's looking thinner. And a little lethargic?*

Or maybe you're neurotic. Just a thought.

Maybe so, but I tucked the notebook in the pocket of my sweatshirt that I'd hung over the main gate and headed to the back of the barn for some fresh hay, the really sweet stuff. The other bums were all inside their shelter sleeping, so hopefully I could sneak some into the corner for Petey and get her to eat it.

Once I got back with a few chunks—what Frankie called *flakes*—I decided the best thing to do would be to drop it into the pen from the horse corral side, where they kept Hildegarde. I wouldn't have even considered it but the cow was currently standing in a far corner of the corral letting Little Augie nurse while he was lying down.

Oh brother.

The cow didn't even look my way as I dropped the hay in, got over the fence the way I'd learned from Frankie, and picked the hay up again.

Y'know, that whole scene with her and Augie is like a metaphor for your past relationship, don't you think?

No! Okay, yes, sort of. But right now it seemed like that had happened to somebody else. Some other Kirsten who wouldn't have tossed hay into a lamb's pen and tried to climb in with it if—

That thought was interrupted by the sudden sense that something large and smelly was behind me. When I turned I found myself looking directly up into Hildegarde's enormous brown eyes.

Make that ticked-off brown eyes.

Even if she hadn't delivered a moo loud enough to start a stampede, I would have tried to leap over the fence just from the sheer indignation that flared her nostrils. I didn't care if her horns *had* been taken off with a chain saw; it was that gigantic head that freaked me out.

I at least had enough of my wits left to straddle the fence. But once I was up there, Hildegarde shoved that head against my leg and I couldn't move. Below me, Petey was bleating piteously and I tried to lean over to at least touch her. But with one leg immobile and my other foot now caught in the lower slat, all I could do was wave one arm blindly in Hildegarde's direction in the hope of connecting with her nose so I could punch it.

The cow was bawling, the lamb was crying, but somehow I still heard a male voice yell, "Man, Hildegarde, no wonder you don't have any friends!"

The big head moved and my back leg released. But there wasn't time to get myself back in balance on the fence. Arms flailing, I went over, barely missing Petey as I fell with a splat into the muddy, poopy bottom of the bums' pen. It was apparently an event not to be missed, because I was instantaneously inundated with curious lambs, all discussing the matter inches from my face.

Above me Andy hung over the fence and grinned down. "How ya doin', Bo?" he said.

I laughed. And then I laughed some more. And I kept laughing until I was barely breathing and Andy was pulling me up by both hands.

"This is a good look for you," he said.

"Shut up," I said, and then threw my head back and laughed even more. The inevitable snort produced a spray of gunk, which drove the hysteria to another whole level.

"I'm just gonna have to hose you down," Andy said.

"Is Petey okay?"

"You didn't squish her. Come on—"

He dragged me all the way up to the area where the vehicles lived, pulled out a hose, and proceeded to do exactly what he'd promised. I didn't know which was making me squeal louder as he turned the beyond-icy water on me and sprayed me from ponytail to hiking boots—the cold, the hilarity, or the fact that the more he squirted the more I looked like I had entered a wet T-shirt contest.

"Stop!" I said. Rather unconvincingly.

"You've still got stuff in your ears—let me get that!"

"No!"

Andy turned off the hose, looked at me, and let out the single most authentic male laugh I'd heard since the boys in my preschool class giggled about farting noises. It was the kind of laugh I hoped I would never hear the end of.

Another hope foiled, however. Andy looked past my shoulder and his face sobered. As far as I knew, only one person could make that happen that fast.

"I've got this handled," Andy said between his teeth.

"I have no doubt," Joseph answered. "But if there's going to be a *this*, son, you'd better be honest with Frankie."

I heard his boots crunch away, spurs jangling behind me. He took the delight of our moment with him.

"I'm, uh—I'm gonna go get changed," I said. I was already backing up.

"Yeah, go," Andy said.

But I wasn't sure he was talking to me.

There is no *this* between Andy and me, I told myself as I half-ran to the Cloister. And I am *not* going to get involved in whatever drama is playing out in that family.

Good luck with that.

Fine. If the Nudnik wouldn't shut up, I could at least—*God, can you do Your thing and keep me out of it? I'm not ready for that.*

Huh. Now that's the first *thing you've said that's made sense.*

I stopped in the doorway and let that whisper one more time. I was still standing there when Emma appeared in the living room, took one look at my soaked-through self, and laughed. Really laughed. As in giggles that bubbled up in the mezzo-soprano range somewhere.

"Let me guess—you fell in the water trough," she said.

"Worse," I said. "You don't want to know."

I wanted to tell her, actually, but as far as I knew she hadn't had a change of heart about Andy, and what was the story without him?

"You're headed for the shower, right?" Emma said, giggles still dancing in her voice.

"Yes—and I won't clog the drains."

"You didn't know," she said. "I was being a witch that day."

Wait! I want to hear that again!

But I said, "It's okay," and went off wondering who this girl was and what she'd done with Emma.

I wondered even more when I came out in clean clothes and still-wet shampooed hair and Emma was waiting with two large mugs whose aroma laughed in the face of Starbucks.

"Where did you *get* that?" I said. "It smells amazing."

"I made it." She handed me a cup. "I'm drinking mine on the porch if you want to . . ."

She let that trail off and exited through the front door. I followed with my mouth watering. I barely waited until my buns hit the seat of the rocker Bathsheba was curled under before I took the first sip. Emma watched, eyes expectant.

"Okay, that may be the best coffee I have ever tasted, ever. And trust me, I drank a *lot* of it in college."

"You consume a fair amount in the army too," Emma said.

"Yeah, but I bet it didn't taste like this."

"Unh-uh. The secret to this is Hildegarde's cream."

It was too late to gag. I'd already admitted the stuff was the nectar of God. And as ecstatic as it was making my taste buds, I would happily die from salmonella.

"Can you taste the hay?" Emma said.

"Come to think of it, yeah." I was suddenly blinking. "It makes me think of sitting in the pen with Petey. But now she's off to kindergarten."

"Ugh. Separation anxiety. I hate that."

I took another sip so I wouldn't blurt out some question that would send Emma skittering back into her den. I liked her being out of it.

I did say, "Thanks for sharing this with me."

"Yeah, well, it's like a friend of mine used to say: 'There's nothing wrong with just improving the moment.'"

"I like that," I said. "There are definitely plenty of moments that need improving."

Emma grunted. "Tell me about it."

I wanted to. Maybe I would have if a white sedan hadn't appeared over the rise in the driveway and fishtailed toward the main house.

"Somebody doesn't know how to drive on a dirt road," Emma said. "Who would come up here in a car like that, anyway?"

"You don't recognize it?"

Emma shook her head.

We watched as the car stopped where the driveway ended. Its brake lights flashed as if it were annoyed by the lack of pavement. Frankie came through the gate and she and the two dogs greeted the driver as he stepped out of the incongruous white Lincoln and used the door as a shield against Norwich and Undie.

"Doesn't like dogs," Emma said. "Shows up driving a stinkin' Lincoln. This guy's lost."

But I found the tabletop with my coffee cup and stood up, already trembling.

"Yo, Petersen."

I turned woodenly to Emma.

"What's wrong? Do you know that guy?"

"Yeah," I said. "It's my father."

> Share this chapter with your friends!
> *I already believed in God. Now I had to accept*
> *that God believed in me. #TheMercifulScar*

Chapter
TEN

Emma stood up like a pole beside me as my graying-blond, too-tanned father spoke with Frankie in words we couldn't hear.

"I take it this isn't a good thing," Emma said.

"I don't know yet," I said.

Her grunt was almost sympathetic. "You want me to go up and see what he wants?"

"No." I lowered myself back into the rocker. "I'll just wait."

"Okay," Emma said. "I'll wait with you."

Bathsheba waited, too, until Sandy Petersen and Frankie started to make their way up the knoll. Then she untangled herself from under my chair and sailed off the porch without touching the steps. She was on my father's heels before he got within ten feet of the house, snapping at the hems of his pressed jeans.

"Knife pleats?" Emma muttered. "Really?"

The group kept moving—Bathsheba snarling and nipping, my father attempting to kick at her and missing, and Frankie commanding, "Off, girl. Off."

"That dog might be worth something after all," Emma said.

I went down the steps and called to Bathsheba. She paused and looked at me, and then went back to setting up for a full attack on my father's leg. I had to go over and grab her by the scruff of her furry neck.

"It's okay, 'Sheba," I said. "He's not going to hurt me."

Well, the jury's still out on that.

Bathsheba grumbled and circled around to sit at my feet. Emma had been right about her worth: my father had been knocked slightly off-kilter by the whole thing, which gave me a moment to take the temperature, the way I always had to when I saw him for the first time in months. It was anybody's guess what it might be—bone-chilling, tepid, or sunny and breezy. I didn't hold out much hope for the latter at that point.

But to my amazement, Dad put his arm around me and tugged me into his side. I heard Emma mumble, "Gee, could ya spare it?" but in my show-no-affection family, a sidearm hug was like killing the fatted calf in anybody else's. He added a disarming smile, too, but it was the eyes that got me. They were looking directly into mine, blue for blue, with no agenda to dart them on to the next thing. He was looking at me, and I melted.

"I'm sure you two could use some alone time," Frankie said. "Emma, you want to come up and help with supper?"

Emma looked at me as if she was waiting for a go-ahead. I nodded to her.

But I also watched her and Frankie make their way down the knoll in the wind that was just kicking up. Frankie put one hand on top of her cap and linked the other hand around Emma's elbow. I felt a tug inside.

My father was literally tugging at my hand. "Let's go in and talk," he said. "It's a little gusty out here for me."

This is nothin', pal. You need to cowboy up.

In a starched Oxford shirt and polished Western boots that looked like he'd just taken them off the rack, Dad did look singularly out of place, not something I could ever have said about him before. He either created the environment he wanted or he simply didn't show up. But he was here and he seemed to want to be, and I couldn't help warming to that.

I kept a firm hand on the still-grumbling Bathsheba until I left her on the porch and led Dad inside. She jumped up onto the rocking chair and peered in the window like a private investigator.

Dad stopped in the middle of the living room and did a survey. "I like what you've done with the place," he said, tongue planted firmly in the proverbial cheek. "What's it got, a five-star rating?"

"It's okay," I said. "You want some coffee?"

"No, I want to look at you." He took me by both shoulders and held me out in front of him. The blue eyes shimmered. "You look better than I expected you to. Nice to see a little color in you for a change. And a little muscle tone."

Are these supposed to be compliments?

I tried to smile. "How did you expect me to look?"

Dad nodded to the two recliners by the side window that neither Emma nor I ever sat in. The way they were arranged called for two people curling up.

I followed him over and sat stiffly, despite the overstuffed arms that invited a true sink-in-and-veg. Sitting and talking was never my father's approach. Usually when he showed up with a smile and a one-armed hug, he followed up by rubbing his hands together and saying, "Okay, this is what we're going to do."

Yeah, watch yourself. He's acting like an actual father.

Just like I'd always wanted him to. But that wanting had gone on for a long time, so I resisted the chair's embrace and stayed on guard.

Dad leaned toward me. "First of all, kiddo, let me just say how sorry I am—"

Say again?

"—that you've been suffering. I had no idea Wes was going to turn out to be a . . . jerk."

Yea, Daddy. Keep that vocabulary clean.

"I should have seen it," Dad went on. "I'm usually a better judge of character than that. Guy's a good actor."

It struck me to ask: "Did Mother tell you we broke up?"

"She did not. I got my information from the little weasel himself. I know this has been tough on you, really tough, but kiddo, you dodged a bullet with that character. A guy who gets his girlfriend's best friend pregnant . . ."

Whoa.

". . . and expects his girlfriend to go on with him as if nothing happened would give you nothing but heartache if you married him. I don't care if he *did* take Clarabelle or Annabelle or whatever her name is to have an abortion . . ."

WHOA.

". . . if he cheated on you once, he'd do it again."

I pressed both hands to my mouth and squeezed my eyes closed, but I was too late to shut out what my father had just marched past me like a funeral parade.

Wouldn't do you any good anyway. Come to think of it, you should've seen this coming.

I should have. I could hear Wes's voice now, saying, "*We took care of that. We took care of everything.*"

That was why Isabel had called him crying that Saturday night.

That was where they were, he and Isabel, all that Sunday while I was preparing for my betrothal like the village idiot. My life wasn't

179

the only one that had been lost because Wes couldn't make a commitment to anything but himself.

My skin screamed.

"Now, let me be clear," Dad said, as if I weren't disintegrating before his eyes, "I did talk to your mother, which is how I knew where to find you. I have to tell you, kiddo, between her and Wes, I can understand why you'd think the world wasn't a place you'd want to live in. She has the emotions of a . . ."

Okay, look, don't go off the deep end. He's gonna talk 'til he's done and then he'll leave and you can—do whatever. For now, just sit there and, I don't know, pray or something.

All I could think of to pray was *Please don't let me lose it. Please.*

My father was indeed still talking and he didn't seem to be even close to wrapping it up. "I'm just so, so sorry I wasn't there for you. I wish you'd called me instead of your mother."

"I didn't call her," I managed to say. "Wes did."

"See? One more reason he's a loser. Did he even know you at all?"

I just shook my head.

"No matter." Dad moved to the edge of the chair and took both of my hands. He turned over my wrists so my red-yarn scar was visible.

What are we, Father of the Year now?

"I'm glad you weren't very good at it," he said with a wobbly smile. "But it's going to be okay. I've already made arrangements to move you to one of the highest-rated private care facilities in California, near the ocean even."

He held up one hand as if I'd made a move to protest. I hadn't moved at all. I couldn't.

"I'm not going to just take you there and leave. I've rescheduled all my obligations for the next few weeks so I can be close by and help you work all of this through." He gave me more of a wink than a smile. "And we'll keep your mother as far out of it as possible, yes?"

Dad waited no longer than a nanosecond for a response.

He ain't no Sister Frankie, for sure.

"I'm going to say this again: I am so sorry I wasn't there for you. I don't know if I could stand it if you took your own life, kiddo. I just don't know."

I might have corrected him then—told him I never intended to take my own life—if it hadn't been for the tears in his eyes. Real tears. "You can get past this, and I'm here to help you. You and me, kiddo."

O-kay, you're thinking this through, right? You might want to go with that praying thing.

Dad glanced at his watch. "It's pretty late in the day to be starting out now and you'll probably want time to pack." He gave me another once-over. "Or maybe not. The clothes you've had to wear up here won't be what you'll want in California. No worries. We'll go shopping tomorrow if you're up for it. So let's do this: since our flight doesn't leave until late afternoon, I'll go back now to my hotel in Conrad—if you can call it that—and I'll swing back up here a little before noon and we'll drive the rental car to Great Falls, pick up a few things for you, and still catch our plane to Santa Barbara. How does that sound?"

"Hello?"

I had never been so glad to hear Frankie's voice.

"It's okay—come in," I said.

I didn't look at my father. He had succeeded in turning me back into a small piece of marble that was about to be picked up and moved. How was I supposed to answer him?

Frankie slanted her head in, and I could hear Bathsheba resuming her grumbling on the porch. "Supper's almost ready," Frankie said. "Mr. Petersen, can I interest you in some lamb kebobs? We have plenty."

"I don't think so," Dad said. "I really need to get going."

Get him to stay. Do it.

"I wish you would, Dad," I said. "They're amazing cooks."

I turned to my father in time to see him regrouping, just behind his eyes.

"If that's what you want, kiddo," he said, "that's what we'll do."

Good job, kiddo. Good job.

Dad hunched his shoulders against the wind as we walked up to the main house, a posture I knew was not amusing him. As she always did, Frankie hooked her arm through mine and smiled into every gust that whipped at our hair and made off with our breath. And just as always, she was able to converse as if we were in a tearoom, chatting over china cups.

"What line of work are you in, Mr. Petersen?" she said.

"I'm in commercial architecture," Dad shouted. "I own a firm in San Francisco with branches in Santa Barbara and San Diego."

Frankie opened the gate and let us pass her into the shelter of the cottonwoods and out of the wind. "Well, welcome to Montana—although I understand MSU is your alma mater."

"Right. Go Polar Bears."

Frankie gave him her husky laugh. "We've come to that, haven't we? Distilling our fine educational institutions down to the stuffed animals who dance at football games."

She laughed again, and if I hadn't felt like I was making my way through some surreal painting, I would have laughed with her. I had always felt that way about the obsession with college sports.

Now, my father, he showed no signs of laughing at all. He put his hand on the back door and said, "Please, after you."

I was surprised, and maybe a little relieved, to find only Andy waiting at the table when we got to the dining room. My guess was that Emma had expressed her opinion about my father and had been packed off to Conrad with Joseph for pizza. I had to wonder, though, why Andy didn't go with them.

He stood up the minute we entered the room and offered his hand to my father. He was freshly showered and shaven. I could even smell a trace of musky aftershave.

"Andy DeLuca," he said.

"Sandy Petersen. Are you a patient here, Andy?"

Oh. My. Gosh.

Andy grinned. "I have always been a patient here, sir. I'm Frankie's nephew."

Being back in Andy's presence, and Frankie's, brought the picture into focus. I caught Andy's surreptitious grin for me as I took my customary seat at the table, and it gave me a pang. I was leaving right when it really did look like we could be friends. Not a *this*, as Joseph had put it. Not a *this* he was supposed to tell Frankie about, but a good-bud thing.

Really? You want to go there right now?

I couldn't. I couldn't see to go anywhere—not with my father's revelation about Wes, and his plan to take me from here and put me someplace else, and the tears in his eyes because he thought I'd tried to kill myself—not with all of that spinning in my head. I scratched at my arm under the table and tried to center.

The dinner was, as always, fabulous, and so was Frankie's way of guiding the conversation along like a piece of silk. Andy wasn't bad at it either, though he punctuated his repartee with sly secret smiles at me.

My father held his own, especially when Frankie drew him out about his avant-garde design for a spa in Palm Springs and his plans for a father-daughter trip to the South of France when I was well enough—at which point Andy raised his eyebrows quizzically at me and I shrugged. Another one of today's surreal surprises.

But as the evening progressed, I also saw Dad's smile become more plastic and his eyes more vague. Once I saw them redden and his closed mouth stretch as if he were holding back a yawn. I looked at Frankie but she didn't seem to notice. Or maybe she was too polite to let on, because Frankie didn't miss much of anything. Still, I hoped she missed that.

Just about the time I knew Dad was going to make an excuse to leave, he leaned back in his chair and looked smoothly around the dining room.

"Well," he said in his confident baritone, "I can see this place has done Kirsten a lot of good. There's a part of me that hates to take her away."

The air froze. It was Andy who chilled it with eyes of ice, not Frankie. Her demeanor was as quiet and intentional as ever as she said, "Would you like to explain that, Mr. Petersen?"

"Of course. I think I owe you that much."

As he filled them in on his plan, I clawed at my arm, though it wasn't enough to put out the fire on my skin. I couldn't look at Andy, but I knew he was searching my face for an explanation that went far deeper than the one my father was giving.

"Please don't take this the wrong way," Dad said. "I'm sure in time your method would produce the same results. I just think a more professional approach will speed things along so she can get back to school."

Is it just me, or did he just make that entire announcement without ever looking at you?

Which meant it had to be blatantly obvious to both of them that my father had formed the rescue plan without consulting me.

Wasn't a heartfelt rescue what you wanted? What you always wanted from Daddy?

I couldn't deny that, especially since my father's reaction to my situation was not at all what I'd been afraid it would be. Yet something crawled up the back of my neck. I didn't recognize it as resentment until Frankie said, "Do you think you two have discussed this enough?"

Her eyes prodded me. I could hear them telling me: *Say exactly what you think.*

"We haven't discussed it at all," I said.

Dad sniffed. "What is there to discuss? Kirsten needs the best and fastest care so an unfortunate incident like that won't happen again." He gave Frankie the synthetic version of his smile. "I don't know what financial arrangements you've made with Kirsten's mother, but I'll pay you for the entire thirty days Kirsten was to be here. That's only right."

Frankie said nothing. It took me several seconds to realize she had no intention of saying anything as long as he was still there.

"Excuse me," Andy said.

He scraped his chair back and left through the kitchen without a glance at me. And certainly not a sly smile.

I stopped scratching at my arm and let the resentment crawl up my neck unhindered. When I heard the back door slam, I turned to my father.

Say exactly what you want to say. Say it.

"It wasn't just one unfortunate incident," I said. "And I wasn't trying—"

"Then all the more reason to get you the best doctors in the psychiatric field." He rose from the chair and kissed me on top of the head. "Listen, we've got a big day tomorrow, kiddo, so I'm going to let you get some rest." He nodded at Frankie. "Sister, it's been a pleasure."

Frankie and I sat without talking as the door closed and Bathsheba growled and the Lincoln's engine purred to life and faded down the driveway. When all was quiet, she drew my arm out from under the table and rested her hand on it.

"I can feel something stirring under your skin," she said.

I was only a little startled. "That's exactly how it feels," I said.

"How much does he know?"

I looked down. "He thinks I tried to commit suicide. He doesn't know about the cutting apparently, which makes sense, since my mother doesn't give him any more information than he asks for and Wes couldn't have told him about the—self-injury—because he's in total denial. He's still telling himself he saved my life."

"Your dad doesn't give you much chance to explain, does he?"

"I will tomorrow," I said. "On the way to Great Falls. I mean, I have to, right?"

"Only you can answer that."

"It isn't that he doesn't care about me. He wasn't the check-your-homework-every-night kind of dad when I was growing up because he was busy building his business—"

And his extramarital affairs, in case you want to throw that in.

"And then after the divorce, my mother took Lara and me to Missouri but he couldn't leave it all in California so I didn't see him much. But he was the one who told me I needed to get out of there, away from my mother's dead-end life, and he said he'd pay for any college I wanted to go to, all four years, room, board, tuition, books, everything. And he did."

My voice sounded defensive, even to me, and it didn't have to be.

Frankie was listening and nodding without a trace of judgment on her face.

"When it got to be my senior year at MSU and I didn't know what I was going to do next, he came back, just at the right time again, and said he'd not only pay for grad school but he'd rent a house for me so I could live off campus and really be able to focus on my work. He even furnished it."

"He's generous."

"I never had to look for change in the sofa cushions like some of my friends did."

"When was the last time you saw him before today?"

I had to speak past the lump forming in my throat. "Almost a year ago. He came to Bozeman to help me get settled in my house. He's been going through a divorce this year so . . ."

We fell silent again. I was just starting to pray that Frankie would say something, anything, when she whispered, "The Lord be with you."

"And also with you," I said.

Frankie breathed in, long and slow as if she were drawing God Himself into her soul. "Father, I hate to see Kirsten go before she has a chance to hear Your voice. You'll go with her, I know that. Please—speak Your voice deeper and louder than her earthly father's. Don't let him drown her out."

Once again she touched my arm and when my eyes opened, she said, "I'll walk you back."

"I'll be fine," I said. "I'll have Bathsheba with me."

She nodded. "I'm actually beginning to trust that dog's instincts."

I was all the way to the gate before it came to me that I would be leaving Bathsheba behind. The thought made my throat ache.

"Listen," I said to her as she lathered my hand. "You're really starting to shape up. You can still be the dog you were made to be after I—"

"You really shouldn't be out here by yourself at night, Bo."

I sucked in air and closed my eyes. The good news was—it was Andy. The bad news was—it was Andy. I wasn't sure I could stand to hear the questions, much less answer them. I wanted to leave it at the giggling, spraying, wonderful hosing-down that now seemed like so long ago.

But he only said, "I'll walk you home," and fell into step beside me. Bathsheba licked his hand too.

You can't catch a break, can you?

No, especially when one of the lambs on the hill cried out for its mother and I thought of Petey for the first time since my father had shown up.

"I need to go check on her," I said.

Andy didn't ask who. He just changed course and saw me to the barn.

At first glance it seemed all was well in the bum lamb pen. The young residents were piled inside the shelter, as still as their grown-up counterparts on the hill. All except one.

In the corner of the pen, near where I'd dropped the sweet hay for her, Petey lay curled in a ball, trembling.

"Petey," I called softly. "Petey, it's me."

She answered in a voice frail as a cobweb, but she didn't run to me.

"Something's wrong," I said.

I climbed the fence in one move and went to her. She looked as frail as she did the day she was born, maybe more so. I cradled her into my arms and carried her to the gate that was always kept closed to prevent escapes. Andy had it open. He looked at Petey and said, "I'll get Frankie."

———

Nothing we did seemed to help. Frankie examined the lamb and gave her a dropper of something, but an hour later it had had no effect. I tried the last of the formula but Petey spit the nipple out. I held her the way she loved to be held, and yet she couldn't seem to sleep. As the night deepened, so did the concern on Frankie's face.

At about three a.m., when Petey was stirring restlessly in my lap, Andy said to Frankie, "What else ya got?"

"I have one more idea," she said. "Would you get Hildegarde into her chute?"

Andy hurried out and I stared at Frankie. "You're going to milk the cow *now*?"

"I've seen this work before," she said. "I don't know if it will this time, but we have to try. We're going to give Petey some of Hildegarde's milk. I think it may have the nutrients that will build her back up."

"If she'll even take it," I said.

"Who's going to turn down Hildegarde's cream?" Frankie gave me probably the only smile she had left. "I just hope she'll give us some. She doesn't like to get off her schedule."

"I want to try to milk her," I said. "I have to do this for Petey."

Without hesitation, Frankie said, "Then let's give it a shot."

Andy had a taciturn Hildegarde ready when I took my place on the tractor seat and put the bucket under her, away from her back feet. As I massaged her udders with balm, I talked to her.

"It's like this, Hildegarde. You're a mother. You know you'd do anything for Little Augie. You even let him lie down to nurse."

"She does?" Frankie said.

"I caught her at it today." A hundred years ago. "I'm not an actual, biological mother like you are, but I love that lamb. I can't just watch her die. I'm begging you to help me—mother to mother."

I handed the jar back to Frankie, took a breath, and put my hands on the two long nipples.

"Will you talk me through it, Frankie?"

She did, voice low and soft and sure. I followed every word with my hands—until a rich white stream sprayed into the bucket.

"Thanks be to God," Frankie whispered. "We just need a few ounces. Then I'll take over and you can go try to feed Petey."

When we had enough, Andy poured it into the bottle he had ready and he and I ran back to the pen. I had to squirt some of the milk into Petey's mouth to get her started, but once she got a taste of Hildegarde's cream she couldn't seem to get enough. What she couldn't swallow drooled down her fleecy chin.

"Look at her chug-a-luggin'," Andy said.

"I think I love that cow," I said.

When Petey fell asleep on the hay beside me, Frankie didn't even try to make me leave.

"We're not completely out of the woods yet," she said. "When she wakes up, there's more Hilda milk in the fridge. We'll know more then."

I did know at dawn, the minute Petey nuzzled me awake with her nose. She still looked fragile but there was no mistaking the voice. She was hungry.

"I'll get you a bottle," I said.

I climbed over the gate and immediately tripped over someone lying in front of it. Bathsheba bounced up from her shirt nest, saliva at the ready, but the pile of person on the barn floor only rolled over and squinted his dark eyes at me. A hunk of black hair fell over one of them.

"How's she doing?" Andy said.

"Good. I'm going to feed her again. Go back to sleep."

He nodded and curled up again. But before I reached the refrigerator, he whispered, "Hey. Bo."

"What?" I whispered back.

"I'm glad you didn't kill yourself."

My breath caught. "I never intended to."

Andy nodded and settled back into his bed of hay. As his eyes closed he said, "Then you better tell your father that."

Share this chapter with your friends!
Don't let any voice speak louder
than God's. #TheMercifulScar

Chapter
ELEVEN

After I fed Petey and made sure she was settled into a sweet new bed of hay, I went to the Cloister. Emma was either still asleep or already gone and the house seemed strangely empty without her.

Now *you start to get attached to this place.*

I turned on the water in the shower to give it the required five minutes to heat up. If my father had shown up a week ago I would have left with him before the dust had settled around the Lincoln and not looked back. A posh "rest home" on the Pacific would have sounded like Utopia compared to moths circling the showerhead and a brainless border collie dogging my trail. Now there were good-byes that would have to be said.

Steam was starting to rise from the shower, so I stripped out of the milk- and drool- and hay-covered clothes and stepped in.

Don't clog the drain.

Right.

You have just enough time to check out those scars.

It wasn't a taunt. In fact, it sounded like something Frankie would suggest, though maybe not in those words. The tone was definitely there, warm and wise.

So I did look down to the early scenes of my attempts to let out the pain. They seemed fainter than they had the last time I'd looked, but they were there, a purposeful puzzle etched on my skin, so many that the scene had become too crowded and I'd had to look elsewhere for relief. As for the one I never looked at, inside my thigh . . .

I shut off the water with a squealy jerk and watched the last of it trail down my jigsawed legs. If it were just as simple as it used to be to let it go—

And let Daddy.

I heard the front door close, which meant I was no longer alone. The pressure was building again under my skin. I had to be by myself.

When I knew Emma was in her room, I threw on some clothes and a jacket and went looking for Frankie. The light was early-weak yet, so she might still be at the house. I tried there first.

I had never gone up to the door without Frankie but I didn't feel like I was trespassing as I pulled it open just a crack and called her name. But a day from now, even a few hours, it *would* be trespassing. Suddenly everything took on a this-is-the-last-time-you'll-do-this feel. It wasn't a feeling I'd ever had before, and I was grateful for Frankie's voice calling back to me from the garden on the side of the house.

"We're out here, Kirsten."

Although I had peeked at the side yard through the dining room curtain once, I hadn't actually ever gone out there. From my brief glance it had seemed pretty enough. Neat rows of green things and a couple of benches.

Now in the Montana early morning I would have sworn it was a garden lifted from an ancient cloister and lightly set down here, Sister Frankie and all. Wrought iron spikes and bars formed its boundaries, keeping the billows of flowers I couldn't name from overflowing into the vegetable garden on the other side. A circle of trimmed emerald grass rounded a concrete cross like the one on the dining room wall, the one we prayed under just as Frankie appeared to be praying now. Sitting on a plain bench next to Andy.

"I'm sorry," I said. "I didn't mean to interrupt."

Frankie beckoned me over with her hand. "It's all right. We were just praying together. Come join us."

Though Andy's eyes were at half-mast he managed the grin. It looked softer and younger than usual. Maybe it was the little-boy way his hair stuck out like a dark version of Petey's hay bed.

"There's room for you," he said.

"With you, me, Andy, and God, that'll make a foursome," Frankie said.

Uh, Kirsten. You're staring.

It was just that I had never put it together that Andy's participation in the blessings and communion was voluntary. I assumed he was being polite, making his aunt happy. But right now there was no indication that he was under duress. The way his hands hung loose and relaxed over his knees . . . he wanted to be there. And so did I.

But I shook my head. "No—thank you—I just came to tell you that I'm going to go up to the shepherd's monument for a little while. You said to let you know . . ."

"Absolutely. I appreciate that." Frankie's face glowed as if she hadn't been up most of the night like I had. I was sure *I* wasn't beaming at the moment.

That is a true statement.

"I know you're a little pushed for time," she said, "so take the green truck as far as you can and then walk the little bit that's left. The keys are in it."

"And we'll send a posse for you when it dies halfway up there," Andy said, brows twisted. "You want me to drive you?"

"No!"

Nice.

"I mean, that's okay. I kind of need to be . . . alone."

"Gotcha," he said.

Well, that little outburst is going to make it easier to say good-bye.

I made a hasty exit and headed down the driveway to the line of vehicles that always reminded me of one of those places where they sell cars for parts.

Kind of endearing, actually.

I wasn't making this any easier on myself. All I could think of as I climbed into the concave driver's seat was how I'd sat with fifteen-minute-old Petey pressing herself into my chest.

"Headed out somewhere?"

I jumped.

"Didn't mean to scare you." Joseph leaned his forearms on the open window frame. "Aren't you forgetting something?"

I tapped the keys dangling in the ignition. "No, I think I have everything. I don't need my driver's license, do I?"

I thought I saw his lips twitch. "Not hardly." He produced the thirty-thirty and reached behind me to hang it from the rack on the back window. "You go, that goes."

"Right," I said. "Are the bears still around?"

"You going up to the monument?"

I nodded.

"They were spotted an hour ago five miles in the other direction. You should be all right. You remember how to use it?"

"Yes."

I squeezed the steering wheel. Frankie was right. I *was* pushed for time. Joseph *would* pick now to get chatty with me.

"You taking this one with you?"

I looked out the window where he was pointing. Bathsheba gazed up at me, eyes anxious, tail in a slow, hopeful wag.

"Do I have a choice?" I said. "Look at that."

"You women and your dogs. I'll put her in the back."

But Bathsheba was having none of that. She leapt straight from the ground through the window and landed next to me, facing front with her ears alert. She did everything but fasten her seat belt.

Oh, wait, there aren't *any seat belts.*

"Don't let her get dog hair on the upholstery," Joseph said as I pulled away.

Frankie hadn't been kidding when she said the truck only had two gears, but somehow Bathsheba and I managed to bounce our way up to the spot where no trucks had gone before. Or at least not one with absolutely no shocks.

As I dutifully slung the rifle over my shoulder before we continued on foot, I felt like someone else. I had no idea who this girl was who talked to a dog and carried a gun and wanted a chance to try praying in that garden. I was definitely no clearer on what that girl was going to do when she reached the monument and stood as if she were naked before the world.

Bathsheba romped off to the hole where she'd flushed out a playmate before. I returned to the shepherd's monument and ran my hand along the rough-hewn stones. There were plenty like them on the ground. I could pick one up and use its time-worn edge to set free this thing that throbbed inside. But that seemed wrong here.

Yeah, I'm thinking it would be right up there with getting drunk on the communion wine, you know?

Cutting had never seemed wrong before. Not until Frankie had run her hand along my arm and said, "I feel something stirring under your skin."

I shivered, but there was no wind. It was in fact so quiet I called to Bathsheba, just to make sure sound still existed. She bounded over to me, soaked my hand, and then raced on to the cliff.

"Careful!" I shouted.

She dropped her haunches to the ground and sat. I went to her and squatted beside her. The sun had not yet done its watercolor wash on the mountains beyond us, and they stood in such sharp, dark contrast to the pale sky that I was sure I could run my arm along the ridge and it would give me a clean incision.

And what would that do for you?

It would probably do nothing. I pulled my hands through my hair, still damp from the shower. All right, think. Think about all the things Frankie said.

"I hate to see her leave before she hears Your voice."

"Listen for bat kol."

"You'll hear God in the daughter of the voice."

All I heard was my own voice, crying out, "I wish You'd just say it, outright! Just tell me what to do! I need somebody to tell me what to do!"

I flung my folded arms across my pulled-up knees and looked down at the tiny-toy ranch. I couldn't see them but I knew the sheep were waiting, still as wax figures in their pen, for Frankie to come and say, "Time to move, woolies." It wasn't the first time I'd envied them.

Somebody is *telling you it's time to move. Or did you miss the part where your father showed up with a plan?*

Then why was I up here, sitting on the edge of a cliff calling to God, instead of packing and saying my good-byes? I had always listened to my father's voice—

When he spoke to you, anyway.

Yesterday he said he didn't want me to die. There were tears in his eyes.

But did you hear them in his voice?

"I don't know!"

Beside me Bathsheba whimpered and pressed her head into my lap. I tangled her fur into my fingers. The quality of the quiet was suddenly soft, and in it I did hear a voice. Not the Nudnik. Not my own thoughts. Not God, I was sure. Just the whisper of memory.

Frankie praying. *"Don't let his voice drown out hers."*

And then my father saying, *"So an unfortunate incident like this won't happen again."* Reducing my pain to a fender bender.

And then the strongest: Andy's sleepy whisper in the barn: *"Then you better tell your father that."*

"Bathsheba," I whispered, "it's time to go back."

———

I went straight to the barn to check on Petey. She was as still as a lamb in a ceramic nativity scene, eyes closed, breath moving gently in and out of her pink nostrils.

Don't start crying yet.

Right. Put that off as long as possible. I stepped outside the barn and looked at the sun, just now clearing the tops of the mountains. I would have time to throw my few things into the zebra-striped bag after I helped herd the sheep and still be ready to talk to my father before we left.

Frankie was just opening the big gate to release the flock when I joined her.

"I'll take the back," I said.

"Andy will appreciate that," she said. "It's been awhile since he's done this."

Of course Frankie would need someone to help her, now that I was leaving. Emma might cut Andy some slack if he was assigned to the job instead of her.

Funny. It didn't seem that much like a job.

Neither Frankie nor Andy asked me why I was there, and I was glad. If I'd had to say I wanted to do it one last time, there would have been no putting off the crying. The thickness in my throat almost made it hard to breathe.

The walk back was silent, and toward the end I broke into a run for the barn so I could check on Petey. One more time.

Joseph was leaning against the corral when I got there, arms folded as if he had nothing better to do than wait for me to show up.

"You better get in there," he said.

I ran, one hand on my throat, and tripped on a chicken squawking across my path. When I caught myself on the gate to Petey's pen, an image of her lying stiff and motionless in the corner was already fixed behind my eyes.

But the lamb I saw was standing up in the middle of her little home, stub of a tail quivering with life.

"Petey!" I said.

What she actually said when she answered, who knew? But in my mind it was clearly, "Mama!" The halting little trot to the gate was proof of that.

"You're okay! Oh, Petey, you're okay!"

I was in the pen by that time, holding her head between my hands. She pulled up her chin and let out a bleat, and I knew the meaning of that one.

"There's still some Hilda milk left," I said. "And we are gonna celebrate."

———

At eleven o'clock Emma escorted my father to the barn, where I was feeding Petey a lunchtime bottle, and promptly disappeared.

I looked up from Petey's wooly head to smile at him, just in time to see the annoyance pinching his brows together. To his credit he made a quick recovery.

"One last time before you go, huh?" he said, nodding at Petey.

I refocused on the bubbles in the bottle. "I'm not sure yet if I'm going," I said.

"Oh, you're going."

My head jerked up as he leaned as far over the gate as he could without falling in. His look was dark.

How is it that this man can be all seven of the dwarves in one twenty-four-hour period?

"I did some checking on this place, Kirsten." His words jammed tightly together. "I don't know where your mother came up with this McKee woman but she isn't a licensed counselor. And that Joseph character they kept out of sight last night . . ." He consulted his phone. "Joseph Maxwell has a criminal record. He did fifteen years' hard time for—"

"Dad!" I said.

"We're dodging a bullet here, kiddo. Is your stuff packed?"

"No."

"Oh, for—"

"I just need to ask you something before I decide, okay?"

He shoved his hands onto his hips. Yesterday's jeans had been replaced by Brooks Brothers slacks, the teary eyes with impatience that was going to cross over into anger if I didn't get this out.

"This facility you're taking me to," I said, "do you know if they treat patients dealing with NSSI?"

"I have no idea what you're talking about."

"Non-suicidal self-injury. It's what I do. Did."

Might again. Get on with this.

"I don't understand this. What—"

"I'll show you."

I set Petey's bottle aside and slid my T-shirt from my shoulders, first one, then the other. Eyes on the scars, I said, "I've been doing this since Lara's accident. There are more on my legs. I do it to release the pain."

"*What* pain? That was seven years ago. Your mother has pro-longed it for herself but you've had every chance to move on."

"I know, Dad," I said. "But I couldn't. So I had to do *this.*"

"You didn't have to. Nobody has to do . . . that." He spit out an expletive that desecrated the barn. "If you needed attention that much, why didn't you tell me?"

"Because you—"

"I don't know what you'd do if you had *real* problems." He stabbed at the screen of his phone. "All right, I'll check with them. What's it called? NCIS?"

"You don't have to check." I let out the breath I didn't know I'd been holding. "I'm not going. I'm sorry you went to all that trouble but I want to stay here and finish out my thirty days. I have two weeks—"

"This is ridiculous. Get up—we have a plane to catch."

"I'm twenty-two years old, Dad. You can't really force me to go."

The words came out so small I wasn't sure he heard me. Nothing in the red fury that hardened his face indicated he did.

"Don't expect me to pay a dime for this," he said, dismissing the ranch with a wave of his cell phone.

"I don't," I said. "I told you, I'm sorry you went to—"

"Stay—just stay here in your convent and do slave labor. But understand me, Kirsten. I am not done with this."

Those were the last words he said before he banged his fist on the pen and left.

Well. That went well.

Among the tearful good-byes I'd dreaded that day, that had never been one of them. But I cried anyway. Without tears. Just dry, sad sobs.

———

I was still in the pen stroking Petey's head between her ears when Frankie found me some time later. She smelled of hay and incense and molasses as she sat down on the hay beside me and, of course, waited.

"Sandy Petersen is a Chinook," she said finally.

"Does that mean jerk?"

She laughed the husky laugh. "No. A Chinook is a very warm wind that comes to us here in the early spring and can make a foot of snow vanish in one day. Amazing." She wobbled her hand. "Actually, it's an extremely dry wind so it only partly melts the snow. It evaporates the rest. Anyway, a Chinook can raise the temperature from twenty degrees to sixty-eight for a few days and fool the uninitiated into thinking spring is here and winter is over. But then it's gone and the temperature plummets again." Frankie ran her hand across my arm. "But at least the snow has melted."

"My father doesn't really love me," I said. "He maybe thinks he does, but it's not the way I need him to. It never was."

"And does that make you want to hurt yourself?"

I looked down at my still-exposed shoulder. "No. I know it won't help."

"That's a start," Frankie said.

"Did you know I haven't . . . hurt myself in twelve days?"

"Have you wanted to?"

"A few times. But I didn't. Doesn't that mean something?"

Frankie didn't answer for a moment. Then she said, "I find more meaning in the fact that you sent your father away." She let her finger hover over the dotted scab on the newest of the wounds. "It looks like something is healing, Kirsten." She closed her eyes. "The Lord be with you."

Share this chapter with your friends!

Sometimes I feel like someone else and I know I'm getting closer to who I really am. #TheMercifulScar

Part
THREE

And after the wind an earthquake, but the LORD *was not in the earthquake.*

1 KINGS 19:11

Chapter
TWELVE

The Nudnik stopped reminding me what day I was on every fifteen minutes. Somehow I simply got to Day Twenty-Two without noticing.

What I did notice were the subtle changes along the way.

Emma started a new routine at the Cloister. Every afternoon before our end-of-the-day chores, she made coffee—with Hildegarde's cream—and we drank it from Crazy Trixie's vintage cups on the front porch with Bathsheba curled up under my chair. Emma officially named it Improving the Moment. Sometimes we rocked and let the wind do the talking, but we did our share too. It started with fathers.

"I'm glad you didn't go with him," she said the day after Dad left.

I didn't have to ask who she meant.

"I'm glad too."

"Sorry, though."

"For what?"

"That he's not the dad you want."

I stopped with my upper lip dipped into the cup and stared at her, cream mustache and all.

"I get that," she said. "Trust me."

"Your dad too?"

"Yeah. In a different way from yours though, probably."

"Is yours a Disneyland dad?" I said.

She gave me her signature grunt. "Not even. He's a retired army officer. We moved all around the world when I was growing up. He was always working so my mom did most of the raising of me and my three older brothers." Another grunt. "And most of the smothering."

That I couldn't relate to, but I nodded and took another sip.

"When my dad retired and we settled in San Antonio—*his* hometown—I thought finally he and I could have some kind of relationship."

"How old were you?"

"Sixteen. I know. It's weird. But I was sick of my mother trying to make me be her clone, which was never gonna happen, and I decided I wanted to emulate him."

"Your going into the army didn't make him happy?"

"It did when I said I wanted to go to West Point. But you don't just sign up for that."

"Don't you have to have a congressman nominate you or something?"

"Yeah, there are all kinds of hoops you have to jump through. You have to show you've done all these activities and get letters of recommendation, only we never lived anyplace long enough for me to get that involved." She shrugged and took a long drag from the mug.

I take it we didn't get into the Academy.

"When I got the rejection letter, my dad said he was going to go to some people he knew at the Point, blah, blah, blah. But the day I turned eighteen, three days after graduation, I went down and enlisted."

"Did he have a meltdown?"

"Oh yeah. Him. My mother. All three of my brothers. I was

persona non grata for about a year. The thing was, I was glad I didn't get into West Point because from day one, I loved boot camp. I was at Fort Leonard Wood in Missouri and even though there was all this yelling and making you feel like you were pond scum, it was the best thing that ever happened to me."

Tha-a-a-t's why she's here. She's a crazy person.

"I actually liked having to get along with people I didn't particularly care for and finding ways to work together. Because in the army, it can't be all about me, it has to be about we."

She looked at me as if she were going to add more to that statement and changed her mind.

"Marksmanship was my thing," she said. "We were required to knock down twenty-three of forty targets on our final test and I knocked down thirty-eight." Emma frowned. "Does this sound like I'm bragging?"

"No. It sounds like you're amazing. No wonder you didn't need shooting lessons here."

She got quiet.

For Pete's sake, what was wrong with that *statement? Seriously, she needs to mark which buttons not to push.*

Emma took in a long breath through her nose and closed her eyes. When she opened them she seemed to have gathered herself together. "Anyway, basic training broke me down and then built me up into something better. But my father's never been able to see that. I got a leadership award at graduation from basic training, and all he said was, 'That just shows me you should've been an officer.'"

"Ouch," I said.

"That's what makes it so hard to accept this stuff I'm going through. He says I need to just get control of myself."

I watched her once again start to slide back into the cave she so often seemed to live in, and I didn't want her to leave. I raised my cup.

"To the healing of father issues," I said.

She stared at the mug for a moment, eyes cloudy, ready to retreat. And then she tapped her cup against mine and said, "Amen to that."

All right, who are you and what have you done with Emma?

But I had a feeling that was the real Emma.

———

The other subtle change—okay, maybe not so subtle—was in Andy. He popped up more often when I was working in the barn or hanging out with Petey and he no longer acted like he was doing something wrong by being there. Our conversations consisted mostly of, "Hey, Bo, how's it going?/I'm good. You?" But at least there were no furtive glances over his shoulder as if he were afraid of being caught at something. No monosyllabic answers. No dark eyes darting to everything but my face. He was still no-nonsense when we went behind the house for target practice again, but he gave me a few of those grins that said, *What could possibly be wrong in the world when you can smile like this?*

I, of course, being me, ruminated so much over why that had changed I was sure I looked like Hildegarde doing a number on her cud. I kept coming back to Joseph's suggestion that Andy be honest with Frankie about whatever *this* he and I had going. Maybe Andy had made it clear to her that we were really just almost-friends. That would've eased her mind.

Um, about what? Why would she care if you two were buds or not?

I kind of hated that question, because on even further cud chewing the only answers I could arrive at were: (a) Frankie didn't think Andy was good for me, or (b) Frankie didn't think I was good for Andy. Even on the most casual level.

You don't think Joseph might've been making something out of nothing? If your father was right and he actually did serve a prison sentence, he might not be the most stable person emotionally . . .

Every time I thought about that I came to the same conclusion: my father wasn't above using everything he could think of to get me to leave the ranch. Including lying. There was no way Joseph had ever committed a felony. Frankie wouldn't let him spend all this time with Emma, and Emma wouldn't be turning into an actual human being as a result, if Joseph were an ex-con. Right?

Why don't you just ask Sister Frankie about all of the above?

Because the other subtle change was in my relationship with Frankie. It grew deeper by the day, and I didn't want to do anything to mess that up.

Our daily routine was marked by chunks of one-on-one time. Our walks back from taking the sheep out and returning to get them later on. Our rides in the truck to go out and fix pumps and water troughs in pastures that I was sure stretched all the way down to Wyoming. The times when we wandered out into the garden after supper on the nights it was Andy's turn to clean up the kitchen.

We prayed—Frankie out loud, me still in the privacy of my head. Most of the time we talked. Okay, most of the time *I* talked and Frankie did those things she did best: she waited and she nodded.

Each time we fell into step or found a bouncing rhythm in the truck's cab, I peeled off another layer. I told her . . .

About my mother's "too nothing" and my father's "too everything."

About growing up trying to impress Dad with stellar grades and impeccable behavior until by the time I left middle school I had an impressive résumé. And about my blonder, funnier, more blue-eyed younger sister testing every limit and getting no more attention than I did.

About my parents' divorce and my mother's reversion to her Missouri roots after twenty-five years as a sophisticated San Francisco banker. And my father's return to his twenties, or so he thought, with a woman barely out of pimples and crushes.

About my one friend in Missouri, Carrie Cowan, who was a year younger than me and practically idolized me—and who started cutting because she found out I did. And about how I had to end the friendship and isolate myself in my guilt.

About the crushing loneliness my freshman year because after settling me in at MSU, my father evaporated from my life again and went off to another project: marrying Pilar.

And about Wes Rordan coming into my life at the beginning of my sophomore year and changing everything. About how I believed that if God really did love me the way Wes did, I could trust Him.

By Day Twenty-Three I felt lighter, as if I no longer had layers upon layers to carry on my body. I'd told Frankie everything.

Not quite everything.

Everything that needed to be told.

Because the thing was, during those eight days I never had the urge to hurt myself at all. The newest scabs had disappeared and with them the certainty that there was no other way to relieve the pain. I could leave in seven days knowing the scars would fade and that no new ones would take their places. That part of my life would be folded up and put away in the trunk of my confused past.

I hope that works out for ya.

Yeah, that tidy wrap-up lasted until Day Twenty-Four, when Frankie stopped nodding and waiting, and started the unfolding.

We had just finished feeding the middle school bums that morning and I went back to the younger bums' pen to do a last check on Petey before we headed out with the flock. The lambs had drained the vats and were all sleeping, tummies bulging, in a pile inside the shelter. All but Petey.

She stood at the trough where I'd dumped the pellets earlier, nose buried in the leftovers, chowing down.

"Look at this!" I said.

Frankie stopped at the gate to Bellwether Middle and grinned. "How *about* that? Ya did good, Mama Kirsten. I think she's going to be okay, that one."

I grinned back and dug into my pocket for my ranch notebook.

"You about have that filled up, don't you?" Frankie said.

"I was about to ask you for another one." I felt suddenly shy. "I guess that means I write down too many details."

"No, I think it means you're working too hard. It's time we changed your rhythm."

She's gonna explain that, right?

"I'm not sure what you mean," I said.

Frankie joined me at the end of the pen and propped a foot on the bottom slat. She rearranged her hat so I could see all of her brown eyes. They were somber.

Uh-oh.

"Did I do something wrong?" I said.

"Absolutely not. You're just ready for the next step."

"Before you go on . . . I haven't told you this, but I haven't hurt myself since my dad was here, and even then it was only some scratching. I haven't even wanted to. I mean, in case that makes any difference in what you were going to say."

"I hope you feel good about that," she said.

"I do," I said, though I was a little disappointed that she didn't seem any more impressed than she had the last time we'd discussed this.

"You have every reason to feel good because now you're in a place where you can look at what made self-injury necessary in the first place. You don't have the triggers here that you had before, but the reasons, the really deep ones that scream under your skin, those are still there."

"I've talked about those, though," I said. "I feel like I've peeled off all these different layers."

"You have. You've worked hard and you've been honest and the top layers are, like you said, peeled away. But what hasn't been peeled away yet you've learned to distract yourself from with work." She nodded at the red notebook I was still holding. "It takes me three months to fill up one of those."

"I thought that was why I was here." My voice was going into that defensive octave I hated to hear myself use. "And I'm liking it finally. Especially taking care of Petey."

"Now it's time to start taking care of you."

Frankie nodded for me to follow her out the gate. My boots suddenly felt like they were made of lead and I was sure it wasn't from the mud and poop molded to their soles.

"I would like for you to do two things," she said. "One, I want you to spend at least an hour of your free time every day in the Cloister doing something to nurture yourself. You've been going at it so hard I don't think you've even noticed what's there."

A manual for this, maybe? Downloadable instructions?

We rounded the barn toward the sheep pen. "That will give you cushions for the tough inner work you have ahead. Which leads me to number two. I want you to start acknowledging how the people in your life have made you angry."

"I thought I already did that," I said.

Look out, Kirsten. The hair's standing up on the back of your neck.

"I've heard sorting and I've heard analyzing and it's all been very rational." Frankie gave me the soft version of her grin. "But I haven't heard any anger and, my dear, I have a feeling there's a lot in there to be angry about."

I tried to focus on the sheep and on keeping Bathsheba from bugging Undie before she incited a dogfight, but I couldn't shake Frankie's assignment. By the time we got to the gate across the public road, I'd already run through the checklist of people in my life who ticked me off. But each time I felt the smallest flame of anger licking at me, the guilt poured in and doused it.

My father was narcissistic and controlling and I hated that. But wasn't he still the one who had rescued me from a dead-end life with my mother and given me the future that I myself had now essentially flushed down the toilet?

My mother was so wrapped up in my sister that I was little more than an inconvenience to her now. But wasn't she the one who came to the hospital and figured out what I had to do to get out of there?

As for Wes, he'd betrayed me with my best friend and tried to hide it. But didn't I partly bring that on myself by being so closed up he had to turn to Isabel for help figuring me out?

And then there was Lara who, the minute she turned twelve and went out and had her nose pierced and lit up her first cigarette, had turned *me* into her personal bodyguard. Actually she wasn't really *in* my life anymore. She wasn't even in her own life.

I crossed her off the checklist. But she still seethed under my skin.

"You're lost in thought."

I jumped as Frankie hooked her arm through mine. "I'm just going to do some inspection on the barn this morning, see where it needs to be shored up. You're free to do whatever. I suggest some time at the Cloister but that's up to you."

That was the very last place I wanted to spend time right now.

That or any other place where I had to be alone with the thoughts she'd stirred up.

"I want to check on Petey again," I said.

She nodded and waited. I let her wait.

Joseph was also waiting—at the barn to talk to Frankie. They disappeared into its shadows and I sat on the top slat of the gate that led into the middle school pen so I could look down at the bums. Even Petey was snoozing from her Grand Slam breakfast. I focused on a rusty nail whose point had worked its way through the wood. Before I realized it, I was imagining it skimming across the palm of my hand.

"Hey."

I had to grasp the slat to keep from jerking from the gate.

"Nice reflexes," Andy said. He joined me on the top slat. "You must be good at pinball?"

"No, I stink," I said. "You?"

"Reek like a cow patty." He gave me a melting grin, complete with nose crinkle. "So, Bo, have I told you I'm glad you decided to stay?"

"I don't know," I said. "That was so long ago . . ."

"Nine days. I needed to find just the right words."

"What are they?" I said.

"Hey, Bo, I'm glad you decided to stay."

Those were definitely the right words.

So right my throat thickened.

"Be sure and write those down for posterity," I tried to say—and choked.

"You okay there?" Andy nudged me with his side. "You need the Heimlich?"

Yes, please.

"No," I said. "I'm good."

"Actually, I was thinking very good." Andy pressed his lips against my forehead.

Um, Kirsten, you're breaking into a cold sweat.

"Is Andy out here?"

Andy didn't move at the sound of Frankie's voice but I slid off the gate and tried to figure out what to do with my arms.

She saw. You know she did.

Above me, Andy chuckled. At least until Frankie got rid of the startled expression on her face and said, "Emma needs some down-time and Joseph's shoulder is giving him trouble, so we're going to need for you to go with him to repair some fence. It'll take a couple of hours, so be sure to bring water—"

"No," Andy said.

It was the first time I had ever seen Sister Frankie at a loss for words. I watched her lips fall open.

"I'll do anything else you want me to do—you know that—but I'm not working with him. I can't."

Andy slid from the gate and was over the outside one before Frankie moved.

This one goes right to the top *of the Awkward Moment list.*

I didn't know what to do. Frankie followed Andy, and I could hear their muffled voices rising and falling just beyond the barn. No matter which way I escaped I'd have to pass them.

But staying here was not a much better option because Joseph emerged from the shadow of the barn and stood staring at his boots. I was pretty sure that wasn't what he was seeing.

Yeah, but when he looks up he's going to see you *standing here gawking at him. Say something.*

"I'm sorry," I said.

I meant something that made sense.

Joseph stared at me for a long, searing moment. "Why are *you* sorry? This has nothing to do with you."

At that point I didn't care if I had to pass the grizzly bear to get out of there. I half-tripped, half-ran to the main gate and somehow managed to get over it so I could take off for the Cloister. By the time I reached the front porch I knew I wanted to cut—and I didn't know why—and that only terrified me slightly more than knowing that it wasn't going to do any good. And where, oh where, did that leave me?

I stumbled over Bathsheba trying to get to the front door, which opened so abruptly I fell straight into Emma. She set me out in front of her by both shoulders and scoured my face with her eyes.

"What the Sam Hill is going on?"

"Don't let me cut, Emma," I said. "Don't let me."

"Okay." Her voice was calm. "First tell me what it is you were gonna cut."

"Me," I said.

Nothing registered on Emma's face at first. Finally she looked at me with soft eyes and waited. I could have been standing there with Sister Frankie.

"It's just so much easier to hurt myself than it is to face the mess I keep making of my life and everybody else's."

"Did you just mess up somebody's life?" she said.

"I will if I—"

Yeah, I wouldn't go blurting out something about Andy . . .

"I just will because I always seem to," I said. "It's *me* I'm angry with—doesn't anybody get that?"

"I might," Emma said. "Tell me some more."

But I pushed past her and shoved open the door to my room and flattened myself to the floor so I could pull the first aid kit out from under the bed.

"What are you doing?" Emma said from the doorway.

I didn't answer. I just grabbed the box and got to my feet. My skin was on fire as I staggered toward the bathroom. Emma got there first and planted herself in the doorway.

"Please move," I said.

Emma shook her head. Her jaw was set like a lockbox. "You told me not to let you cut. This is me not letting you cut."

"I have to," I said.

"You don't want to or you wouldn't have told me to stop you."

"I don't *want* to—I *have* to!"

"Why?"

"Because if I don't break my skin I'll break my heart. I'm afraid I'll die, Emma. Please."

My voice sounded desperate, even to me, but I didn't try to push her out of the way.

Yeah, I'm not thinking that's gonna happen. Good choice.

"I think I get that," she said, and she stepped aside.

"Thank you," I said.

I set the box on the toilet seat and waited for her to leave. She didn't.

"I promise I'm not going to kill myself," I said.

"I know."

"So . . ." I looked pointedly at the door.

"I'm staying," she said.

I had never cut in front of anyone before, but I wasn't sure I could convince Emma that she didn't want to see this. Particularly since she didn't actually seem to *want* to see it. There was no perverse curiosity in her eyes as she watched me disassemble a disposable razor and wash my hands. In truth, she looked like she might throw up.

"Don't try to grab me and physically stop me," I said. "I could slip and slash an artery by mistake. That's what made everyone think I was suicidal in the first place."

"I know you're not suicidal," Emma said. "Or you wouldn't be here. Besides, I don't see that in you."

I tossed the razor blade onto the towel I'd spread across the sink and looked at her.

"How is it that you get it?" I said.

"I get what it's like to need an outlet for stuff you can't look at." Emma pointed to the blade that still lay on the towel. "I actually kind of envy you."

"What?"

"I can't see myself doing this. I get queasy when I have to get a shot. But at least you let it out, even if it's only temporary. All I seem to be able to do with my pain is bury it."

"Is that why you have nightmares?"

She didn't look like she was going to scurry back to her cave, but I didn't push it by adding, *And why you freaked out that day the bear killed Petey's mother?*

"That's what they tell me."

"Does it help?"

Emma grunted. "For about seven seconds. Then here comes the guilt." She pulled a Band-Aid from the first aid kit. "I wish they had these for our insides."

"Yeah," I said.

I dropped the blade in the trash can and folded the towel. Emma closed the box.

"Coffee?" she said.

"With cream," I said.

> Share this chapter with your friends!
> *I wish they had Band-Aids for our insides.* #TheMercifulScar

Chapter
THIRTEEN

We had just finished improving the moment when Undie and Norwich heralded Frankie's arrival on the porch.

"May I ask a favor of you two ladies?" she said.

We said yes in unison. I didn't know about Emma, but I'd had enough of my own thoughts for now.

"I need you to take some things in the truck up to where Joseph and Andy have gone with the auger to repair some fence." She only grinned with her eyes. "They left without the posts."

A little distracted, were we?

"Sure, we got this," Emma said.

The grin spread to Frankie's face.

See? I knew you two would learn to play well together.

Emma drove and I rode shotgun—almost literally, since Frankie handed me her thirty-thirty before we left—with Bathsheba in my lap, drooling out the window. Fortunately we never went fast enough for her saliva to blow back into my face.

When we'd gone past the gate at the south pasture and were

crawling in low gear up a roadless hill, Emma said, "I bet she sent the two of them up here to duke it out."

"Andy didn't want to go," I said.

"And I'm sure Joseph didn't want to take him. He's being as stubborn as Andy now."

I didn't see that *coming.*

"I don't know what could've gone down between them," I said. "Frankie said Joseph was like Andy's dad when he was little."

Emma gave me a deadpan look. "An issue with a dad couldn't possibly be the problem."

"Oh yeah, huh?" I pulled some Bathsheba hair out of my mouth and let it go out the window. It gave me a minute to consider whether I ought to ask the next question.

"Spit it out, Petersen."

"I just did."

"No, I mean whatever it is you're dying to say."

"Promise you won't throw me out of the truck?"

"Ask it already!"

"Okay, okay." I shaped the words carefully. "Has Joseph ever said anything to you about being in prison? Because I'm wondering if that has anything to do with Andy's issue with him. I mean it's none of my business—"

"Sure it is. They're family."

Is it just me or wasn't she the one who said you were being nosey in the first place?

I didn't remind Emma of that.

She took off her ball cap and stuck it back on. "Joseph said to me one time that we've all done things we aren't proud of but we have to accept God's forgiveness or we never get past them. He said that was what got him through a prison term." Emma pulled the truck to the crest of a hill and stopped. "He didn't tell me what he was in for and I didn't ask. But he's not a criminal. Not in here."

She pressed her hand to her chest. I nodded and hoped my disappointment wasn't smeared all over my face.

Don't you hate it when your old man's right?

The fence Andy and Joseph were working on was at the bottom of a hill. Following Emma's lead, I rolled several poles that looked like large pencils down the slope before joining them on foot. Rotted fence posts lay in a pile, looking almost grateful to be relieved of duty. The holes that had been augered out went as deep as the silence between Andy and Joseph.

Awkward Moment alert.

"So what happened?" Emma said.

My stomach lurched until I saw she was pointing to the fence.

"Bull went through it."

Joseph bit off the ends of his words and spit them out like they were cigar tips. Andy didn't say anything at all.

"You bring the dibbler?" Joseph said.

"It's probably in the truck," Emma said.

"We're gonna need that and the shovel and the rest of the poles."

"I'll get them," Andy said. His voice sounded rusty.

But Joseph shook his head. "I need you to place the poles."

I refused to look at Andy, though I imagined his face resembled one of the Black Angus steers about now, and hurried up the hill behind Emma. Actually, hurried didn't quite describe it. Huffed and puffed and heaved like the bull that charged the fence—that was more accurate.

"Good for the glutes and thighs," Emma said when we got to the truck. She narrowed her eyes at me. "As if you had either one."

"Are you serious? I have body envy every time I look at your figure."

She grunted.

By the time we got back to the fence, laden with tools I couldn't have named even on a multiple choice, Andy had placed the gigantic pencil-poles next to the holes they were apparently going to be stuck into.

You guys have fun with that.

"Em, you're with Andy," Joseph said. "Kirsten, you're with me."

"Whatever it is we're doing," I said, "I guarantee you I've never done it before."

Joseph let one side of his mouth go up. "Well, fancy that."

He was going to hold the pole in the hole, he said, and I was going to use a long metal pole—the dibbler, he called it—to push the sod back in so the pole would stand upright.

I got a great idea: you *hold the pole and he does the dibbling.*

I was about to suggest that when Joseph said, "Doc says it'll be two more weeks before I can do anything with this arm. Besides"— he shrugged the sinewy shoulders—"I think every woman ought to know how to set a pole. You can't tell when you'll need it in your skill set."

I can. How 'bout never!

I was supposed to start with the dibbler end to push a layer of soil into the hole. That sounded easy enough, until I tried to lift the thing.

Yeah, you're gonna need to work on that upper-body strength.

No wonder Emma did those push-ups every morning. Somebody could have mentioned that might come in handy.

"Now use the tamper end to press that soil in there nice and tight," Joseph said.

I pressed.

"You're gonna have to do it harder than that. Lift and then jam it down. Lift and jam."

I tried.

"That was pretty puny. Don't just use your arms. Use your whole body."

Suddenly I would have loved to have used my whole body to shove Joseph headfirst into the hole. I felt more uncoordinated than I had since I'd tried to hook a sheep, and now I was showing my extreme inept spastic clumsiness in front of Andy, while without looking I knew Emma had one pole secured and was working on her second, still perspiration free.

And somehow that just ticked. Me. Off.

I lifted the pole and jammed. I was doing just fine with the sheep. Lift. Jam. Why was I now being held responsible for things I wasn't even capable of doing? Lift. Jam. Things that weren't my fault in the first place. I wasn't the one who rammed through this fence. Dump in more soil. Lift. Jam. I was sick of not living up to people's expectations. I was sick of it always coming back on me and my loser-ness. Sick of having anger I had no right to feel because apparently everything was my fault to begin with. Jam. Jam. *Jam.*

"Hey."

I stopped jamming and looked at Joseph. *"What?"*

He nodded at the hole, which was no longer there. "I think you've killed this one."

I could feel the blood surging through my veins. "You got another one?"

"Come on."

Joseph led me to the next hole. "What's this one's name?" he said.

"This one's Michelle," I said.

"All right. Have at her."

Each of the four more poles I secured in the ground that day had a name. Michelle. Sandy. Wes. Isabel. Each one received the wrath of the dibbler and the wrath of Kirsten. Whenever the guilt began to slow me down, Joseph said, "You're not gonna get it done that way," and I let the rage return. Lift. Jam. You hurt me. You hurt me. You hurt me bad. Jam. Jam. *Jam.*

When we got to the last one, Joseph stood the pole upright in the hole and looked at me, brows raised. There was only one more name, but I couldn't say it.

"I've got nothing left," I said, and handed the dibbler to Joseph.

The unearthly strength seeped out of me and my legs wobbled. The muscles in my throat let go and an unbidden sob was set free. I tried to run from it, down along the fence, away from Joseph and Emma and the anger I'd left in those holes. Sob after sob burst from the throat I'd depended on to hold them back. I couldn't see, I couldn't control where I went, I could only weep . . . right into a pair of sweat-damp arms.

They held me there only long enough for the sobs to stop rocking me. When Andy let go, I looked at my own arms to make sure I hadn't cut them somehow, because the rush of relief I felt was cutting-real.

"I'm sorry," I said.

"For . . . ?"

"Andy!"

Joseph's bark was sharp. Andy's face hardened, as if that were the only way he could keep from barking back.

"There's not enough wire in the truck. Need you to drive back and get more."

Andy gave my hand a squeeze and turned to go. By then Joseph had almost reached us. When Andy swerved to get around him, Joseph stuck out his arm.

"What you two do is none of my business," he said.

"I'd have to agree with that," Andy said.

What's that noise? Oh, it's teeth grinding.

"But I can't be part of keeping secrets."

"Look, I talked to Aunt Frankie. She's cool with our friendship." Andy spread out both hands. "What do you want me to do?"

"I want you to be honest. Things being kept in the dark just about ruined my life, and if you're not careful, son, they'll ruin yours." Joseph looked hard at me. "Like I said earlier, that has nothing to do with you. But if there's something more than friendship going on between you two, you better come clean with Frankie."

"We're adults," Andy said.

"Then act like it. Because you know what's at stake here, Andy."

I am so confused.

Emma arrived, winded, and bent over at the waist to lean on her knees.

Or to avoid looking at this *Awkward Moment.*

"Em, why don't you stay here with me and we'll get started with the wire we have. Kirsten can go back with Andy."

Emma raised only her head and looked at me, forehead furrowed. I nodded at her.

Andy didn't say anything until he and I and Bathsheba were in the truck. She didn't sit on my lap but scooted herself next to the window so I had to slide closer to Andy. He smelled warm and perspire-y and musky.

No. No getting high on his scent. Absolutely not.

I pulled Bathsheba onto my lap and moved back toward the door. Andy started the truck down the other side of the hill.

"Joseph is overreacting," he said.

"Is he?" I said. "That doesn't sound like Joseph to me."

He barely reacts at all if you ask me.

Andy waited until the truck lurched over a rock before he went on. "That first day you and I were sitting in the pen together—the day Petey was born—Frankie told me I shouldn't distract you from the work you were here to do. She didn't tell me in so many words to stay away from you. She just asked me to be considerate of you." Andy looked across the seat at me and grinned. "That's been harder than it sounds."

So correct me if I'm wrong, but this guy was way ahead of you.

Andy tried to downshift but the truck gave an asthmatic protest. "Do you know she's had this thing since I was three? It's twenty years old. She needs to give it a rest."

Yo, could we get back to that whole harder-than-it-sounds thing?

He found a gear that worked and opened and closed his hands on the steering wheel. "Here's the thing. *I'm* the one who's distracted by *you*. Have been ever since I saw you dump that hay bale ten minutes after I showed up—and that just doesn't happen to me. At least it never has before." He wiped one hand on the top of his thigh. "I came back here to figure out why I just flunked out of graduate school, and now . . ." He stole a glance at me. "I'm not sure I *care* why."

Andy stopped the truck just short of the gate that separated the sheep from the public road. They grazed a few yards away, completely uninterested in us. Bathsheba whined restlessly and jumped out the window.

"Alone at last." Andy's grin softened. "Before I go making a confession to Sister Frankie, I guess you better tell me whether *you* have anything to confess . . . about me."

Tell him you think he's hot. Do it.

I would have, if hot had been all of it. But I wasn't even sure what it was. I was so caught off guard I could only stammer, "I like you. I do—"

Andy smiled, but the hand he put on my shoulder was clammy. "If you're going to say like a brother, just nod and I'll drive on and pretend this conversation never happened."

"No! I just didn't know you felt . . . I haven't even thought this all through . . . But, Andy, the thing is, I only have six days left here."

"You're allowed to stay more than thirty days. Emma's been here for three months."

"I have a lot of work to do in six days." I spread my hand on my chest. "In here."

Andy pulled my hand away and pressed it between both of his. "I'm no Sister Frankie, okay, but from what I saw up there just now, you're getting a lot of stuff out. Only you're just getting started, am I right?"

I had to nod.

He grinned. "I'm not trying to sell it just so you'll stay, but if you need more time here all you have to do is ask. And that would be no problem for me."

I closed my eyes and felt like I was falling, in that weightless, eager way you fall when you know you're going to land on a pile of pillows. A cushion? Didn't Frankie tell me I needed a cushion? Someplace to rest when working on the pain was too much?

"Hey, Bo."

I opened my eyes.

"I'm sorry. I shouldn't be making this harder for you." Andy squeezed my hands. "What do you need?"

Say again?

I did want to hear it again. Because search as I might through my memory, I was sure I would find no time when anyone had ever said, "Kirsten, what do you need?" It was an unfamiliar question I didn't know how to answer. Except to say—

"Support?"

"Done. I'm already praying for you." He tried to stifle the dimples. "Not to mention the fact that I have already saved you from a killer cow, pulled you out of the bum pen, taught you how to fire a weapon—although I have to say I don't see you ever shooting one beyond target practice."

You did not just giggle.

"I know, right?"

"How does this sound to you?" Andy said, still holding on to my hand. "I'll tell Frankie I'm supporting you in your work here—"

"And I'm supporting you. I don't want to feel like a project. This can't be one-sided."

Way to grow a backbone, Kirsten.

"I'll tell her that, but I know she's going to say that's a distraction for you."

"We can't leave that out, though. I want her to have the whole truth."

Andy brushed the tip of my nose with his finger. "That right there—that is why I like you so much. One of about fifty reasons." He put the finger to my forehead as if he was going to brush back a strand of my hair, but he pulled back. "I'm also going to tell her that I'll do my best to keep my hands off you."

Rats.

It was hard not to protest. I wanted his arms around me again. Sometime. Soon.

He kissed me on the forehead and whispered, "Last time. For now."

When he climbed out of the truck to open the gate, he turned back and said, "I'm serious. I don't want to get in the way of what you're trying to do up here."

Get in the way?

No, he wasn't going to get in the way. For all I knew as I sank against the lumpy, rode-hard back of the seat, Andy DeLuca was *part* of the way.

Hmmm . . .

Frankie and Joseph had to go into Conrad for a meeting that night, which meant Andy wouldn't be able to talk to her until at least morning. Still, I fell asleep cocooned, not just in Andy and Emma and Frankie and Petey and Bathsheba and now maybe even in Joseph, but in a soft kind of safety that felt like maybe it could be God.

"Thank You," I whispered.

———

The next morning as Frankie and I went about our barn chores I couldn't tell whether Andy had talked to her or not, but it wasn't long before it was apparent that someone else had.

"I understand you confronted some anger yesterday," she said as we let ourselves into the sheep pen.

"Does Joseph tell you everything?" I said.

"He told me you kicked tail up there at the fence." Frankie smiled at me over the top of the gate. "I figured out the rest. Good work."

I waited until we were at the top of the hill, looking down over the flock, before I said, "You know what *I* figured out?"

She absently patted the top of Avila's head. Her brown eyes were right on me.

"I figured out that it always comes back to me. I can vent for days about my family, but I'm the one I'm angry with."

"Because . . ."

"Because most of the mess of my life is my fault."

"It's your fault that your father treats you like chattel?"

I felt my eyes widen.

"It's your fault that your mother disregards who you are? It's your fault that the man you loved turned out to be a two-timing freeloader?"

Frankie paused, but I couldn't say anything.

Don't look at me. I got nothin'.

"Kirsten, you have a right to be angry with just about everybody who has had an important place in your life."

"Except Lara."

It was out before I could stop it, and I wanted to, because Frankie grabbed on to it as if she'd been waiting for its appearance since the moment she met me.

"But you *are* angry with your sister, aren't you?" she said.

"Sometimes. But I shouldn't be."

Frankie curled her fingers lightly around my wrist. "We don't do *should* here. We work with what is. We work with what we hear from God."

She let go of me and made her way through the flock with Avila. I stayed at the top of the hill, but I didn't watch for sheep that didn't get to their feet. I could barely stay on my own.

I thought I had at least *felt* God. Wasn't that Him, cushioning me in safety the night before? I felt the hair rise on the back of my neck. Why was it that every time I thought I was getting it, Sister Frankie had to come along and stir it up with a stick?

By then Frankie had the gate open and the flock was starting to move. I didn't want to follow today.

You know, you only have five more days and then you could leave.

Even with the promise of Andy, that sounded better than staying here and being angry with my sister. I had no right to be angry with Lara.

But she had every right to be angry with me. If only she could.

———

I might actually have planned to leave behind the beginnings of family I'd found at the ranch if staying meant I had to do what Frankie wanted me to do. I might have, if it hadn't been for what happened the next day.

All five of us were cutting out wethers for processing, which I quickly gathered meant the young castrated males were going to be turned into lamb chops. I would have had a hard time with that if they'd been cute and fluffy like the bums, but they were far beyond cute. They were even rowdier than the middle school crowd.

"They act like frat brothers," I told Andy as we formed a line in the barn with Emma, Frankie, and Joseph to keep them from hurling themselves back into the flock we'd just separated them from.

"That's why it's easier to send them off to become kebob meat," Andy said. "By the time we're done doing this, you're going to want to slaughter them yourself."

I started to protest, but one of them chose that moment to break from the pack and try to charge through us. We all stood with our knees bent, arms out like basketball players, ready to step in the way of whoever came our way. This one came *my* way and bowled me over on his way through.

"Grab him, Kirsten!" Frankie called out.

I did my best, arms reaching up from the ground, hands grasping at wool. I was able to grab on to the now panicky frat boy but I couldn't stop him. He dragged me all the way out of the barn and through the open gate into Bellwether Middle School. I didn't let go until he swerved to miss an equally panicky ewe and swept me into a pile of flaked hay. Five eighth-grade lambs came over to investigate. So did Andy. He was laughing almost as hard as I was.

"You okay?"

"Yes, no thanks to the Lambda Lambda Lambda pledge over there."

Andy let out a guffaw and reached a hand down to help me up, but I smacked it away and scrambled to my feet.

"You're supposed to keep your hands off me."

"Why did I make that promise again?" he said.

When we got the Lambda pledge back to the barn, his brothers were already in the trailer, bodies pressed together as if they were absorbing each other's fear.

"Do they know where they're going?" I asked Frankie.

She laughed her husky laugh. "You've been working with sheep for how long and you're asking that?"

"Oh yeah," I said. "Is it ever hard for you, though? You've taken care of them all this time and now they're going to be . . . processed."

"Our job here is to feed the world," Joseph said. He set the latch on the trailer and looked at me with an unusual kindness in the lines of his face, as if he were talking to a young child. "We're just feeding the world. You ready, Em?"

She climbed into the front seat of the truck with him and they pulled away with the trailer.

"I'm going to let the rest of these sheep back into the pen," Frankie said. "You two just make sure I don't leave behind any stragglers, okay?"

I nodded, but I was staring at Andy. His dark face was ashen.

"Are you okay?" I said when she was gone. "Andy?"

Although he shook his head, I knew from the distant horror in his eyes that it wasn't me he was answering. Nor was I the target of the "No!" that shot from his lips before he tore through the open gateway as if demons seen only by him were clawing at his back. He disappeared with them around the corner of the barn.

I knew what panic looked like when it roared out of its cage, and I knew it was impossible to beat back alone. Anxiety rising in my own throat, I took up the chase through the gate.

Andy was sitting up against the barn wall when I found him. His knees were pulled to his chin, arms wrapped around them, face buried. The only thing not held tightly in a ball was his hair, which stood out in startled spikes as if a hand had just raked through.

I sank down beside him and waited. I wasn't doing my Frankie imitation. I just knew fear like that could take awhile to retreat to its hiding place. No sense in churning it up again.

Bathsheba joined us and sat on the other side of me, silent except for the ever-present rhythm of her panting. It might have been my imagination but as Andy's breathing slowed, so did hers. Finally he lifted his head.

"That was—I don't know, it was . . . weird."

"You've not had a panic attack before?" I said.

Andy shook his head. "It freaked me out but it wasn't like panic. I remembered something." He squinted with all of his face as if he were trying to peer into it again. "What did Joseph say to you?"

"I'm sorry?"

"When you asked if it ever bothered them to take the lambs to be processed—what did he say?"

"Um, something about our job here is to feed the world."

Andy squeezed his eyes closed. "He said that to me when I was little. I didn't know it until I heard it again just now, but I saw it so clear."

I wasn't sure how that could have led to the abject fear I'd seen in his eyes, but I didn't ask. Judging from the shudder I felt go through him, he was afraid of the answer. Bathsheba whimpered.

"We were coming up the driveway in the truck," he said. "We'd been to the processing plant . . . and I asked him why we had to leave the guys there . . . I called them the guys."

It wasn't hard to conjure up an image of a chubby preschool Andy giving human attributes to the lambs he'd grown up with. Guys. That went beyond precious.

"And he said the same thing to me. He said it was okay because we were feeding the world. I can see his face."

Kindness in the lines, just as I'd seen it, I was sure. So why—

"And then it changed and—" Andy pushed the heels of his hands into the sides of his head. "Something bad happened. Something really bad—but I can't see it." He rocked forward. "I don't want to see it, Bo."

My throat ached for him. "Then don't," I said. "Don't go there yet."

He nodded and tipped sideways until his face and shoulders were in my lap. He didn't cry. He just lay there until the memory that had seized him seemed to ebb away and leave him limp. I looked down to find my fingers smoothing down the frightened spikes in his hair.

"Thank you," he said.

"I didn't do anything."

"I know. That's what I needed you to do."

Having no clue what to do turns out to be the right thing to do. How often does that *happen?*

True. But I wasn't as calm as Andy now seemed to be, curled up with his head in my lap.

"Just a thought," I said. "But shouldn't you talk to Frankie about this?"

"Probably." He sat up, but he kept his face close to mine. "But I don't want to do that yet. I need to try to sort this out."

"I'm just thinking about what Joseph said about secrets."

"Maybe I just don't want to know what it is yet." A trace of his grin went through his eyes. "I'm gutless."

"You are *so* not!"

"No, I'm serious. I don't have the courage you and Emma have to look your stuff in the face."

You gonna let that one go?

"I'm not that brave either," I said. "I know how hard it is."

Andy put a hand on top of mine. "Then it's like we said: we'll support each other. Okay, Bo?"

"Okay," I said.

He squeezed the fingers he laced through mine. "That promise didn't last long, did it?"

"What promise?"

"The one where I was going to keep my hands off you."

I met his smile with mine. "I'm okay with that," I said.

And again I say, Hmmm.

Share this chapter with your friends!

We don't do should here. We work with what is, with what we hear from God. #TheMercifulScar

Chapter FOURTEEN

The Nudnik could *hmmm* all she wanted about Andy, but at lunchtime the next day as I was walking back to the Cloister I knew one thing for sure: I had learned something from him.

I learned that it was okay to let yourself break down. I was envious of his ability to give in to his pain, even if he didn't know what it was, and curl into a fetal position and shove his hands through his hair. With someone sitting right next to him.

You could probably do that too if you'd been raised by Sister Frankie.

It didn't strike me until I was standing with the refrigerator door open, gazing at the bowl of dewy grapes and the hunk of artisan cheese and the jar of Hildegarde milk with its three-inch layer of cream, that in a way I *was* being raised by Sister Frankie. So why wasn't I doing what she said I needed to do?

Good question.

I closed the door and leaned against it. "You *are* angry with your sister, aren't you?" she'd said. And then she'd followed up with: "We don't do *should* here. We work with what is. We work with what we hear from God."

Okay.

But I couldn't do it here in the Cloister. I still wasn't where Andy was, able to fall apart where someone might see. There was only one place to go for this.

———

Bathsheba—my cushion—and I reached the shepherd's monument just after noon. Down on the ranch the air was starting to simmer but up here the wind—always the wind—blew off anything that hinted at oppression. I leaned against the tightly fixed stones with Bathsheba at my side and gazed out over the vast expanse and was once more aware of my complete powerlessness over . . . anything.

As much anger as I'd let out, jamming my parents into the holes with the soil, they were never going to change. At least *I* couldn't change them. Maybe that was why I hadn't jammed Lara. She *couldn't* change. Frankie may have been right that it wasn't my fault my mother and father treated me the way they did. But where Lara was, that *was* my fault.

"I don't have the courage you have to look your stuff in the face."

I startled, setting a small landslide of loose pebbles in motion. Had Andy followed me?

Nah. You're just freaking.

Andy was nowhere in sight, but I'd heard his voice so clearly in my head, like an echo of yesterday's conversation.

"Courage?" I answered him now, out loud. "I don't have the courage to face hidden memories."

But they're not hidden. Your skin never forgot.

That made me want to run, just like Andy did. Maybe I would have, if Bathsheba hadn't pressed her head into my lap and sighed. Then I could only sit there and remember.

Remember how one night I talked my irrepressible, silky-haired eleven-year-old sister to sleep like I always did, with a story about a princess named Lara who was the favorite of her father the wise king and her mother the loving queen. And how it seemed like she woke up the next morning and said, "I'm twelve and I'm going to have my nose pierced."

Overnight the clever charm I'd always admired turned to cunning. Overnight the laughter that kept our household from being a morgue transformed into contemptuous secret snickers at all she was getting away with. Overnight "Please tell me a story, Sissy," was replaced by "You'll cover for me, Sis."

"And I did," I said to Bathsheba.

For a year I made sure our parents never knew that she was smoking in the gardening shed no one ever went into except the landscapers. Or that she did get a friend to pierce her nose and put in the tiniest of studs she could cover with makeup at home. Or that she stayed up until two every morning chatting with pubescent boys online.

It wasn't all that hard to keep it from them. They might not have noticed even if I *hadn't* sprayed the inside of the shed with Lysol and bought Lara makeup out of my babysitting money and rolled up a towel and put it in front of the crack under the door so no one could see the light from the computer at one a.m.

Even if you'd told Mother and Dad . . . would they have cared?

Maybe I could have rationalized it that way if Lara hadn't turned thirteen and entered my sacred space: the church youth group.

I shifted my weight from one sitting bone to the other, but Bathsheba showed no signs of moving. I scratched behind her ears and elicited a deeper sigh.

You're not going anywhere. You might as well continue.

Pointless as it seemed, I remembered me at fifteen, driven to perfection in school and at home.

Somebody had to make up for Lara. Right?

All right, so now it seemed stupid, but what else was I supposed to do? The thing was, that youth group—they called us the Hugh Crugh because our youth pastor's name was Hugh—was the only place where I had ever been allowed to be what my mother would have called silly, and yet at the same time ask questions ("Does *God* expect me to be perfect?") and own up to the fact that I was afraid ("What if God does and I'm not? What then?"). There, as a member of the Hugh Crugh, I came as close as I had ever come to being a me I could like.

And then Lara became a teenager and burst on my scene and took away my freedom to be that person.

Can I just mention that you have never actually put all this together before?

"It must be your influence, 'Sheba," I said.

She snored in a most unladylike fashion and dug her muzzle further into my lap.

At that point I had seen just how charismatic Lara could be. Within two weeks she had all the kids in the Crugh with even a flicker of rebellion in their spirits following her around like she was the Pied Piper of Hellions.

If Lara wanted to turn a skit about Hosea and Gomer into an R-rated performance, they were right there with her. Until I intervened before they took the stage.

If Lara got it into her head to roll up the waistband of her skirt after her arrival so that the hem hit her just below the butt cheeks, she had ten other girls in the restroom with her following suit. Until I stood in the doorway and made them all unroll.

If Lara got up a petition for allowing guys and girls to "show physical displays of affection" during prayer circle, she had promises for twenty signatures before she even got the thing printed out. Until I tore it up and told her that next time I would make her eat it.

You should have.

Yeah. Frankie could say all she wanted to about not doing shoulds, but I was so loaded down with them I wasn't sure I could ever get out from under.

I *should* have told Hugh when Lara decided to forget the petition and take matters into her own hands and sneak out during movies to make out with whoever behind the church and then sneak back in before the credits rolled. The only one she left alone was Ralph. She didn't overlook him because she knew I had a terminal crush on him. It was because he was, as she put it, too Christian for her.

The shoulds continued.

I *should* have told my parents when I smelled alcohol on her breath after one of those rendezvous. I *should* have told them before—

"I can't."

Don't stop now. You're almost there.

"I *can't*! Bathsheba, get up. Please!"

I all but shoved her off my lap and somehow got to my feet and ran. Behind me Bathsheba whined but she followed me, down the slope on the far side of the monument, down where I stumbled to a stop and cried out, "Why did you listen to me, Lara?"

My voice was stolen as always by the wind. But this time something came back.

Bat kol? Could it be?

But it was Bathsheba, now back up the slope behind me, barking. Furiously. Like Avila.

I whirled around, nearly losing my footing on the slant. And I gasped.

The grizzly bear cub was at the top, the shepherd's safe monument forming a backdrop behind her. It was wagging its head and baring its teeth at my dog.

In that frozen moment, before the panic and the terror, I realized two things.

The mother bear couldn't be far away.

And I had forgotten to bring a gun.

"Bathsheba!" I screamed. "Bathsheba, *come!*"

She didn't. As the cub began its descent toward her, she only bared her own teeth and snarled and growled as I had only seen her do one other time. One other time when I'd had to physically remove her.

Don't be an idiot!

I opened my mouth to scream for Bathsheba again, but I knew as focused as she was on keeping the cub at bay, she wouldn't even hear me.

But that cub's going to hear you and so is its mother. That dog is the only thing keeping them from attacking you *right now.*

I couldn't leave her. I couldn't leave Bathsheba. Once more I screamed for her but she didn't look my way. The cub did. And he looked nothing like a teddy bear.

Run! Run, you fool!

I did—down the slope—skidding as I went because it was far steeper than I knew. The ground was loose and small rocks gave way under my feet and took me downward at a pace I couldn't keep up with. I felt myself trip—watched myself roll—heard the hill following me in big angry clumps.

And in my tangled, horrified mind I saw myself hurtling off the side of the mountain, into the endless expanse below.

But I slammed into something—a rock formation that didn't give way to the avalanche behind me. Pain soared up my back as I batted at the dust and tried to see Bathsheba. She was still snarling from some guttural place. She was holding her own, right?

The wind snatched the dust and I tried to stand. But what I saw paralyzed me against the rock. The grizzly cub ran, faster than its chubbiness should have allowed, straight at Bathsheba. With a swat of her paw, she sent Bathsheba over the ridge. Out of sight. And went after her.

Get out of here! Get out*!*

I found my body again and stood in a moment of awful indecision. I couldn't leave my dog. I couldn't just run away and leave her.

The yelp and the quiet after it made the decision for me.

Traversing this time instead of tearing blindly downward, I ran. I ran until I nicked the side of a rock and went down. The blood rose at once to the surface of the scrape, but it only struck more fear in me. I got up and ran again, in the direction I hoped would lead me to the road. I had lost my bearings completely. I could only run and hope.

I did reach the road, which meant I had only a mile to go before I got to the ranch, but my legs were too heavy to run anymore. I trudged, head down, along the side until a vehicle pulled up. And still I kept walking.

"Are you all right?" someone called.

I shook my head and walked some more.

"Ma'am! Are you all right?"

What part of no don't you understand?

Let him help you.

I looked up to see the wildlife conservation truck backing toward me. The face that came into view out the window was creased with concern.

"Where you headed?"

"Bellwether," I said.

"I'll take you."

I shook my head. "Will you please just go up and get my dog? The bear has my dog."

My voice broke into pieces. And there weren't enough horses and king's men to put it back together.

———

Andy met the truck as it pulled into the driveway. Frankie, Joseph, and Emma were there, too, but no questions were asked. My wildlife rescuer must have called them while he was driving but I couldn't have testified to that. All I could hear was Bathsheba's last yelp.

And all I could say as Andy carried me into the house and Emma cleaned and bandaged my leg and Joseph made tea was, "I shouldn't have left Bathsheba. Please go find her."

"You need to tell us what happened," Frankie said. "Just take it slow."

There was no taking it slow. It all came out on its own in bursts I couldn't hold back. Every one of them ended with, "You have to go find her!"

"Okay, Bo," Andy said finally. "I'll go."

"I'll drive," Joseph said.

I didn't have to look at him to see what he was forcing himself not to say: *What were you doing up there without a gun?*

"I left you a note," I said.

"Note didn't give me a chance to tell you that bear was sighted a half mile from the monument this morning."

"All right, you two go," Frankie said. "And be careful. Please."

I heard Emma mutter, "Shoot the stupid bear."

"He's mad at me for not taking a gun," I said when they were gone.

"He's not mad—"

"But what would've been the point? I couldn't have taken that cub down. I have no power over anything."

Frankie eased me back into the tweedy chair and sat on the low table to face me. "You are absolutely right," she said. "You have no power *over*. You only have power *to*."

"Power to what?" I said.

"The power to pray." She touched my cheek. "The Lord be with you."

"And also with you," Emma said.

I wasn't sure what words they prayed as we sat in a clump with a frightened Mary above us. At first all I could hear was my own sobbing and Bathsheba's snarling attempts to save me. When that subsided, I only knew that God was in the room. Because Frankie was holding me in her arms and Emma was crying with me.

———

When Joseph and Andy returned an hour later, I ran out to meet them. Andy lifted Bathsheba's body from the front seat of the truck, wrapped in his jacket like a swaddled baby.

"I'll get a grave ready," Joseph said.

Andy started to follow him with the bundle but I stopped him. "I want to see her."

"No, you don't, Bo."

"I have to," I said. "Let me see her."

Andy shot Frankie a look but she nodded.

So Andy knelt beside the truck and lay Bathsheba down and unfolded the jacket from her face. It was perfect. Still the prettiest dog face on the ranch. Still shiny-furred and black-nosed. If only she would sigh and snore and drown my hands in her happy saliva.

"I'm sorry," I whispered to her. "I'm sorry I took you up there. I'm sorry I didn't protect you. I'm so sorry."

Joseph dug a grave close to the Cloister and Frankie arranged three smooth stones at its head. Then they all stood silently as I covered

Bathsheba's still-wrapped body with dirt. When I could no longer see her, Joseph said, "I used to think you were a good-for-nothing dog, Bathsheba. But I've changed my mind."

"You brought joy to Kirsten," Frankie said.

Emma grunted. "You made me laugh."

"You saved Kirsten's life." Andy slid his arm around my shoulders. "And for that we will always, always be grateful to you."

"Amen," Joseph said.

I would have said amen, too, if I could have.

———

I couldn't sleep that night. I knew I wouldn't be able to before I even considered crawling into bed, so I dragged a quilt to one of the recliners instead. Emma appeared before my back even hit the cushions and handed me a steaming Crazy Trixie mug.

"Tea," she said. "Joseph's blend. With Hilda's cream, of course."

I nodded my thanks and cradled it between my hands. She had a cup too.

"You don't have to stay up with me," I said.

"Yes, I do."

"Why?"

"Because I promised I wouldn't let you cut, and it seems to me like you might be primed for it tonight."

"I'm afraid I might get there," I said. "All I can think about is that if I'd waited to actually tell somebody where I was going, I wouldn't have gone up there with her. And if I'd had a gun—"

"Didn't you hear what we all said at the grave? About Bathsheba fulfilling her purpose here and, hello, saving *your* life? And by the way, they've had two dogs and a cat die since I've been here, before you came, and they never had a funeral for any of them. Just so you know."

"That just makes me feel *more* guilty."

"Oh, for crying out loud, Petersen, when are you going to give up this whole control thing? It's not all about you."

I wasn't quite sure what to do with that. Especially when she leaned her curly head back and laughed.

"What could possibly be funny?" I said.

"Me. Telling *you* to give up control when I'm over here hanging on to it like a third-world dictator. Seriously, can you believe I said that?"

She laughed again, an infectious kind of wheezy thing that made me laugh with her.

"Can I ask what you're trying to control?" I said. "You don't have to tell me, but . . ."

"They keep saying I need to tell *somebody*, and maybe I would if I could even think about it without going into some other dimension." She looked at me almost sheepishly. "You've seen me do that."

"And you've seen me hold a razor blade over my arm. What's the difference, really?"

Emma grunted. It was a sound I was starting to like.

"I think I'm trying to control the memory for one thing. I get so far and then I can't go any further."

"Are you serious?" I felt my eyes widen. "Because the same thing happens to me."

I didn't add, *And to Andy too.*

"Then you probably don't want to hear it." Emma shrugged. "You've got your own stuff."

"Actually I do want to hear it," I said. "As much as you want to tell."

Emma nodded. Her gaze drifted just above my head.

"After graduation from basic training I moved to Advanced

Individual Training at Signal Corps School, Fort Gordon, Georgia. Then I trained at Fort Bragg as a signal corps paratrooper."

I blinked. "You realize, of course, that I have no idea what any of that means."

"It just means I was training to be combat support."

"Combat," I said. "You mean, like, in Afghanistan?"

"Not just like in Afghanistan—*in* Afghanistan. I found out about an hour after I got there that support was a euphemism. Almost every mission on the battlefield is potentially a combat mission. As part of a signal station I could find myself in unfriendly territory that had been friendly the day before, only somebody had decided to go after a unit's signal assets or the front had shifted."

I nodded my head like I knew what she was talking about. It didn't seem to matter whether I understood or not. Just saying it seemed to be helping her.

"I'd had the same training as men: what to do if you get hit with chemical agents, what to do if the enemy sends a squad around to attack, what to do if it looks like your site is about to be overrun and you have a choice between shooting back or taking an axe to the gear and burning all the crypto." Emma nodded at me. "And that was okay, you know? I didn't want to be stuck in the rear echelon. And since a lot has improved for female soldiers since the beginning of the Iraq war, the guys in the unit I was assigned to integrated me into their band of brothers—"

She licked her lips and did battle with some tears that gathered at her lower lids.

"Do you need to stop?"

"No," she said. "It's just . . . that's the first time I ever realized the reason that meant so much to me is because I never got that kind of acceptance from my own brothers."

"That's good, then," I said.

"Yeah. I think so." She blinked at the tears. "So anyway, I served with them for a year. During that time I flew from one forward operating base to another on CH-47 Chinook helicopters and I was shot at and mortared on a regular basis." She tilted her chin at me. "And I always found ways to stay focused and deal with it. That's when I learned how to pray."

I waited, Frankie style. But Emma sat up straight in the chair.

"That's as far as I get, and then I feel all this pressure in my chest and I can't do it anymore. My entire second tour is just like this faraway dot I can't reach. Joseph keeps telling me I will, that I have to keep relying on Christ to guide me through this. But sometimes I wonder if it'll ever happen."

"Does it have to?"

She looked down at her hands. "I used to ask that. When I was addicted to Ambien because I couldn't sleep. When I was anorexic. When I had headaches so bad I thought I was going to explode and got addicted to Vicodin too. They call it PTSD."

"Post-traumatic stress, right?" I said.

"Yeah. I've come a long way since I've been here. Especially since I arrived during lambing season and Frankie was, like, up to her earlobes in ewes and lambs so she asked Joseph to see to me for a week. Turns out he'd had it, too, from Vietnam, only they didn't call it that back then. They told him he was lazy and a drug addict."

I wondered if maybe drugs were what landed him in prison, but I didn't stop her to say that.

"Anyway, he got me, you know? And like I said, he and Frankie have brought me so far. *God* has brought me so far. But for somebody with post-traumatic stress disorder, it would probably help if I could remember the trauma."

She sagged back into the chair and sipped her tea and basically signaled the conversation was over. She looked drained.

I fell asleep in the chair, and when I woke up Emma was curled up on the couch. Still making sure I didn't cut. Even with all she had to deal with, she cared that much.

Wonder what would happen if all three of you could dig up your pasts from where you've buried them.

Would we find mangled selves like Bathsheba? Or could we possibly be made whole like Sister Frankie?

And even Joseph. Somehow he must have overcome the secrets that he himself said had almost ruined his life.

There was hope in that. I tried to cocoon myself in it.

Share this chapter with your friends!
You have no power over. You only have power to. And power with God. #TheMercifulScar

Chapter FIFTEEN

The next day, Friday, was my twenty-eighth day. I didn't need the Nudnik to remind me that I had some decisions to make in the last two.

Frankie didn't say that was why she thought I should take the day off. She said something about staying off my leg, even though my injury was nothing more than a scrape.

Yeah, you've done worse things to yourself.

But I insisted on at least doing my chores and helping herd the sheep. If I did only have two days left, I didn't want to miss anything that might be in them. Once we headed down to the barn, though, Bathsheba's absence was like a stake through my heart. I would have given anything for a handful of good-morning slobber.

On the way back from the south pasture, Frankie said they'd start the process of bringing in alfalfa the next day.

"The leaves are the most palatable part and they have the most nutrition," she said. "So you want them to remain on the stems as the hay dries before you bale." She nodded as if I already knew. "It's all about timing, isn't it?"

I said I guessed it was.

"Putting up enough hay for winter—thirty-five hundred bales— is an all-consuming job for Joseph and me, and, thank heaven, for Emma. That means I won't be around as much." She tilted her head back to look at me from under the cracked bill of her ball cap. "You okay with just early-morning and after-supper talks for us?"

"I'll be fine," I said. "I still have Petey to watch over. I can do anything else you need me to do for the sheep."

The inevitable, comfortable arm slipped through mine. "Actually I'd like to leave you and Andy in charge of the herding. You two can also buck hay as we bring it in. How does that sound?"

All day alone with Andy. How does she think *that sounds?*

"You think I can handle it?"

What—the sheep or the guy?

"I have complete faith in you," Frankie said. "But remember I do want you to spend a minimum of an hour a day at the Cloister, nurturing Kirsten."

"I will," I said.

Frankie tilted her head at me. "And how will you do that?"

"I'm sorry?"

"What will you do to take care of yourself?"

"Um, I don't know. Yet."

"I'll take that for now," she said.

She headed back to the house and I went to the bum pen for another look at Petey. She liked a nice scratching between the ears after her breakfast had digested. Andy was waiting for me there, grinning like that cat from *Alice in Wonderland*.

"Sounds like it's gonna be you and me, Bo," he said. "You okay with that?"

Do sheep have prehensile lips?

I wanted to say I was, but I was nervous too. I had the falling feeling again, as if I were floating toward that pile of cushions.

And this makes you nervous because . . .

Because I'd fallen there before, and the cushions had fallen apart.

So let's do that again just to make sure it's still a bad idea.

"Bo?" Now *Andy* looked nervous. "Something wrong?"

"No," I said. "Not wrong. Just scary."

Andy ran his hand over his mouth. "Did I grow fangs or something?"

You're giggling again.

"You did not grow fangs. It's me I'm afraid of, not you."

He was visibly relieved. "Tell you what," he said. "How 'bout we take this one day at a time?"

"We only have two of those."

"One hour at a time?" Andy's hands flexed as if they wanted to touch me. He shoved them into his pockets. "I don't want to push you, Bo. I just want to enjoy you. Support you. See where it goes. Is that scary?"

"No," I said. "Not at all."

Did you feel that?

I did. It was me hitting the cushions.

———

Frankie sent us out alone that evening to herd the sheep back. I had spent my hour in the Cloister earlier, pacing and trying to figure out how I was going to ask Andy the one question that needed to be asked. Emma told me during Improving the Moment time that if I didn't get out whatever was wearing a path in the floor, she wasn't going to make me any more coffee.

So I asked him as we walked out to the pasture.

And with such poise, I might add.

"Did you tell Frankie what you remembered?"

Andy leaned down and pulled up a stem, which he stuck in his mouth. "No. I haven't remembered anything more so . . . I'm still sorting."

"It's totally your call," I said. "But Emma's told me some things and I've looked at some things. And even though neither one of us is probably where we need to be, y'know, it helps."

"When I'm ready I'll tell her," Andy said.

He didn't use a this-is-none-of-your-business tone, but the stem between the teeth was a clear signal.

"Okay," I said.

And then I wondered if we weren't both playing hide-and-seek with our pasts.

———

I didn't have to wonder long.

The next morning before Andy and I headed up to the sheep pen, Frankie told us we needed to move what was left of the old hay into the barn to make room for the new stuff outside.

"Dress light and drink a lot of water, Kirsten," she said.

"I'll take care of her," Andy said.

The look Frankie gave us both clearly said I was to take care of myself.

So I put on enough sunscreen to cover everybody on a Waikiki beach and buttoned a cotton shirt over a tank top and had two bottles of water from the barn pump with me as I climbed into the truck with Andy.

"You've seen me try to buck hay before," I said. "I'm probably not going to be much help."

"Define help," he said.

"Uh . . . I do half the work?"

"Nah, see, you need to rethink that."

"I do."

"Yeah."

Andy steered the truck up into the baling area with one hand and gestured with the other.

Had I mentioned that I really liked his hands?

It's come up, yes.

"If I had to lift something that weighed eighty pounds," he said, "and I could only lift seventy-nine, but you could lift one, wouldn't that be helping? Wouldn't we get it done?"

"Yeah."

"So just because you can't do as much work as I do doesn't mean you won't be helping." He stopped the truck, shoved it into park, and gave my upper arm a playful squeeze. "Besides, you might be surprised."

It turned out I was. Three weeks before I had barely been able to lift a hay bale by its strings, much less toss it to a person in the back of the truck. But that day I was bouncing bales up to my hips and thrusting them out to Andy's waiting arms, one after another.

Of course I was also sweating from places on myself I didn't even know existed. The sun beat down relentlessly and the wind was someplace taking a nap. I unbuttoned the shirt I was wearing over the tank top, but as my mother's Missouri relatives would say, I was still burnin' up.

You're gonna have to lose that shirt. It's either that or pass out where you stand.

Or let Andy see the scars.

You don't think he knows?

Maybe he did. Maybe he'd figured it out. But knowing wasn't the same as seeing. Having to look at the places where I had cut and sliced and carved into myself could be a deal breaker. Not that we *had* a deal of some kind. But if Andy never grinned at me again or called me Bo, I wasn't sure I could handle that. Not after losing Bathsheba.

But what if it isn't a deal breaker? What if he doesn't run off screaming like he's seen Godzilla? Won't that tell you something?

I closed my eyes to make sure that was actually the Nudnik talking. But maybe it didn't matter. They were questions I suddenly had to have the answers to.

While Andy rearranged the last of that truckload of bales, I slowly pulled off the cotton shirt. The tank top was scoop-necked and came just to the top of my jeans, but it covered better than most swimsuits.

Not that you've worn one in seven years.

Still, I felt as if I had just stripped completely down to my skin and was standing there naked. But naked or no, I had to get back to work.

Are you noticing anything? Like . . . you just revealed all and the sky didn't come crashing down?

I was actually aware something else had been peeled off with my shirt. A layer of aloneness maybe? Because it came to me that I was no longer by myself with my secret.

We bucked an entire truckload of hay, had it piled over the edges of the truck bed, before Andy looked at me. I could suddenly feel every one of my scars as if it was freshly added to the roadmap etched on my skin. He just grinned at me and said, "Somebody's gonna have to ride on top to make sure it doesn't fall off."

"That's my job," I said.

I always rode back to the barn up there with . . .

Bathsheba.

I could almost feel her paw on my leg, the way she'd pressed it there as if she were making sure I didn't tumble over the side. Right now her fur would be lifting and falling as we bounced, and her tongue would be hanging out like a long elastic spatula. I put my hand to my face to wipe away her dog drool and realized it was my tears.

I tried to smear them off when the truck rocked to a stop at the barn, but Andy was there lowering the tailgate before I could get it done.

"Don't," he said. "Come here."

I crawled to the edge of the pile and let him lift me down. His arms stayed around me.

"Let the tears run down," he said. "Then you won't have to do this anymore."

He ran a gentle finger over the spiderweb of scars on my shoulder.

I had never slept with anyone. I didn't know what it was like. But I did know that with that tiny gesture, Andy had just made love to me.

———

I lay awake all night, my twenty-ninth night at the Bellwether Ranch. I heard Emma's bad dream and Avila's alarmed barking and the ceaseless wind that kicked up at midnight to rattle the old windows and slap the blackberry bushes against the glass. But it was the unmade decision that kept me from falling asleep.

I sat up amid the yellowed quilts that had provided such safety for me and hugged my legs to my chest. I'd been so sure that at thirty days I would leave, ready or not. I even thought when I started to admit my anger that I could take it with me and deal with it . . . somewhere.

My face fell to my knees. It wasn't just that I didn't know where somewhere was that made me doubt now. It was Lara. How could I urge Andy to talk to Frankie about *his* nightmarish memories when I couldn't even talk to my*self* about things I hadn't forgotten and probably never would? The bear cub encounter, losing Bathsheba, uncovering my scars and my secret for Andy—it had all distracted me from what was still left to face.

Lara. Lara and my guilt and the anger I couldn't bring myself to feel.

I fell back against the pillows, but the bed didn't cocoon around me. Could I continue to chip away at that in Bozeman? The summer semester was half over and I couldn't slide into a studio without an approved project anyway. I definitely couldn't go back to my house, not with the painful memories waiting in the very cracks in the walls. Chances were that as furious as my father was with me, he'd probably already gotten out of the lease and sold the whole IKEA shebang on eBay.

You could always go back to Missouri. Lara's there. You wouldn't be able to get away from her—

"I can't," I whispered.

Then it looks like you were right. You're powerless.

I clawed my way out from under the covers and stumbled out to the front room, where I could pace like Aunt Trixie, back and forth across the feet-worn floor.

I couldn't be powerless, not after thirty days of the hardest work I had ever done. Sister Frankie even said I wasn't.

She said you had no power over—

But that I did have the power to. The power to pray.

You don't think she's still up.

Did I need Sister Frankie to pray with me?

Well. No. Maybe not.

259

I pulled a throw pillow from one of the recliners and set it on the floor in front of the window that overlooked the porch. There I knelt and folded my hands on the windowsill and closed my eyes against the slap of the wind and the last mutterings of the Nudnik and the faint, faint cry of my skin.

"God," I whispered, "I need to hear Your voice. Please."

———

Day Thirty dawned bright blue and as I squinted out the kitchen window I remembered how invasive that light had seemed to me on Day One. Now it glared at me as if to say, "Why haven't you made a decision?"

Cut the girl some slack. She still has twenty hours.

Frankie had told Andy and me the night before that we'd be handling the morning chores on our own so she, Joseph, and Emma could get an early start in the alfalfa field. Andy and I had agreed to meet at 6:30 and it was only 5:45. I *had* made one decision before I fell asleep around two and I had time now to carry it out.

I called my mother.

You sure you're ready for this?

If I wasn't it was too late now. She answered on the second ring.

"Kirsten?"

"Hi."

"This is a surprise."

It didn't sound like it was an unpleasant one, so I didn't hang up.

"Are you still at that ranch?" she said.

"I am."

I heard her let out a long breath. "I'm glad to hear that. I was afraid your father took you out of there."

"I would have let you know," I said.

"I should have called you, but—" She cut herself off with another sigh. "Frankly, I assumed you wouldn't speak to me."

"Why?"

"Because I told your father where you were. He called here right after he talked to Wes—I guess Wes called him?"

"Yes."

The scumbag.

"And you know what a bully he can be. He threatened to bring me up on charges of gross negligence—"

"It's okay," I said. "I get it. He came up here and tried to bully me too."

"And he wasn't successful." Now she did sound surprised.

"No, I stayed. But this is the last of my thirty days and I need to figure out what's next." I took a breath. "How would you feel about my coming home for the rest of the summer? Just until school starts."

"You're better, then?" she said.

How subtle.

"Are you asking me if I'm still cutting?"

"Are you?"

"No. I'm not."

"So that's done."

Does she want it written in blood? Oh . . . sorry.

"I could help out with Lara."

There was a silence so dead if I'd been in the same room with my mother I would have checked her pulse.

"I'm not sure what you could do, Kirsten," she said finally. "We have our routine down. I have help when I need to go out."

In other words, you're still an inconvenience.

It wasn't that bad, was it? She wasn't completely dismissing me.

But she's not begging you to come home either.

That was the truth, and suddenly that truth burned in my throat.

"I'm your daughter, too, Mother," I said. "And if I could just hear that you care whether I come home or not, that would be great."

My mother's pause was only long enough for her to blink. "Of course I care, Kirsten," she said. "You don't have to take that tone with me."

There it was—the heart of the anger that now roared in my ears.

Don't take that tone. Don't be honest. Just make it so no one else has to face what is.

My mother sighed yet again. "Well, when would you be coming?"

"I'll let you know," I said. And I hung up.

I was halfway through with my incensed stomp to the barn when Andy caught up with me.

"This walk is about a five on the Richter Scale," he said.

I stopped so abruptly I almost fell over my own hiking boots, and I jabbed at the shoulder he'd kissed with his finger the day before.

"I made that cut with a calligraphy pen my old boyfriend gave me," I said. "It felt like that pen was the only thing left that loved me. And now I think maybe I was right."

I know I told you that but it's a little dramatic for this moment, don't you think?

No, I did not think that. What I thought was that I'd just said exactly what I felt. Out loud. To someone I cared about. And now it wasn't stuck under my skin anymore.

Andy was slowly shaking his head. "That pen's not the only thing that loves you, Bo."

I tried to look away, but he caught my chin and turned it back to him.

"I know this has to be totally your decision," he said. "And maybe I don't have the right to give my input. But, Bo, please don't leave. Not yet."

I closed my eyes and rested my forehead on his chest. "I'll get back to you on that," I said.

Because he was right. For the first time in my life, something *was* my decision. And if I was going to make the right one, there was one more person I had to talk to.

————

Although Joseph and Frankie worked until sunset, they still prepared communion just as they always did on Sunday night. Frankie was just taking the bread out of the oven when I joined her in the kitchen. She pulled off her mitts and looked into me with her wise brown eyes.

"Is this going to be a celebration dinner or a farewell supper?" she said.

"I got angry today," I said. "I got angry and I expressed it to the person I was angry at. Okay, my mother. I did it, and she shut me down."

She waited. When I didn't go on, she said, "There are two reasons for that, I think. One, you're the one who's changing, not your mother. None of your work here is guaranteed to make the situations themselves better. Just you."

"Okay," I said.

"Two, the voice of God isn't in the anger itself. That just shakes things loose so you can look at them. You're just now starting to look."

"I don't think I can look by myself."

"There's no need to."

Go ahead. Ask her.

"How long can I stay?" I said.

"As long as it takes, my friend."

One more. Get it out.

"How will I know it's time to go?"

The grin I counted on wrinkled her nose. "You'll hear *bat kol.* So"—Sister Frankie scooped the bread up into a white towel and set it between my hands—"will you carry this to the table? We have some celebrating to do."

I still wasn't sure I would ever hear God or even *bat kol.* But I did know the voice that whispered to me before Emma and I left the main house that night. I was putting on my boots by the back door when Andy was suddenly there, in that way he and Frankie both had, putting his lips close to my ear.

"You're loved here, Bo," he said.

I had no trouble sleeping that night. I was back in my cocoon.

Share this chapter with your friends!
It came to me that I was no longer by myself with my secret. #TheMercifulScar

Part
FOUR

And after the earthquake a fire, but the Lord was not in the fire.

1 Kings 19:12

Chapter
SIXTEEN

We were a week into July before I realized I'd stopped counting days: days I'd been on the ranch and days since the last time I'd hurt myself. But without that as a frame, I found myself sticking closely to the rhythm of Bellwether.

I got up early to make notes in the (second) red logbook. Prayed on the pillow in front of the window. Put my heart and soul into Petey and the other sheep. Improved the Moment every afternoon with Emma, dutifully showed up for target practice twice a week, gathered with the family for supper, stopped by Bathsheba's grave to whisper a good night.

Through it all I listened for *bat kol*. Sometimes I thought I might have already heard it. In Bathsheba's barking to save me, telling me I was worth dying for. In Petey's devoted bleating, telling me I was worth living for.

And surely there was something sacred in my time with Andy. I had never felt so at ease with a guy, not even with Wes in our early days. What I had taken for comfortable with Wes was merely me fitting into the folds of his life. It was so different with Andy.

For starters, we had conversations that went far beyond flirting and into our ideas, our doubts, our truths.

Our exes.

Okay, so I told him about Wes and he told me about Cara, the long-legged beauty with the trendy-messy bun who transferred in his junior year and who had a fatal flaw: "She knew something was building up in me and she thought if we just had sex I'd feel better. She left me when she finally got that I wasn't going to do it."

I also told him about Lara, but when I came to the night of her accident, my mental tires screeched. Andy, too, ran into a wall when he tried to talk to me about Joseph.

We got onto that subject one day when we were walking back from taking the sheep out and there was time to start from the beginning.

"I don't remember him myself," Andy said, "but Frankie and my grandfather always talked about Uncle Joe who I was supposedly pretty attached to until I was three. My mother died around that time . . . I barely remember her either. And then Joseph left and didn't come back until I was eighteen and away at college."

"Where did he go?" I said, although I was afraid I already knew.

"Prison. I didn't know that until I was probably ten and I overheard Frankie and my grandfather talking about Joseph refusing parole. I wanted to know what that meant, which is when Frankie told me he'd done something he thought was right but the court thought it was wrong and he had to go to jail."

"Did you ever ask what it was?"

Andy shook his head. "Something about the way Frankie said it—I don't know, I just thought I wasn't supposed to ask. I know now, of course, she would have told me. She'd tell me today if I asked her." Andy's face darkened. "But I'm not sure I want to know. Maybe that's why I can't remember."

"So what happened when Joseph came back?"

"It was the end of my freshman year at MIT. When I came home for the summer and saw him here, I had this visceral reaction." Andy worked his shoulders as if he were feeling it right then. "All this stuff just started churning in me and I felt, I don't know, just sick."

"But you still didn't ask Frankie about it."

"I didn't really feel like I could then. Her dad, my grandfather, had just died, like, a year before, which left her with nobody to help on the ranch except some losers she hired who tried to make off with a bunch of her cattle. Joseph coming back was like a godsend for her and I didn't want to mess that up." Andy shrugged. "I talked myself into thinking I was just turned off by him because prison had taken its toll on him. He was completely closed off and when he did say something it was more like snarls than actual words."

"He's come a long way then," I said.

"I know. I didn't come home that much until I graduated, and by then he'd obviously done some serious healing. He tried to get a relationship going between us."

We'd reached the barn by then, and Andy leaned on the main gate. His gaze was so far away I wasn't sure whether he was talking to me or himself.

"I couldn't blame how I felt about him anymore, but the stuff started messing with me again. It was like I was a different person, y'know—angry, depressed. That's just not me and it freaked me out because I didn't know why it was happening . . . except that somehow it was connected to him." Andy almost grinned at me. "Don't say it."

"What? 'Why didn't you talk to Frankie?' *That* it?"

"That's the one." He lost his attempt at the grin. "She was working with young women by then, had two of them staying here, and she was involved with all that. She would've dropped everything to help me if she'd known what I was going through, but I wasn't sure I wanted her to. 'Course, she noticed something was up with me—I mean, that's just Frankie, right?"

"Right."

"So I made an excuse to go back to Cambridge. I was going to bury myself in grad school." His grunt sounded a little like Emma's. "It ended up burying *me*. I couldn't numb the pain, and I couldn't explain it, and I sure couldn't focus the way I needed to. I was on a fellowship and I flunked out." His gaze drifted back to me. "So here I am, feeling like a jerk because I can't stand to be around a prince of a guy who has probably done more for my family than any three people could have."

"Have you thought about asking *him* if he knows why you'd feel that way around him?"

Andy turned to me, so quickly and so full-on I took a step backward. Frustration took hold of his face.

"I don't know how to explain this to you, Bo. I can't talk about it—not to him, not to Frankie—because every time I even think about doing it, it's like something is trying to rip me apart." He closed his eyes and sagged against the gate. "I guess I'm afraid if I confront Joseph, I'll end up torn in two. Do you see?"

"Yeah," I said. "I do."

The only time during those structured days when I felt adrift was that hour every afternoon I promised Frankie I would spend in the Cloister nurturing myself.

It wasn't that there was nothing to do. In a cabinet in the den I'd never opened before I found shelf after shelf of every supply known to the art world. Van Gogh would've been impressed. I also discovered a table that pulled down from the wall; it bore the marks of painters and sketchers and writers who had been there before me, probably trying to express aches as deep as mine. On further investigation I uncovered an easel folded up behind the couch we never sat on. Within five minutes the entire area could be turned into a studio.

I let it all stay out because it made the room look alive, but the thought of working with any of it brought up too much guilt over the fact that I was not currently back at Montana State designing a building that would somehow change the world.

Those discoveries did inspire me to explore the hitherto unopened closets in the rest of the Cloister. The double one in the kitchen I'd assumed was a pantry was actually an impressive library containing mostly poetry and the stories of the female mystics. The cabinet where anyone else would have kept the cereal bowls held a collection of enough candles and soaps and scrubs to open a small spa. And in the broom closet, *voilà*: two guitars, a flute, and a saxophone.

Too bad I didn't paint, read for pleasure, or play a musical instrument.

Pretty depressing, isn't it?

I wasn't the only one who thought so. The second week of July, on a Thursday, I was languishing in one of the recliners and contemplating my decidedly uninteresting personality when Emma slammed into the house and flopped into the chair opposite mine.

"Did she tell you to nurture yourself?" she said.

I burst into guffaws. She sat there staring at me until I could breathe without gasping.

"You done, Petersen?" Emma said.

"Yeah." A few more giggles leaked out.

"You want to fill me in so we can both play?"

271

"I'm sorry—it's just—this whole self-nurturing thing isn't working for me either, and when you said that . . ."

I went off into another gale. Emma still didn't seem to see the humor. She got herself out of the chair and padded around the room in her socks, sighing and then mumbling about how she should be out in the field helping Joseph instead of doing a craft project—and then picking up the sighing again. It would have continued to be comical if I hadn't done much the same thing myself on a number of occasions.

"Okay, look," I said, "before both of us turn into Aunt Trixie, I think we ought to at least try to improve the moment."

"I don't want coffee." Emma's voice was sullen as a three-year-old's.

"Then how about a spa?"

She stopped pacing and gave me one of her deadpan looks. "Do I seriously look like somebody who knows how to do a spa?"

"Okay, no," I said. "But I do. Do you have a bathrobe?"

"There's one hanging on the back of my door. I've never worn it."

"Go put it on and meet me in the kitchen in fifteen minutes."

If there was one thing I did know how to do, it was set a scene. I gathered pretty much everything from the spa cabinet and found enough tablecloths to drape the room into shape. I rolled towels into an inviting pyramid, lit candles on every surface, and warmed several washcloths in the toaster oven. Just as I finished sprinkling lemon oil on them, Emma appeared in a white terry cloth robe that, cinched in at the waist, made her look like Jennifer Lopez.

"This is great," she said, "but it's way too girly for me."

"It's not girly," I said, "it's nurturing."

I coaxed her into a chair, propped her feet on another one, and went to work giving Emma the ultimate spa treatment.

She fought everything at first. Why did she need to have her heels pumiced? Who cared if her elbows were as soft as a baby's behind? What did I think I was going to do with that jar of gunk?

Somewhere between the mud facial mask and the tea tree oil foot soak, her sense of humor kicked in.

"Do you know what my army buddies would say if they saw me like this?" she said as I was wrapping her feet in hot lavender-scented towels. "'You're going soft, Velasquez. You're gonna be worthless as a puddle of mayonnaise after this.'"

"They'd say 'a puddle of mayonnaise'?"

"No. I cleaned it up for you. So where's *your* spa treatment?"

"This is all about you. Next time you can treat me to something." I paused, loofah in hand. "I guess if we don't know how to nurture ourselves, we can at least nurture each other. Which, by the way, you've been doing every afternoon with the coffee and cream. I've gained, like, five pounds since I've been here."

"You could stand to gain about ten more. I thought you were anorexic when you first showed up. Anorexic and all about yourself." Emma looked at her feet. "I was totally wrong about that. I'd take you in my unit anytime."

I think you just got nurtured.

When Emma had been softened and smoothed and pampered in every way I knew how, I put on a bathrobe, too, and we had coffee in our recliners.

"We oughta take a picture of this," Emma said. "Prove to Frankie that we nurtured, already."

I took a long look at Emma, and I nodded. "I *should* take a picture of you. No makeup, but your skin is like cream. You're pretty, Emma."

I expected a full-scale protest but she looked into her mug and her eyes glistened.

"Somebody used to tell me that," she said.

"A guy?" I said.

"Yeah. Buddy of mine in my unit. He's the one who introduced me to the real Jesus, not the one that got preached at me growing up. We used to pray together."

"And he thought you were pretty."

Emma's grunt was unconvincing. "Yeah, but you have to remember it's not a glamor gig over there. Anybody who's not a guy is pretty."

"What was his name?"

"Patrick."

"Do you still keep in touch?"

Emma shook her head. And continued to shake it. Until she stood up and said, "I can't talk about this anymore."

"Okay," I said.

She started for her room, but she turned around before she reached the den. "I know you, Petersen," she said. "You're going to sit there thinking it's your fault that I'm upset. Just so you know: it's not. That's the most I've been able to talk about Patrick. Joseph will probably nominate you for a Medal of Honor for that, so don't go taking yourself on a guilt trip. Are we good?"

Say yes or you're gonna be court-martialed.

"We're good," I said.

"All right. And tomorrow it's my turn to pamper you. I'm taking you on my favorite hike."

No, see, pampering *means—*

"Sweet," I said. "I'll be ready."

———

Emma was true to her word. When I returned to the Cloister just before noon the next day, she was tucking sandwiches into a backpack that, judging from its bulges, was already filled with enough food for an entire brigade and whatever else one needed for Emma's Favorite Hike.

"What do I need to bring?" I said.

"Nothing. I've got this."

Now would be a good time to ask if we're headed for boot camp.

Emma hiked the backpack over her shoulder and gave me what I could only describe as a satisfied look. "I think you're gonna like this, Petersen."

I thought so too. Even if it *was* like boot camp.

From the number of orders Joseph gave us before we left in the truck, I wouldn't have been surprised if that was where we were actually headed.

"There's been no sign of that grizzly and her cub," he said, "but both of you carry. We clear on that?"

"Yes, sir," she said, smile twitching.

He squinted at her. "You have plenty of water?"

"Yes."

"Cell phone?"

"Yes."

"I better give you a flare—"

"We're going on a hike, Joseph, not mobilizing for Iwo Jima."

"Don't get wise, Corporal," he said.

I decided I never liked Joseph better than when he was bantering with Emma.

"He loves you like a dad is supposed to," I said when we were finally on our way to the trailhead.

"I know I would have gone back on the pills if it weren't for him," she said. "Him and God."

We drove in a different direction than I'd been before, to the hills north of the house. Emma called the area Four.

"Where you take the sheep is Ten," she said. "Frankie owns Two through Five and Eight through Ten. Thirty-eight hundred acres."

"Have you seen them all?" I said.

"I was going to try to, but then I found this spot where I'm taking you and I figured I'd found heaven, so why look any further?"

Emma drove until what she called a road ended in a pile of flat orange and tan rocks that looked as if a cave child had left them there when he was called in for supper.

"We'll hike in from here," she said. "This is where it gets good."

She slung the backpack over her shoulder and I did the same with the thirty-thirty. We'd walked about a quarter of a mile before I noticed Emma didn't have her gun.

"Be nice to me or I'll tell Joseph you left your rifle in the truck," I said.

Emma slowed and looked over her shoulder at me. "*Don't* tell him," she said. "I'm serious."

"O-kay," I said. "I was actually joking."

"Not even a little bit funny, Petersen."

I kind of thought it was.

Emma's words chilled the air for a few more steps, and then she stopped and let me catch up.

"I'm not trying to be a jerk," she said. "I carried a gun so much in the army. I'm just trying to get away from all that."

I bit back the question, *Have you told Joseph that?* Everybody's answer to that kind of query seemed to be an unqualified no, so why did I keep asking?

Emma nodded for me to follow her. The trail was mostly a path of trampled-down grass bordered by thin yellow lilies and star-shaped pink flowers clustered at the tops of their leafless stems. It followed a long narrow ribbon of water that gleamed in Montana's afternoon sun. I'd heard Joseph say water was like gold to a rancher: rare and valuable. The cottonwoods and huckleberry bushes seemed to think so too because they grew greedily along the banks, showing off their greenness against the stark weathered beauty of the rocks and the summer-faded grass.

"See how lush it gets right up here?" Emma said, pointing.

"Yeah, it's like an oasis."

"Exactly. There's a spring there."

"It feels cooler up here."

"That's because it is. The perfect spot for our picnic—and I am talking epic perfect—is right around this bend—"

Emma stopped in front of me. Everything about her was so suddenly on guard I fully expected antennae to come out of her head.

"What?" I said.

"Shh!"

I couldn't have said anything if I'd wanted to—I saw the bear ambling toward us on all fours. With a smaller, thinner version of herself trailing behind her.

The cub's deceptively soft face I knew. It was forever branded in my brain. Yet he fanned up far less fear than his sharp-nosed mother, wide with rolls of heft, the fur around her mouth wet with purple juice as she moved in a Z-pattern, sniffing the ground.

Emma slowly slipped a hand behind her back and motioned for me to retreat. I could hear Frankie in my head: "*The best thing to do is back slowly and quietly away. They aren't usually aggressive with humans . . .*"

I held my breath—not hard to do since I was barely breathing anyway—and imitated Emma's every step. Frankie still whispered from my memory . . . "*A grizzly can move at thirty-five miles an hour, so you aren't going to outrun it. Just a calm, slow walk.*"

Slow I could do. Calm was out of the question. My heart slammed against my chest wall and every nerve shrieked for me to flee. Only the sight of Emma, backing soundlessly away from the bear, kept me from freezing on the path.

The bear's heavy movement stopped and I almost did, too, but Emma waved for me to keep going. The bear stopping was good, wasn't it? That put more distance between us and her until we could get to the truck—

The grizzly's head came up, rippling the two large muscular humps on her shoulders, and I could hear her snorting at the air. Her eyes, tilted up at the outer corners, narrowed and searched. Until they found Emma.

Emma stopped and closed her fingers into a fist behind her back. I kept moving, no longer even trying to pull off calm, but she tightened the fist insistently and I knew I was supposed to stop too. It was the single hardest thing I'd ever done.

The bear was still on all fours, but she was now swaying her head. The snort-like sniffing had turned into blowing and the agitated neck strained toward Emma.

Frankie must've been wrong. That's *aggressive.*

What had Frankie said exactly? "*They aren't usually aggressive . . . unless you have food.*"

OhmygoshEmma—the backpack.

"She wants the food," I whispered. "Give her the backpack."

Emma hesitated . . . then nodded. Moving at half-speed she pulled the pack from her shoulders and the bear watched, still wagging her head and huffing.

Set it down gently, Emma. Set it down—

Brave, calm, military-trained Emma probably would have . . . if the bear hadn't suddenly risen on her back feet and clacked her teeth.

Emma's arm jerked and haphazardly flung the backpack—straight at the cub.

"The cub," Frankie's voice screamed in my ear. *"If she thinks you're endangering her baby, all bets are off."*

Now towering over us, the bear lowered her head and laid back her ears. Everything in me did freeze then. Everything except the image of my Bathsheba, beside herself with fear and courage, being smacked over the side of the mountain like a plaything in a cruel game. That part of me, that part that could still move, grabbed the gun from my shoulder and shoved it into Emma's hands.

"Run," she said between her teeth. "Run!"

I would have argued but Frankie's most urgent words of all screamed in my head. *"Run like your life depended on it. Because it would."*

So I ran, already blanching at the shots I knew were coming.

Except they didn't.

Still stumbling forward I looked over my shoulder. Emma stood in the middle of the path, the rifle poised at her shoulder, aimed at the grizzly's head. But even from behind I could see that Emma was almost paralyzed. The only thing moving was the tremor that made its way up her arms.

"Emma, shoot!" I screamed.

She didn't.

"Shoot her!"

The bear advanced but the gun was still, held in the hands of a statue that threatened to crumble.

If the bear didn't tear it apart first.

My mind screamed, *Run, Kirsten! Run!* and I did, straight for Emma. With the bear close enough for me to hear her jaw popping, I snatched the gun from Emma's hands. My own hands shook as I pulled back the lever. Beside me, Emma covered her eyes and gave a tortured cry. I shoved her behind me and groped for Frankie's voice again.

"... *shoot until the gun was empty ... it would have to be in her neck or head.*"

The gun that had always seemed so heavy in my hands was now a mere toy against this animal whose eye was larger than the barrel. I pointed it without bothering with the sight. She was closer than any target I had ever shot at.

I can't do this! I can't do this!

Yes, you can. Frankie said ... shoot until the gun is empty.

I moved my finger to the trigger and squeezed. The shot cracked Emma's statue.

"*Patrick!*" she screamed. "*No!*"

The mother bear wagged her head, eyes furious. I'd done nothing but tick her off. I pulled back the lever and once more squeezed the trigger, and again Emma screamed Patrick's name. On my third shot she went to the ground. The bear was still standing, still coming for me, lessening the distance between us and horror.

Three more rounds. I only had three more chances.

I jammed the lever back and tried to take aim at her chest. The shot didn't seem to faze her but I didn't wait. Again—*cha-ching*—just the way Andy had taught me—I fired and saw the bear flinch, as if I'd attacked her with a slingshot.

One more. One more and then we had to run.

With Emma bordering on hysteria, screaming for Patrick, and the bear so close I could smell her hungry breath, I fired my last round, into the front of her neck. The gun was empty. The bear gave a hideous roaring gasp. Emma's screams went on, painful and raw. I could do nothing but grab her and run and hope that one of those shots gave us enough time to get to the truck.

"Come on—run with me!" I cried.

Emma let me pull her only a few steps before she clawed at my arm and cried, "I can't leave Patrick! I can't leave him!"

"We'll come back for him!" I said.

In that moment that Emma wavered, I got her around the waist and pressed her against my side and ran, hard, clumsily, but away from the grizzly. Emma sobbed and wailed all the way, and when we reached the truck and I let go of her long enough to get the door open, she tried to stumble back to the path, still screaming Patrick's name. I hurled myself after her and brought both of us to the ground. The gun bounced away with a spray of pebbles—and Emma froze, eyes bulging at it.

"It's okay," I said. "We'll come back for Patrick, I promise. Come on, Corporal. Let's get you in the truck."

By the time I pulled into the driveway I was starting to believe Emma and I *were* on a battlefield. She rode with her upper body folded into her legs, hands behind her neck, and cried and cried and cried for Patrick. When Andy jerked the door open, I was crying too.

I hadn't been able to call ahead to Joseph and Frankie because it had taken all I had to keep the truck on the road and hold on to Emma in case she tried to eject herself. Now I said to Andy, "She thinks we're in Afghanistan. Call Joseph."

"Let's get her in the house first."

It took both of us to carry the struggling Emma inside and get her into one of the wide armchairs. Andy made the call while I tried to wrap her in a throw, telling her I was a medic, but she kept straining to get up, insisting hysterically that she had to get back to Patrick. The only thing we had going for us was that she was wearing out and her trembling arms had turned to noodles.

Frankie arrived first and went straight to her as if no one else was in the room. She took Emma's face in her hands and spoke to her in a voice that would have soothed the wretched bear herself. Frankie was here. It was okay.

"You were strong enough to survive the real trauma, Emma," she said. "God brought you through it. You're strong enough to let God bring you through the healing too."

She said it again, and then again, until Emma blinked as if she were waking up in a strange place.

"You're safe," Frankie said.

Emma looked around, eyes searching, I was sure, for something she recognized. Her gaze found me sitting on the table next to Frankie. With a cry, Emma came forward in the chair and threw her arms around me. And sobbed.

I held her, but I didn't know what else I should do. I was sure my face looked helpless as I stared over Emma's head at Frankie.

"It's all right," Frankie said. "That's a healing kind of weeping."

It did seem that the longer I held Emma, the less she shook, in spite of the sobbing that no doubt came from some dark place.

When Joseph arrived, sprouting alfalfa from his shirt and mopping rivulets of sweat from his neck, Emma slid from my arms into his and began to babble as if a dam had broken inside her. I wasn't sure I should be there, but when I whispered that to Frankie, she patted my leg and whispered, "I think Emma wants you to stay."

I wasn't sure about Emma, but one look at Andy and I knew I shouldn't leave him. His face was ghostly.

"I saw it again, Joseph," Emma said. "I saw it all today. I was there and it was happening again."

"It didn't happen again," Joseph said. "It's never *going* to happen again—not if you get it out."

Emma closed her eyes. I knew she was seeing the pain, and my heart broke.

"We were just trying to save the Afghani children—Patrick and me—the area where they lived was about to be occupied. All we wanted to do was move the mother and babies to safety. That's all!"

"And what happened?" Joseph said. "Tell me what happened."

Emma curled over herself as if she were in physical pain to match the torture in her memory. "I got a mother and two children out and Patrick told me to go on and he'd get the rest." She opened her eyes and clung to Joseph with them. "I was holding a toddler and pushing the mother who was holding her baby and I heard . . . I screamed for Patrick to get out of there and I saw him running toward me with a baby. And then"—Emma pulled her arms around herself and gasped as if the memory had ripped her breath from her—"and then the mortar hit—and then he wasn't there. There was nothing." She trembled toward silence. "All they ever found was his dog tags."

The cry I heard next was my own. Frankie took my hand and led me out to the kitchen. Behind us, Emma was once again sobbing in Joseph's arms.

"That was hard to hear," Frankie said.

"I hated it for her. Wasn't it enough the first time without having to go through it over and over?"

Frankie brushed back a tendril of hair that was tear-stuck to my face. "You are the soul of compassion, my friend. So hang on to this: we have been praying for Emma to be able to get this out for over four months. This means she's free to begin to heal. And that's of God, Kirsten. Hard as it is, this is good."

"Okay," I said.

But if that was what it looked like to finally face the thing that trapped your soul, I wasn't sure I could do it. I wasn't as strong as Emma.

"Kirsten?"

283

Frankie gave my hand a shake.

"I'm sorry, what?"

"Did something happen on your hike that might have triggered this?"

I sank against the kitchen counter. "Oh, Sister," I said, "you have no idea."

Chapter
SEVENTEEN

Emma stayed at the main house that night. Frankie offered me a room too so I wouldn't have to be alone at the Cloister, but I declined. I'd just spent a half hour convincing the wildlife conservation people that if I hadn't shot the bear, both Emma and I would have probably met the same fate as the contents of the backpack they found the cub devouring a few yards from his mother's wounded body.

Obviously very concerned, the little ingrate.

Joseph finally intervened on my behalf.

Intervened? He practically escorted them out at gunpoint.

"You said yourself the animal will probably live," Joseph told them. "The girl saved you six more weeks of chasing the two of them down with a tranquilizer gun."

Then he actually did all but escort them out at gunpoint.

By then I was so tired my bones ached and I just wanted to be by myself. No one seemed to be concerned that I might go to the Cloister and break out a razor. Even if I'd wanted to, I didn't have the energy.

I missed Emma the minute I walked in the door, but other than that the silence welcomed me. That and the promise of a hot shower and a cup of Joseph's blend with Hildegarde's cream to help me breathe away the tumult that had been today.

My, my, look who's self-nurturing.

Who would have thought, huh?

I barely had my sweats on and my tea brewed to perfection when someone tapped on the front door.

Look first. If it's Ranger Rick, climb out the back window.

I absolutely would have, but it was Andy who stood under the porch light, shoulders hunched as if the first blizzard had just hit. I couldn't tell whether his chill was from inside or out. I slipped out to join him and handed him my tea.

"You look like you need this more than I do," I said.

"No—"

"Your teeth are chattering. Drink it."

He cupped his palms gratefully around the mug and took a sip that made him wince.

"Yeah, it's hot, but it'll warm you up. You want a blanket?"

Andy shook his head, but he did take the rocker I offered him. I let him sip until his shoulders sank away from his earlobes.

"I'm sorry I can't invite you in," I said.

"I know the rules. It's okay."

I curled into a ball in the rocker facing him.

"If you're too cold—"

"I'm fine." I smiled at him. "I live on a sheep ranch in Montana. This is nothin'."

Andy tried the grin, but it wavered. "Is that what it takes to get free, Bo?" he said.

"You mean Emma?"

He nodded.

"I was asking myself the same thing," I said. "I didn't get very far though. It scared me too much."

"It *terrified* me."

He did look haunted. Dark smudges formed half-moons under his eyes and his skin was pallid. And yet there were still those shoulders and that strong jaw.

"Whatever it is, you can handle it," I said. "You've got family, you've got God . . . you've got me."

"That's a lot."

"And you've got you," I said. "I should be *half* as strong as you are."

"You're joking, right?"

"No," I said.

Andy put the mug on the porch floor and leaned into the space between us, his hands on the arms of my chair. "Who took down a grizzly bear and brought home a woman in the middle of a PTSD crisis and stood up to the wildlife inquisition all in one day?"

"That's different," I said.

He looked around as if he were clueless. "You gonna explain that to me?"

"I don't know."

"Yeah, ya do, Bo."

His eyes held on to mine.

"That was all outside of me. I guess I can handle anything if it's not about me." I pressed my hand to my throat. "It's this stuff that I wimp out on."

"Is that where it lives, in your throat?"

"Yeah."

"Mine's right here." He pumped his fist lightly against his chest. "I can't tell you how many times this past year I thought I was having a heart attack."

"That's why I used to cut," I said. "To try to let the pain out."

"I get that."

Andy rocked back and ran his hand through his hair. I'd been right about the cause of the spikes. They stood up on his head in boyish disarray.

"Cutting doesn't work anymore," I said.

"Neither does denial."

"Then I guess that answers your question. What Emma went through today—that *is* what it takes to get free."

"It took her a long time to get there."

"She had three months on us."

Andy grinned. "So do we just hang out for a couple more months and see what happens?"

"I don't think so."

"I was afraid you were gonna say that." He scooted forward again until our knees were touching. "You want to pray with me?"

"I'm not very good at it yet," I said.

"What does that even mean?" He put up a hand. "Never mind. I know that's the default Bo Response to anything she's not perfect at. I got a flash for ya: there is no perfect way to pray."

"Then . . . the Lord be with you," I said.

———

We prayed long after the sun left us in silhouette. Andy prayed out loud more than me, although I felt moved to murmur along. When we left our prayers with God there were still hours of night left and we spent them talking and being quiet so Andy could point out the sounds for me. A coyote's yip. Avila's guardian bark. A low moan from Hildegarde.

"Doesn't she ever sleep?" I said.

"Too ornery. Speaking of sleep, don't you need to get some?"

"You can go if you're tired," I said. "I just want to sit here for a while."

So he sat with me and we talked more and listened more. Somewhere between the whispers and the silences, Andy tilted my chin up with his finger and kissed me. It was a whisper and a silence and a prayer . . . and I didn't want it to end.

When the sun stretched its first sleepy arm over the mountains again, Andy left. I stayed on the porch and watched Montana wake up and notice that Kirsten Petersen was in love. It did take note. That had to be what made those orange tongues of sunlight wag in the sky. They spoke as Andy did, with a warmth that assured me it was going to be okay. I could do this.

When I stood up I whispered one more prayer: "If You'll help me, I will."

———

Over the next four days, deep into the middle of July, Andy and I spent every possible moment together, as well as some we coaxed out of the impossible. Kisses were stolen behind towers of hay bales, hugs among the sheep. It was the looks I treasured the most though. The grins tossed back and forth in the barn. The secret smiles exchanged across the supper table. The soft, open eyes that simply met and crinkled and made the rest of the world disappear.

But we didn't meet on the porch at night again. I wanted to keep our romance away from Emma, who was mourning the loss of Patrick inside the Cloister. The quiet weeping, the waves of memory, the emptiness where her grief had once been stuffed away—that all had to be hard enough without us building a new love right under her nose.

Emma's and my Improving the Moment time was also sacred, and Andy got that. I told Emma I didn't expect coffee and talk to improve these sad moments, but she said somehow they did. She still made the coffee and we still rocked side by side and I still marveled at her strength.

"You saved my life," she suddenly said one afternoon. "A soldier never forgets that."

That pretty much says it all.

It did. So I just nodded and took the hand she offered me.

———

It was Joseph who helped Emma most, that was clear. Every time she came back from riding on horseback with him somewhere on those thirty-eight hundred acres, she seemed a little more sure, even in her sorrow. Every time Andy saw them, he grew a little more troubled.

"I'm really trying to remember, Bo," he told me more than once. "But I still don't get why I can barely look that incredible human being in the eyes."

We got part of our answer one afternoon about five days after Emma's breakthrough.

Andy and I were bucking hay and I was getting a little cocky about the whole tossing thing. Even I could see that I'd developed some biceps on my previously scrawny arms. So I decided to impress Andy with a one-hand-on-the-string pitch and only got the bale as far as the tailgate. It bounced off, broke open, and split into an inviting pile on the ground.

"That is screaming to be jumped into," Andy said.

I howled and beat him to it, but he was there before I got the next giggle out. Holding me around the waist with one steel-band arm, he grabbed a hunk of hay with the other and dropped it over my head.

I shrieked, "You are *toast!*" and rolled away from him. I now had the perfect behind-his-back opportunity to get him good. Still shrieking, I wrapped my arms around both of his and held on tight. Obviously I wasn't going to keep him pinned for long—he would have me doing a somersault over him any second—

"Let me go!"

"Are you serious? A lightweight could get out of this!"

He had to say it a second time before I realized his voice was thin and frightened.

I pulled my arms away and watched his face writhe. He was having another memory, but unlike Emma, he didn't hold it back. The pieces came out in a torrent of images.

"A man picked me up and held me too tight—he held me all wrong—he didn't know how to carry me—I was screaming—"

"'Let me go,'" I said.

As he'd done before, Andy pulled his legs into his chest and held on. "Bo," he said.

"I'm here."

"It was so real. It was so real and then it got away." He looked at me, eyes still bright with fear. "I couldn't tell if it was Joseph holding me. But it was Joseph yelling."

"What was he yelling?"

"Stop. He was yelling stop." He shoved a hand through his hair. "It's so confusing. He was yelling and I was crying and someone was under—I don't know. I can't see it." Andy crossed his hands over his chest. "It just hurts, Bo. Right here. It hurts."

I pulled his head against me and rocked him, there in the hay with the remains of our play still stuck in our hair. That was how Frankie found us.

Busted.

I hadn't heard from the Nudnik in days, but it didn't surprise me that she spoke up then. She was always there when the guilt kicked in.

Andy sat up but he didn't move away from me. Frankie perched on a nearby bale and surveyed us with her brown eyes.

Maybe not busted but definitely about to get a sermonette.

"We're all adults," Frankie said. "So I think it's time we were honest with each other."

"Me first." Andy's voice still shook a little but his grin was strong. "I care about Kirsten," he said. "I care about her too much to hurt her."

Frankie pulled in her chin. "I would never suggest that you would, son."

"What you see here is her helping me deal with some memories I've been having that I can't quite wrap my mind around."

There's the kiss of death right there. "Why didn't you come to *me, Andy?*"

But Frankie didn't say anything. She nodded and turned to me. Even the Nudnik fell silent.

"I care about Andy too," I said. "He's good and he's honest . . ."

"Well, don't stop now," Andy said. "You're on a roll."

Frankie closed her eyes and smiled.

What does that look mean? C'mon, what does that mean?

"I don't doubt for a minute that you two care about each other," she said. "I saw the potential for that the first time you met, right on this spot. And even if I had thought it wasn't a good idea for you to explore a relationship, it wouldn't be my place to try to stop you."

Andy grinned. "You'd give your input though."

"Only because *I* care about *both* of you. And that's why I'm going to give it now." She leaned over and put a hand on each of ours. "Please take your time. If this is of God, it will stand that test."

"I'll take that input," Andy said. He looked at me. "You, Bo?"

"Yes," I said. "Thank you."

"You're more than welcome." Frankie stood up and seemed about to go, and then she turned back to us. "By the way, you don't have to sneak behind the bum pen to kiss her, Andy."

"I know that," he said. "It's just more fun that way."

"Incorrigible," she said. "Completely incorrigible."

Andy still waited until she was gone to kiss me, and the sigh I hugged out of him was long and real. But Frankie's words had thrown me off balance again. *"If this is of God . . ."*

I'd never thought of anything I did as being of God. This . . . the this we'd danced around for weeks . . . could this be so real that it was of God? Meant to be? For me?

———

The next afternoon during the free time I'd fallen into the habit of spending with Andy, I went to the Cloister instead and among the art supplies I found a sketch pad and a fine-tipped black marker. I tucked the pad under my arm and the pen over my ear and went out to the side porch.

Neither Emma nor I ever spent much time there because it looked out on nothing but high bushes that were several years past their trimming date; they reached over the roofline like neglected children allowed to run amuck. Seeing the bunkhouse and beyond wasn't my goal. I wanted to be outside and not *be* seen, and this was the perfect place.

I opened the sketchbook to its first white, pristine page and smoothed my hand over it. I was no stranger to such pads; I'd roughed out many a design in them, filling up several every semester from sophomore year on. I waited for a minute to see if any waves of regret or longing would wash over me, but I felt only the Nudnik saying, *Oh, for Pete's sake get on with it.*

I uncapped the pen and let it write across the top of the page . . .

Lara

What I was going to do after that, I had no idea. So I wrote BAT KOL, hoping an echo would tell me what to do. Then I wrote, OF GOD. And THE LORD BE WITH YOU. And LET US PRAY.

And then I wrote, LARA, WHY DID YOU LISTEN TO ME *THAT* NIGHT?

The pen stopped. My mind didn't.

So many times I'd nagged her, pleaded with her, begged her not to go. Not to sneak out. Not to pour vodka into that soda can. She had always tossed her silken head and laughed her elfin laugh and said, "You won't tell. You'll cover for me."

Why that night did she change her mind and do what I told her to do?

You're not ready for this yet.

I looked down at the paper. LARA was dripping down the page, racing after my tears.

"What do you mean, memories?"

The voice was so close I looked to see if Joseph had joined me on the porch, but I was still alone.

"He said he was having memories he couldn't wrap his mind around and Kirsten was helping him."

That was Frankie's voice. They had to be standing more than thirty feet from the Cloister, but the breeze blew their words up to the porch.

"You think he's remembering . . ."

"What else could it be?" Frankie said.

Two things became crystalline in my mind. This conversation was not meant for me to hear. And if I got up and went into the house, they would know I *had* heard. The floorboards would creak and the back door would groan like an arthritic old woman. I sat still and squeezed my eyes shut.

Like that's gonna keep you from eavesdropping.

"I can't help thinking we made a mistake by not telling him, Joseph. But he never asked."

"Probably afraid of the answer."

"Aren't we all afraid of the truth sometimes?"

"Look, Frank, it is what it is," Joseph said. "Whatever he remembers, whatever we end up telling him, it was all for him. He'll see that."

"Unless he saw Ronnie that day and that's what he's blocking out."

"What?"

"I've just always wondered, Joseph, what if he saw her?"

"There's no way he could have seen her. She was under my truck."

The breeze blew a pause across the hillside. Then Joseph said, "Trust me on that, Frank, because *I* have *no* trouble remembering that day."

I let Frankie's reply fly past me as I held on to Andy's words. *"Something was under—I can't see."* Was that something under Joseph's truck? Ronnie? Who was Ronnie?

"You going to tell him now?" Joseph said.

"Not unless I have to," Frankie said. "I have to believe this is all coming to him as he's ready. The question is, are you?"

"I guess I'll have to be, won't I?" I could imagine Joseph pushing up the brim of his hat with two fingers. "You still want to ride up to Five with Emma and me?"

"Yeah. We need to clear our heads."

I waited until I could no longer hear Joseph and Frankie murmuring to each other before I started to tangle with any of that. Even then I got up and peered through the bushes first to make sure they were saddling up with Emma outside the bunkhouse.

Joseph had told me twice to my face, "This has nothing to do with you." But there was no erasing it now. Andy, my Andy, was about to remember something that had been hidden from him his whole life, and in a way even Sister Frankie now doubted was the way it should have been done.

I didn't want him to remember it alone.

———

Andy was standing at the bum lamb pen, leaning over to pet Petey, when I got to the barn. He looked up at me as if he knew I'd be coming. His face was flooded with something just realized.

"I was three years old," he said.

I went to him and he folded me against him. My chest threatened to split in half, just like his.

"A few minutes ago I overheard something I wasn't supposed to hear and I'm sorry," I said. "But maybe it will help you. Only . . . I don't know, Andy, maybe you should ask Joseph. He'll tell you so you can—"

Andy pulled me in tighter. "No. I'd rather hear it from you."

"Wrong," someone said. "You're going to hear it from me."

I wrenched my neck to look behind us. The voice belonged to my father.

He was like a snapshot standing there, as if he'd posed for the moment. He'd made no attempt to look Western this time. The knife-pleated jeans had been replaced by dress slacks, the shiny boots by wingtips. Even his face was on the Corporate Setting: eyes in charge, brow confidently smooth, mouth ready to do business. For the first time since I was seventeen years old I didn't feel an expectant rush because my father had arrived on his white horse.

All I felt were his last words snapping in my mind like alarmed fingers: *"I'm not done with this."*

"Dad," I said, "what . . . what are you doing here?"

"I came to get you out of this place," he said. "And I'm not leaving without you this time."

My face was already immobile but somehow I shook my head. "I'm not going, Dad. I'm sorry you came all the way out here, but I told you—"

"And now I'm telling you."

It wasn't so much what he said that stunned me, but the way he delivered it. Without anger. Without urgency. Without any emotion at all.

Unless you count smug as an emotion.

That was it. And it stood up like nettles on the back of my neck.

"I've done some research on this place," he said. "It's been crawling with loonies since day one."

Until then Andy had remained shocked-still, and why wouldn't he? He'd just been knocked from one disturbing dimension into another. But now he let go of me and stepped forward.

"I'm sorry, Mr. Petersen," he said, "but you don't get to walk in here and insult my family."

"I'm thinking about *my* family, son," Dad said.

How are you not throwing up right now?

"My daughter has spent, what is it now, six weeks, on a ranch that's been run by . . ." He counted on his fingers. "Two hippies with arrest records—that's the good Sister Frankie's parents . . . Frankie's wacko twin sister, Ronnie—that's your mother, Andrew, who ran off and married a guy with a boatload of money and then ran away from *him* and for all practical purposes kidnapped her unborn kid—that's you—and hid him here thinking she could pretend none of it ever happened."

"Dad, stop," I said.

"I'm just getting started, Kirsten. Do you want to know why Joseph Maxwell went to prison?"

"Let Joseph Maxwell tell him."

How Frankie and Joseph got to the barn's main gate without us hearing them I couldn't begin to know. But they were there now, both of them gray shadows of the people I'd seen galloping off less than thirty minutes before. Frankie's eyes were large and stark, not moving from my father as she let herself and Joseph through the gate.

"Sister," my father said, as if she'd just joined us at a table at Ted's Montana Grill. His insensitivity rattled in the barn.

"This is not your story to tell, Mr. Petersen," Frankie said.

"Fine," my father said. "Let's hear his version."

"No," I said. "We shouldn't be here."

I marched to him and motioned to the gate Joseph had just closed behind them, all without looking at my father.

"You're right, kiddo," he said. "This is a family affair."

He looked at the gate latch as if he expected me to open it. I climbed over the bars and waited, arms folded, on the other side. My pulse pounded in my neck.

My father fumbled over the latch until, with a muttered epithet, he gave up and climbed without grace over the gate. The sole of his wingtip slipped on the last rung and he stumbled forward almost into my arms. I stepped aside.

"Don't pull an attitude with me, Kirsten—"

"Bo! Please . . . I need you here."

I turned to look at Andy. He was still rooted to his spot by the bum pen, his face the color of Petey's wool. Nothing on him moved except his mouth, begging me not to make him do this alone.

I looked at Frankie but her eyes were closed.

It's on you.

I climbed back over the fence. Without turning around I said, "Dad. You can go wherever. I'm staying here."

"Kirsten—"

"*Go,* okay?"

He swore. The desecrating words hung in the air as his footsteps popped across the rocks and disappeared.

"I'm sorry," I said.

But no one seemed to hear. Frankie and Andy watched only Joseph, and now as I returned to my place beside Andy, so did I. I could feel Andy's agony seething from his skin. I could see Frankie's in her eyes. But it was Joseph whose very being seemed to suffer as he began to tell the story that had buried itself in Andy's memory.

Share this chapter with your friends!

There is no perfect way to pray.

#TheMercifulScar

Chapter
EIGHTEEN

It was actually Andy who started. With his gaze slanted to the ground he said, "I was three years old. You and I, Joseph . . . we were coming back from the processor. It was good. It was a good moment, and then it turned bad."

He gave Joseph an imploring look that tore through me. It seemed to have that same effect on Joseph.

"I'll tell you why, son," Joseph said. "But you need to know that once I do, you're going to have some demons to wrestle with."

I watched Andy swallow as if it hurt. As if everything hurt. "I'm already there," he said. "I need to hear."

Joseph took one more reluctant breath. "Ronnie was out there in the driveway. But you weren't excited to see her like you usually were. You knew as soon as I did that something wasn't right with your mama."

Andy nodded. "She was arguing with somebody."

"Right. Gabe DeLuca. I'd never seen him before but I knew the minute I looked at him he was your father. The only thing we had going for us was that *he* didn't know he was your father."

"He didn't know I existed," Andy said.

"That's right."

"Your mother wanted it that way, Andy," Frankie said. "She was afraid of him."

"And from what I was seeing, she had every right to be." Joseph shook his head. "He had her backed up against the side of his Porsche and he was just before backhanding her across the face. Bad choice to make in front of me."

Even now anger seared through Joseph's eyes. I didn't want to hear the rest of this story, but Andy found my hand and clung to it with icy fingers.

"I told you to get down on the floorboard," Joseph said. "I didn't want him seeing you, because one look would tell him you were his kid. Same hair. Same stocky body. Same everything except the soul that had been taken over by the devil."

"I didn't do it, though," Andy said. "I got out of the car and ran to her."

"Are you remembering, Andy?" Frankie said.

I knew the answer. I could feel the memory clenched in his fingers.

"She smelled like cinnamon."

"Yes, she did," Frankie said.

"And he knew who I was."

"He did," Joseph said. "Knocked the sass right out of him. That gave Ronnie a chance to motion for me to take you inside the house, and I did." Joseph's voice caught. "And I will regret that until the day I die."

If you want to get out of hearing where this goes, now could be your last chance.

Want to? Every cell cried out, "No! You can't hear this!" But do it? With Andy's courage breaking down in the palm of my hand?

I put my other hand over his.

"I took you inside," Joseph said, "and I tried to calm you down, but you were crying for your mama like you'd never done before. And then we heard other screams."

"Hers," Andy said.

"You got away from me and bolted out the door—"

"He had his hands around her neck . . . he was shaking her . . . and shaking her."

"Son—"

"And then he dropped her and kicked her under your truck . . . like she was a dead dog . . ."

Frankie let out a cry. With both hands pressed to her mouth she said, "Oh, Andy—oh baby, you saw. I didn't know you saw."

Andy didn't seem to be able to say any more. What was there *to* say after that? What more horror could there be? I wanted to pull him into my arms, but I was afraid if I did he would crack into tiny pieces that could never be put back together again.

"Should I go on, Frankie?" Joseph said.

It was Andy who nodded. I bit my lip to keep from screaming, *No! No more!*

"Before I could get out there, DeLuca grabbed you and went for his car."

"He didn't know how to hold me right," Andy had said that day in our hay pile. *"I was screaming, 'Let me go!'"*

"I shouted for him to stop," Joseph said. "And I went after him. But he had you in one arm and he used the other one to pull out a forty-five. I knew from the look in his eye he'd shoot me if I so much as blinked, and I'd be no good to you dead, Andy. You know that, right?"

Andy managed to nod.

"He peeled out of there with you in the car, and I was banking on him not being able to take the dirt roads in that Porsche like I could in the truck. My gun was hanging behind the seat and I jumped in to take off after him . . ." Joseph's voice weakened. "And then I remembered Ronnie was under it. I knew she was . . . I knew she was gone, but I couldn't run over her body." The sinewy shoulders sagged as if he were carrying a burden he could never put down. "By the time I moved her, DeLuca was long gone with you. Took me hours to find him, holed up in Choteau in a motel that doesn't exist anymore. They tore it down after that night."

"I was still screaming," Andy said. "I never stopped screaming."

"And I thank God for that every day. When the guy who managed the motel told me DeLuca was there, I was going to get the police and come back. But when I heard you screaming, all the way out to the office . . . and I heard DeLuca telling you to shut your mouth . . ."

Andy let go of my hand and pressed both of his to the sides of his head.

"We can stop right here, son," Joseph said.

"No, Uncle Joe," Andy said. "We got this far. I have to know."

Do you, Andy? I wanted to say. Do you need to be ripped in half? *Let him get free, Kirsten. Ya gotta let him get free.*

"I couldn't handle that," Joseph said. He took in a breath and set his face. "I kicked in the door . . . saw that DeLuca was across the room from you . . . and shot him in the chest. Three times."

One for every time Andy jerked beside me.

"Then I grabbed you and I brought you back. Your grandfather had just come home and found his daughter. I told him to call the police and have them take me away—but not to let them touch you. You were home and that was where you needed to stay."

"And that, ladies and gentlemen, is why Joseph Maxwell went to prison. Because you don't gun down a rich man and get away with it."

My father was on the other side of the gate again. This time I didn't pause to catch his pose. I hurled myself past Frankie and past Joseph and over the gate, into his face.

"Let's go," I said.

"Did I not say that thirty minutes ago?"

I led him straight to the rented Lincoln parked on the grass and yanked the driver's side door open.

"Please go," I said.

"Let's do it. Get in."

"I'm not going anywhere with you." I hit the top of the door with the heel of my hand. "How *dare* you come here and . . . *smirk* at this family's tragedy?"

"Because I don't want it to become *your* tragedy."

"You don't give a rip about *me*. If you did you'd know that this place, this family is the best thing that has ever happened to me."

My father put his hands on top of the door too. I started to move mine but he planted his on top of them, and they baked right into my skin. The smugness was draining from his eyes, leaving behind glints of anger.

"How would you know what the best thing is for you, Kirsten? You're a mess. I looked into this cutter thing, and as I understand it you've got something seriously mental going on."

I wrenched my hands away. "I am *not* a cutter. I am a person who used to hurt myself so the inside pain would make some kind of sense. The pain *you* inflicted on me. You and Mother and—"

"There you go. It's just like you to blame everybody else for your so-called pain."

"Then the nut doesn't fall far from the tree," I said. "Only the difference between you and me is that I'm trying to do something about *my* self-destruction. And now you've probably even ruined that for me. I don't know how I'm going to face those people after what you just did."

For a wretched moment I thought he was going to hit me. I watched his nostrils flare as he stared, options flipping through his eyes. Which one to choose that would put Kirsten firmly back under his thumb.

He chose shrugging. "So don't face them. Leave. Right now."

"Like *you* always do when the going gets tough?" I shook my head. "I'm done with that, Dad."

And then he did hit me, with the last words he said before he climbed into the Lincoln: "Then I'm done with *you*."

I stood there until I could no longer see the car or the dust that rose and fell behind it without a trace of remorse. It wasn't only that I wanted to make sure he was really gone. I just didn't know what to do now. I couldn't go to the barn to the family my father had just brought to its knees. Andy had to know about his parents eventually, but it shouldn't have come out the way it did. I wanted to put my arms around him and comfort him, support him the way I'd promised I would. But I was going to have to wait until he came to me. If he came.

I climbed the hill to the Cloister, intending to wait for Andy on the porch. But Emma met me at the door and pulled me inside by the wrist. She was obviously frantic.

"What's going on, Petersen?"

"Everything," I said.

And then it was my turn to cry in *her* arms again. Without asking a single question she cried with me. They were tears of solidarity.

———

But the solid feeling was short-lived.

For the next hour, no one came to the Cloister, including Andy. Emma made coffee early and we sat on the front porch not drinking it, until Andy's Jeep flew down the driveway. We watched until the speck of him turned onto the public road and disappeared over the rise.

"You don't have to tell me what's going on," Emma said. "But—"

"I can't," I said. I repeated Frankie's words: "It's not my story to tell." I couldn't help thinking that my part in that story was over, now that Andy had driven away without a word to me.

We were still waiting when Joseph and Frankie brought the sheep in, Joseph on horseback, Frankie walking with her head bowed.

"Should we go help with evening chores?" I said.

Emma shook her head. "When we turned back on the horses—when we saw that Lincoln driving up here—Frankie and Joseph told me to come here and stay. But if you want me to, I'll at least go check on the supper situation."

"I'm not hungry."

"This thing," Emma said. "It's bad, isn't it?"

"Yeah," I said. "It is."

Emma reached over and rested her hand on the arm of my rocker and we waited some more. Finally Frankie came around the side of the house with the dogs and put one foot on the bottom step. Undie and Norwich sat on either side of her, tails unnaturally still, as if they knew now too.

"Can you ladies make do with sandwiches or something here tonight?" she said. "Joseph needs me."

Emma was immediately on full alert. "What's wrong with Joseph?"

Frankie's eyes went to me.

"I haven't told her," I said. "I am so sorry, Frankie. I had no idea my—"

Frankie put her finger to her lips. "First things first." She turned to Emma. "I'm going to let Joseph tell you when he's ready. But don't worry. He's going to be okay. You can pray for peace for him, all right?"

After one last, full look at me, Frankie hurried off with the dogs at her heels. It was a look that said, *Not a word, please.*

I had no intention of telling Emma anything. But why couldn't

Frankie tell me where Andy went? Why couldn't she reassure me that *he* was going to be okay?

"Will you be all right alone, Petersen?"

I looked back at Emma, who already had the screen door open.

"Yeah."

"No offense," she said, "but I have to go to my room, because if I stay out here with you I'll badger you until you tell me what's going on with Joseph."

"I'm sorry—"

"It's okay. I get it. Just let me know if—you know, whatever."

I nodded and waited for the door to close.

"Just tell me this one thing."

"Emma, come on, please?"

"This has something to do with your father, doesn't it?"

"No," I said. "That's the point: it doesn't. He just *made* it about him."

"So what does that have to do with—" Emma cut herself off and closed the door behind her.

After her bedroom door slammed I went inside and got my jacket and my cell phone. When I returned to the porch, the vacant chair rocked in the wind. Like I needed that reminder that I was completely alone. And yet I wasn't. I didn't need Emma out there badgering me as the hours passed, because I did a fine job of that myself.

I should have remembered my father saying he wasn't done when he left the last time.

Today I should have pushed him out before he had a chance to tell Andy anything.

I should have told Frankie that Andy was having disturbing memories even though he asked me not to.

I was ten shoulds into it when I remembered Frankie saying

they didn't do *should* there at the ranch. *"We work with what we hear from God."*

"*If* I heard from You," I said to the night, "I promise You I'd work with it."

———

I had probably just nodded off when my cell buzzed in my jacket pocket. I jolted forward and juggled the phone like a bar of soap trying to bring the screen to life. There was a text from Andy. I'd waited all night for it, and now I read it with fear lapping at my throat.

Driving 'til something makes sense, it said. *No matter how long it takes.*

I closed my eyes, but not fast enough to block out his final sentence: *You might not want to wait for me.*

———

When the sun found me, I was still sitting in the rocking chair trying to think of nothing and thinking, instead, of everything. Frankie found me there when she came by to fetch me for chores.

"Kirsten?" she said. "Have you been here all night?"

I nodded.

She sank into the chair that had mocked me for hours. "We're worried about Andy, and I won't lie to you, there is reason to be. He has never done this before—never taken off and not let me know where he is, what he's doing . . ."

So they didn't get the same text you did.

No.

So Andy only wanted you *to know.*

Yes.

But I couldn't leave it that way. I couldn't keep another one of Andy's secrets from Frankie, or I would be covered in should-haves for the rest of my life.

"You need to see this," I said, and handed her my phone.

Frankie glanced over the text and gave the cell back to me. For a moment she closed her eyes, and then she stood up. Undie and Norwich circled nervously.

"I'm going to ask you and Emma to start on the chores," she said. "I'll meet you after I talk to Joseph."

"Okay," I said.

She left the porch at a brisk walk and headed toward the bunkhouse. I was almost inside the Cloister when she called back to me.

"Thank you," she said. "You did the right thing."

That didn't help much—because I knew Andy wouldn't say it was the right thing. If I ever heard from him again.

Emma and I didn't talk much while we fed chickens and lambs and got some milk out of Hildegarde, who was even more cantankerous than ever, as if she, too, knew the beautiful balance of Bellwether had been turned on its head. When I told Emma about Andy's text, she gave me a sympathetic nod, but there were no tears of solidarity.

And definitely not when we were setting the pail next to the pump and Joseph roared past us in his truck. Emma left the milk sloshing and ran after him, calling out his name like an abandoned child.

Joseph's brake lights flashed and he lowered his window so Emma could lean in. Between the wind and the impatient idle of the truck's engine I couldn't hear what they were saying, and yet I wasn't surprised at what Emma reported when she stumbled, arms hugged around her, back to the pump where Frankie had now joined me.

"He's going to go find Andy and bring him back," she said. "And he won't let me go with him." Her dejection was palpable.

"He's right," Frankie said. "This is between Andy and Joseph."

"*What* is?" Emma said. "What *this* are we talking about?"

Frankie put a hand on her shoulder. "Something that happened a long time ago and needs to be resolved."

Emma wrenched herself away, her eyes on me. "No. I think it's about something that happened just yesterday."

I looked at Frankie, begging her with my eyes, but she deflated like a sad, forgotten party balloon. "There is nothing more I can tell you right now, Emma," she said. "I'm going to the garden to pray. If you'd like to come—"

Emma was already gone, but not before I saw the pain that shot through her eyes. She might be angry with me, but the fear of losing Joseph trumped that. Trumped everything.

When I turned back to Frankie she was gone too—walking her steady walk toward the main house. I wasn't sure if the invitation to come and pray with her was meant for me. If it was, it seemed like a reluctant one.

My hand reached automatically down to my side and groped for a furry head until I remembered that Bathsheba wasn't there either.

Or anyone.

I looked down at the half-filled pail, forgotten next to the pump. Nothing was the same today, my forty-ninth day. Nothing but the loneliness and the guilt I'd brought with me, the feeling that once again I had done something horribly wrong. And I was never going to be able to make it right.

Share this chapter with your friends!

I am not a cutter. I am a person who hurt myself so the inside pain would make some kind of sense. #TheMercifulScar

Part
FIVE

*And after the fire a sound of sheer silence . . . Then there came
a voice to him that said, "What are you doing here, Elijah?"*

1 Kings 19:12–13

Chapter
NINETEEN

Three days passed with no word to anyone from Andy, and even Frankie couldn't seem to find a peace about that. In the times when we normally talked—walking back from the pasture, coaxing milk from Hildegarde—she fell into deep quiet, often in the middle of a sentence.

She did keep us to the work rhythm, she and I tending to the sheep, Emma doing what she could for the cattle. She hired the Cunninghams' two sons to bring more alfalfa, and we three women bucked the hay, largely in sweating silence.

Or it might as well have been silence.

Granted, Frankie assured Emma in front of me that my father was not the reason this was all happening. And Frankie told me privately after a vacant-feeling communion Sunday evening that the whole situation was bound to come to a head sooner or later and I had no reason to blame myself for the way it had.

But you still do, the Nudnik whispered that night as I wrestled with the quilts.

Of course I did, because what Frankie didn't *have* to say wagged at me like an accusing finger in the spaces between the lines. If I hadn't gotten involved with Andy in the first place, I wouldn't have been with him when my father came back with his heinous report. Andy wouldn't have heard it from him; he could have remembered just as Frankie had told Joseph he should: as it needed to come to him. Now Andy was out there running after reasons he might not find before he tore completely in half, just as he'd been so afraid he would. The burden of that was almost intolerable.

It might actually *have* been, if not for Petey. She didn't need individual care from me anymore, but I liked taking her from the bum pen in the afternoons and letting her romp in the grass outside the barn. She had indeed learned from her fellow bums how to be a sheep, and I loved watching her trot along and suddenly stop to munch a tuft of something and then raise her fleecy chin to call for assurance that all was still well.

"You're good," I'd say to her. "I'm watching you."

Guess that's what parents are supposed to do, huh?

I wasn't sure how I would know that. My mother was only now doing it with Lara . . .

As for my father, what had he ever assured me of? That I was hopeless unless he arrived in his armor to save the day? That I couldn't possibly know how to figure out my own life? When I did try, he went to cruel lengths to show me that he was right, and I was wrong.

Hate to say this but that pretty much brings you right back where you were when you came here.

And that was nowhere.

I could hardly see Petey now for the film of disappointment in my eyes. How could I have lived and learned and fallen in love on this ranch for fifty-two days and still be nowhere?

"How can that be, Petey?" I said. "There has to be a somewhere for me."

She let out a tiny bleat. And I knew the one place that could be.

———

Monday, when the deafening silence again dropped over the Bellwether after the morning work, I hiked all the way up to the shepherd's monument, hoping with every muscle-burning step that somewhere would be waiting for me.

But by the time I reached the monument I didn't need the Nudnik to ask me what I'd been thinking. There was nothing here but the absence of Bathsheba's shadow chasing—and the sight of the tiny ranch below, longing for Andy and Joseph—and the refusal of *bat kol* to ever, ever echo for me.

It all ached so hard I couldn't hold it in. I crumpled against the shepherds' stones and let their jagged edges abrade my back, but they gave me nothing. There *was* nothing here except the vast emptiness that went on and on and on above the ragged mountaintops until I cried out to it: "What am I doing here?"

It didn't answer, not even in a whistle of wind or the trip of a pebble. Not even in a thought I could cling to for warmth. It whispered only a still, small question . . .

What are *you doing here, Kirsten?*

I couldn't move.

"Nudnik?" I said.

She didn't have to answer. I knew the words hadn't come from her sideways tongue. Or from some memory of Frankie's wisdom, or even from my own yearning. It was in me, but not in me, and all I knew was that it wanted a reply.

I got to my feet and went to the ridge and stood at its edge. The stillness waited for me.

"I'm here because I want to be free," I said. Out loud. "I didn't know that when I came and now I do." I swallowed hard but it didn't hold back the words. "I'm just so afraid."

I forced my gaze to the frozen tumble of rocks beyond me, stopped on their own path and forever suspended in the fear of falling.

"I'm afraid if I let it all go, there will be nothing left of me."

Still the silence. Open and soft. Like a cushion inviting me to fall . . . to the place where Lara waited.

She was always waiting. Always waiting but never able to understand. I didn't understand either. Why did she have to pick *that* night to listen to me? Why couldn't she have done what she always did: the *opposite* of what I told her to do?

I inched my toes over the edge. All the other times that I had seen her about to flout yet another rule or dance on the precipice of adolescent danger, I had done everything to stop her but handcuff her to me. Everything except tell our parents that she was smoking and drinking and piercing and making out with the boy du jour behind the Sunday school building every chance she got.

But that night, the night of the back-to-school party . . . I wore the red flats and the black skinny jeans I'd saved for and bought by myself . . . that night when I'd tried to curl my corn-silk, mermaid-long locks so they'd bounce against my back when I walked. It hadn't exactly worked, but I still felt pretty. I wanted to be pretty that night, for Ralph.

I closed my eyes. Why was I doing this? What if I couldn't?

Then what are you doing here, Kirsten?

Going back. I was going back to that night because there was nothing else left to do.

Lara and I arrived together and as usual she darted off someplace the minute we walked into the Hugh Crugh room. Which was fine because again, as usual, she outshone me like Venus does your average run-of-the-mill star. And besides, I'd told myself I wasn't going to spend the whole time trying to keep track of her. Ralph had just gotten his driver's license and I had my heart set on a ride home. And maybe a sweet kiss on the cheek.

I ran a hand across my chest where I could still almost feel the tender throb of that teenage innocence. I had wanted so little . . . while Lara wanted it all. And grabbed it, no matter who it belonged to.

My hand balled into a fist. I had to force myself to release it.

Oddly Lara didn't take center stage that night and I wouldn't have noticed if she had. I was looking for Ralph but going all out to make sure it didn't *look* like I was looking for Ralph. I could see my fifteen-year-old self so clearly. I pretended to be engrossed in the details of my friends' mall escapades, though my peripheral vision was on high alert for a glimpse of him. I threw my head back in bell-like laughter, hoping my drooping-but-still-alluring curls would cascade down my back and enchant him.

A similar laugh bubbled up my throat now as I saw myself dipping my first pink-polished toenail into the pool of flirtation. I had been so naïve and so shyly eager. And so trusting.

The laugh died.

Forty-five minutes into the party I still hadn't seen Ralph, and both my hair and my hope were wilting. I made a few not-so-subtle inquiries as to his whereabouts. "It feels like somebody's missing," I said to everyone there, one by one. "Is it Maggie? No, she's here. What's-his-name . . . Ralph, maybe?"

I tried some variation of that on one person too many: the freshman with the George Clooney wannabe haircut who, with his own brand of cluelessness, said, "Ralph's out in the parking lot with your sister."

The scene, until now so clean and sweet and skinny-jeaned in my memory, rose up before me like a specter. I backed away from it until I skidded on a spray of pebbles and fell, bum first, among them. Their tiny points pressed into my hands, and the images pressed into me.

Of the party dizzying around me as I shoved and pushed and elbowed my way out.

Of my brand-new red flats sliding on the hallway floor, careening me into the wall against the banner that said, "Bear one another's burdens."

Of jamming my hands against the bar to open the door to the parking lot—and stopping and squeezing my eyes closed and telling myself that Ralph had followed Lara out to bring her back in—because he was "too Christian."

And the image of stepping out to help him. So we could save my sister together.

I punched my fists against my eyes now to push it all back, but it was too late. It was all there: the silhouettes of their two heads in the Subaru Ralph's father had let him use for the first time . . . a new voice in my head saying, *Get your little wilted self back inside. You do not want to see this* . . . another voice, Lara's voice, teasing, "Go ahead, Ralph. You know you want to." And the long kiss. The one I'd hoped would be for me.

Hands behind me now, I crabbed back until I hit the shepherds' stones again. Pain clutched at my throat like strangling hands. This— this pain—was why I couldn't look. I couldn't stand this pain.

"I can't!" I screamed to no one there. "I can't!"

And then I did. I looked at myself, standing beside the Subaru with my dying mermaid hair sticking to my face, pounding on the window until Lara lowered it. Even now I could smell the alcohol oozing from her breath and from the seat where it had spilled out of the can Ralph held in his hand.

I never looked at Ralph's face. Not then, not now. I could only stare at my sister with her kiss-tousled blondeness and her road-mapped blue eyes and her unsurprised mouth that said, "Hey, Sis. I was just breakin' him in for ya. You can have him next."

"I don't want him," I heard myself say in a voice that belonged to someone whose innocence had just been slapped away.

"Oh," Lara said.

She giggled over something that only seemed to be funny to her and Ralph, who joined in as if on cue. It wasn't funny to me. Hand to my throat—just as it was now—I stepped back from the car. Lara hung the top half of her body out the window.

"If you don't want him, I'll take him," she said.

She tried to twist her head around toward Ralph and banged it on the mirror. More giggles, high-pitched and ugly.

"Take him," I said. "Take him far away so I don't have to look at either one of you."

One more giggle, one that had already been halfway out, faded between us, into the mist of an almost-rain. She tried to focus her eyes on me.

"That's a good idea," she said. "Ralphie, we should go far away. You drive and we'll go far away."

The engine started with no hesitation. Lara was still watching me, brows pinched together as if that would help her understand.

"We're gonna go, Kirsten," she said. "Me and Ralph, we're gonna go."

"So *go*!" I said. Because in that moment I hated her little-sister blue eyes and the stud in her nose and the load I'd been carrying for her for two lost years.

"You won't tell?" she said.

It had never been a question before, and I answered it. I answered it in a venom-filled voice I could still hear in my head.

"I won't tell," I said. "Because I don't *care* what happens to you. Go!" She did.

"She never, ever listened to me before! Why did she listen to me then?"

I let my scream fall dead on the stones around me and I folded my arms across my knees and I let my head fall onto them. And I cried.

I cried and I cried and I cried until there was nothing left but rasping breaths and my own voice calling out, "How can I live with this, God?"

The still, small question didn't wait this time. *Why are you here, Kirsten?*

My answer didn't wait either. "I'm here because I need You!"

It was the only answer I had. Perhaps the only one I had ever had.

Silence settled again, this time fleece-like over the place I'd just emptied. I wrapped myself in its wooly silence and went back to the ranch to wait.

———

If Emma was at the Cloister, she was shut up in her room. But I didn't knock. I was sure my face was a blotchy, swollen mess for one thing. And I was tired in a way I'd never been, tired on the inside somehow, and I wanted to sleep. Take a shower and then sleep. I didn't even bother to vacuum the moths out of the bathtub; we were practically on a first-name basis at that point anyway.

"Just clear me a space," I said to them. "I'm comin' in."

I turned on the faucet for the wait-five-minutes-for-hot-water ritual and slipped out of the jeans that were so stiff with ranch detritus I could have stood them in the corner.

Is it just me or are you in a weirdly good mood all of a sudden?

Good mood? I wasn't sure I even knew what a good mood was

anymore. But I did feel . . . lighter maybe? Had I gotten free? Was that it?

You'd feel a whole lot *lighter if you'd shave those legs.*

That was probably true. My blonde leg hair was pretty much invisible most of the time, but when I propped my foot up on the side of the tub, I saw that my shins currently resembled a bathroom rug.

That isn't the half of it. Check out those thighs.

I stepped back on my right foot and examined my left thigh.

"Come on, it's not that hairy," I said to the moths.

I could still see the fading remnants of my early cuts, although as I ran my fingers across them I could no longer feel them. Their ridges had become flush with my skin. Even that one—

I stopped, hand on my inner thigh. I was looking at the place I promised I would never look at again after the night I cut into it. The first time ever, in flesh I promised myself I wouldn't see again.

Until now, when I couldn't look away from the word I had carved there the night I learned about Lara.

I was screaming before I hit the bathroom floor, screaming what I had held in my throat since I watched those letters bleed.

"It's my fault she can't walk! It's my fault she can't *think*! It's my fault she'll never be Lara again! It's my *fault*!"

I didn't know how long I screamed that way before someone had her arms around me.

"Why is it your fault, Kirsten?" she said. "Tell me, my friend."

I told Frankie everything, there on the cold bathroom floor clutching my jeans and her sleeve and her over-and-over assurance that it was time to set myself free. It poured from me, until I reached the place where the Subaru jerked across the church parking lot in fits and starts and slid out onto the wet road.

"I still had a chance to run after them and stop them," I said to Frankie. "But I didn't."

"Could you have stopped them, really?" Frankie said. "Lara had never listened to you. She still wasn't listening to you when you told her to go. She was listening to a self who was screaming for attention from your parents, not you." Frankie bit her lip. "I'm sorry, Kirsten—this is your story. Go on."

"There's nothing more to tell," I said.

Frankie waited.

"Okay," I said. "Yes. I went back inside and tried to pretend that nothing had happened. I didn't know the word *surreal* then but I see now that's how it was. I felt like I'd turned into somebody else and I had all these weird feelings . . . like I wanted to go in the bathroom and cut my hair off. And I kept having thoughts like *At least she's not here to cramp your style. Too bad she took your guy with her, though. Bummer.* It was all just strange."

Frankie still waited. She didn't come to my rescue, and neither did the Nudnik.

"Then Hugh found me sitting in a corner tearing up a napkin and he took me to his office and told me there'd been an accident. Lara was in critical condition."

"And Ralph?"

"He only had minor injuries. He had a seat belt on. Lara didn't." I shuffled my feet back and forth on the floor. "Of *course* she didn't. She never wore it unless I told her to. And I didn't tell her to. So . . . when he lost control and hit a light pole, she was thrown from the car." My voice choked to a whisper. "And landed on her head. That's it. That's all."

"Is it?" Frankie said. "Because I'm still seeing this."

She touched the hand I had wrapped around my throat. "Something is still choking the life out of you, my friend, and if you don't let it go, it will."

"I *can't.*"

"I know," she said. "You can't, but God can. So let's pray it out, you and me, okay?"

I sagged against her and nodded and she prayed . . . asking God to open my throat and ease the pain out into His hands so I didn't have to fight it anymore. Frankie prayed and I breathed and she prayed and I felt the breaking loose of what was lodged in the lining of myself. It came out in broken pieces.

"We thought she was going to die . . . there was so much brain damage . . . my father kept saying, 'Let her go' . . . but they saved her . . . they saved her and I was so relieved . . . they said I could see her and I was ready to tell her I was so sorry I didn't stop her . . ."

Frankie prayed some more and another piece tore free.

"But she wasn't Lara anymore. She looked at me but she wasn't in her eyes. She moved her mouth but all that came out was a moan . . . and drool she couldn't wipe because her hands wouldn't do what she wanted them to do. I told her anyway, but she didn't know. She still doesn't know, because she can't know anything."

Frankie stopped praying out loud and held me, and I could feel the prayers through her skin. That was the only reason I could let the last piece go.

"I never told my parents I even saw her in the parking lot with Ralph, and he never told them either. I never saw him again."

"He left the church?" Frankie said.

"No, we did. My father threatened to sue Ralph's parents and Hugh and the entire United Methodist Church. We wouldn't have been welcome back there anyway." I tilted my head back and let my jaw drop open, just so I *couldn't* hold it back anymore. "My parents fought every minute Lara was still in the hospital. My father said my mother should have known Lara was running wild and my mother said how was she supposed to know when Lara seemed the same as always to her? And how was she supposed to focus on her daughter when her husband was running wild himself? She blamed him—he blamed her—and I couldn't tell them I was the one to blame."

"Do you blame yourself for their divorce?"

I sighed from someplace. "Not entirely. The worst fights were over what to do about Lara when she left the hospital. My father wanted her put in a facility where she could get professional care. He never said it but it was there: he thought they should have let her die so she didn't have to live the rest of her life like a mentally handicapped three-month-old." I shook my head. "My mother wouldn't have it. She insisted she was going to bring Lara home and take care of her, herself, with no help from anyone. My father even went to court over it, but the judge said since Lara was a minor, her parents were still responsible for her and unless she was being abused he couldn't intervene. But they never *were* responsible for her."

"So you tried to be."

"And I failed."

Frankie nibbled at her lip and nodded for me to keep talking. By then I didn't have the energy to put on the brakes anymore.

"My mother watched the nurses and figured out how to take care of Lara. Everything but actual rehab. In the meantime, my father went out and designed another high-rise. The day they brought her home in a wheelchair with her head fastened into this metal thing because she couldn't hold it up, my father just walked out the door and got another lawyer."

"A divorce lawyer."

"Yeah. When Mother was served with the papers, she didn't even shed a tear. She never cried over Lara either. She just made arrangements with my grandparents in Missouri for them to move into a senior retirement place so she and I and Lara could live in their house, the one my mother grew up in. The state paid her to take care of Lara and my father paid child support but none of us saw him for eighteen months—until he came to tell me he was going to take care of college for me. He didn't see Lara then. I knew he couldn't even look at her." The energy I thought was gone surged again. "But I had to look at her every day. I had certain things I was supposed to do for her—feed her dinner and read to her at night and sometimes I just wanted to scream, 'Why am I doing this? She doesn't even know what I'm saying!'"

I stopped because I was screaming again.

"I'm sorry," I said to Frankie.

"No need to be. Go on, Kirsten. There's more."

I *was* almost to the end. But the only way I could get there was to cry it out.

"I left her, Frankie," I said between heaving breaths. "I left her so I wouldn't have to look at her every day and see the way she was when I told her I didn't care what she did. I just went off to college so I could . . ." I searched Frankie's face.

"So you could have the life your sister could never have."

"Only, you know something?"

She shook her head.

"I haven't had a life since."

"Because you didn't really leave Lara," Frankie said. "You've carried her with you in all those scars."

She was looking at my left thigh, where my hand rubbed the word I'd kept hidden from everyone. Even myself.

"What does it all come down to, my friend?" she said.

"It comes down to this," I said.

My hand shook as I pulled it back and showed her the thin crooked letters of the word *SHAME*.

Frankie closed her eyes, but not before I saw my pain in them.

"I carved it there after I saw Lara that first time," I said.

I felt my head being coaxed onto Frankie's shoulder. "I told you *bat kol* can come in strange and unexpected ways. It was there all along, the root of your suffering in your own writing. Now it can heal."

"How can it heal when it was my fault and it will always be my fault?"

Frankie's arm tightened around me. "You may have had some small part in setting the events of that night in motion, Kirsten. There are things you could have done differently so perhaps the accident wouldn't have happened. More than likely it still would have. But whatever your share of the blame . . . why do you think we celebrate our communion and pray in the garden and go on with the work we've been given to do? Because we're all forgiven. There is no shame, Kirsten. There is only God's love."

I didn't say anything for a while. My body was sinking into a cushion where breathing was the only business required of a throat. I did finally murmur, "My scar is *bat kol*?"

"Any way God can, God will," Frankie said.

"Then please do," I whispered.

The arms of sleep joined Frankie's and wrapped themselves around me too. I made my final nestle into its cushion.

Share this chapter with your friends!

There is no shame. There is only God's love. #TheMercifulScar

Chapter
TWENTY

I was still swathed in my quilts the next morning, trying to figure out how I'd gotten from the bathroom floor to the bed, when I heard Emma squeal like a little girl and pound across the front room to the door. By the time I got up, pulled on a pair of sweats, and made it to the porch, Emma was running barefoot down the hill toward the bunkhouse. Joseph stood at the bottom, his arms out waiting for her.

I laughed out loud when she jumped into them and buried her bed-head in his shoulder. Joseph held her and her bare feet dangled above the ground. It was the way a daddy should greet a daughter.

But the next thought snuffed out my laughter. What about Andy? Did Joseph bring him back? Or news of him?

Or nothing?

I turned to the other side of the porch and leaned out to view the driveway, but no Jeep had tucked itself between the trucks and tractors. My heart began a slow decline that continued when Frankie didn't come by for me at six, and Joseph and Emma were still talking outside the bunkhouse, she in Joseph's jacket, listening intently to whatever he was telling her. If it was the story of Andy's parents' deaths, I was glad she was hearing it in a better way than Andy had. At least there was that. I hurried on to the barn, murmuring a *thank You* and a *please bring him back* and a *please show me what to do next.*

Frankie wasn't there, either, so I fed the chickens and both sets of bums, all the while listening to Hildegarde complain that she had full udders and, by golly, somebody had better come relieve her or all Hades was going to break loose. When I was finished with everything else and Frankie still hadn't appeared, I found a clean bucket and straightened my shoulders and went into the corral.

Uh, what do you think you're doing?

Merton and Sienna shied to the other side, ears down as if they had the same question.

"I'm going to milk this cow," I said. "I'm all you've got, Hildegarde, so let's get it done together."

Her huge brown eyes roamed as if she were actually looking for other options. When she apparently saw none, she blew the air out of her enormous nostrils and let me lead her into the chute, where I had a bale of the freshest hay ready for her to nosh on.

"I would really like to do this without including Little Augie," I said as I massaged her udders with balm. "There's just no reason why we need a man for everything. Come on. Cowgirl up."

The milk was squirting out, white with the promise of cream, when Frankie joined me and lowered herself onto the hay bale I always used for a seat. It was obvious her attempt at a smile was brave at best and that her prayers that morning had come with a side of tears.

"You have no idea how much I appreciate this," she said.

I did my imitation of her and nodded.

"I thought you'd want to know that Joseph found Andy in Reno."

I squeezed too hard and got a correctional groan from Hildegarde.

"He's fine. Physically. He wouldn't come back with Joseph, though. He says he has something he needs to do."

I heard a tremor in her voice that made me afraid to ask what that was.

So . . . yesterday was all for nothing then? You're still going to hide from the things you don't want to know?

"May I ask what it is he needs to do?" I said.

"You have every right to," Frankie said. "And I would tell you if I knew. But maybe Andy told you himself."

I stopped milking and looked up at her. "I swear to you I haven't talked to him. I would have told you."

"No, no . . ." Frankie sank her hand into the pocket of her jacket and pulled out an envelope. "I meant in here. Andy asked Joseph to give it to you." She stood up. "It looks like Hildegarde's given all she's going to give this morning if you want to take some time alone to read it."

I folded the envelope in half and slipped it into my own pocket.

"Kirsten."

I looked up again. Frankie's eyes were full.

"You are under no obligation to tell me what it says. But if you need me after you read it, you know where to find me."

"Okay," I said.

"I mean it."

Frankie closed her eyes, and I knew it was my turn to wait. When she opened them, she said, "This stirring up of my own past these last few days has reminded me how easy it is for anyone to be brought low by the memories that haunt them. I let it pull me down—and away from you and Emma, and I'm sorry."

"It's—"

Frankie put her finger to my lips. "It's not okay. I've left you two to struggle through this on your own when everything we stand for here is strength in God and community. I'm still here for you, my friend. No matter what is in that letter."

———

I didn't read it right away. I left it in my pocket while we herded the sheep, and when I returned to the Cloister I hoped Emma would be there so I would have a reason to put it off even longer. But the house was empty and I was left alone with a letter I didn't want to read because I knew it would say what I always heard. *I'm done with you.*

Again . . . what was yesterday for, then?

To show me that getting free wasn't the end of it. That now I faced a lifetime of looking the truth in the face before it had time to burrow under my skin.

The sky was grumbling and cloaking itself in gray clouds, which could mean a downpour or a-few-spits-and-call-it-good, but to be on the safe side I decided against the porch and curled up in one of the recliners. I could hear her saying, *For Pete's sake, Petersen, read it already.*

Andy's handwriting was strong, not surprisingly, and it raced urgently across the paper.

Dear Kirsten,

Kirsten. Not the Bo I longed to hear. I placed my hand on the bottom of the page so I couldn't scroll down to the inevitable end.

I don't think it's fair to leave you hanging, so I'm writing this so you'll have the big picture. That's what we both tried to see all summer, isn't it? The big picture of our lives?

330

I found myself nodding.

Let me start with what Joseph told me—about what happened after he turned himself in for killing Gabe DeLuca. (I still can't think of him as my father.) His lawyer told him he would never do time for the shooting. He said Joseph knew I was in danger and no jury would convict him for saving me from a guy who was obviously disturbed. (Yeah, I really, really can't think of the man as my father.) The lawyer told Joseph he didn't even see the DA bringing charges.

But he wasn't factoring in the power of the DeLuca family and the entourage of lawyers who descended on Conrad to make sure Joseph went down for what he did to one of their own. They wanted Murder One, which would have meant life in prison, but the DA offered them a deal. Joseph would do fifteen years for manslaughter and the DeLucas would agree to give sole custody of me to Frankie and my grandfather. They took it, which shows me Gabe didn't try to take me because I was his son. He just wanted revenge. (Have I mentioned that I cannot and never will be able to think of him as my father?)

I stopped reading so I could wipe my palms on my jeans. Hope fluttered somewhere just above my shoulders. If Andy could hold on to his sense of humor as he told this story that had the potential to rip him into confetti, maybe he was still all right. I turned back to the paper, which was now limp with my sweat.

Joseph refused all visitors while he served his term, but Frankie and my grandfather kept tabs. He was the model prisoner and probably would have been released years earlier than he was but he would never petition for parole. He didn't tell Frankie this until after he served out his sentence, but he was afraid the DeLucas would take him down the minute he was released.

I *knew* the word *surreal* now and this more than qualified. How was this the life of people I loved?

The day Joseph got out of prison, Frankie was there to pick him up but he almost didn't go with her. That's when he told her about his fear. He didn't want to bring trouble to her. The only way she was able to convince him to come back to the ranch was by telling him how bad things were here. You know about that. He said Frankie prayed, right there in her beat-up truck in the parking lot of the Montana State Prison, and he knew he wasn't going back to the ranch just to help her and save the Bellwether. He knew it was the only chance he had of ever being healed.

I had to stop and wipe my nose before I read on.

I want you to know that I apologized to him today for shutting him out instead of manning up four years ago. He gets it. Of course. He's Joseph. What he didn't get was why I can't come back to the ranch yet. Even though I could hear you saying I should, I couldn't tell him why. I'm only telling you because I got so used to sharing everything with you. It doesn't feel like it's happening unless I tell you. Anyway here it is: I'm going to San Francisco to find the DeLucas and set them straight on the kind of man Joseph Maxwell is. I have to do this.

Oh, Andy. No.

I don't know how long it's going to take, so I don't know if you'll still be there when I get back. And I don't even know who I'll be by then because I don't think I've even scratched the surface of what I have to face. I just know I have to face it on my own. I know you'll get that.

"No," I said. "*You* don't get it, Andy. You *can't* do this alone."

Thank you for the way you were always there for me. I'm trusting you to keep this between us.

I was shaking my head before I even got to the signature, a simple *Andy.*

I can't do that, Andy. Because it doesn't belong between us.

My phone was in the bedroom and I started across the front room to get it. I owed it to him to text him and tell him what I was going to do and at least give him a chance to tell Joseph and Frankie himself. But if he didn't, I had to, or he was going to get himself killed.

Finally *you figured out what yesterday was all about.*

I didn't make it as far as the bedroom before someone knocked with a firm hand. For a crazy moment I hoped it was Andy, but it was Joseph I opened the door to.

"I'm sorry," I said. "Emma's not here."

"I know," he said. "I came to talk to you. Got a minute?"

I stepped out onto the porch. "Pick a rocker," I said.

"I'm not staying that long. You got the letter?"

"Right here."

He only glanced at it, still unfolded in my hand, but I saw the longing in his eyes.

"I just wanted to say I'm sorry I couldn't get him to come home with me," Joseph said. "I know you mean a lot to each other. If he changes his mind, it'll be because of you—"

"He's going to San Francisco, Joseph. He's going to look for the DeLucas and tell them they were wrong about you."

Joseph lowered his head to look straight into my eyes.

"It's in the letter. If you want to read it—"

"Dear *Lord* in heaven," he said.

"Yeah," I said.

———

Joseph left early the next morning to catch a flight to San Francisco. Emma, Frankie, and I stood on the porch of the Cloister and watched him go. But Frankie allowed no silence this time. She took my hand and Emma's and said, "We will do this together."

Every moment of that day seemed deep as we cared for the animals and ate our meals around Frankie's table and prayed together in the garden. When Frankie walked us back to the Cloister that night, we shared Emma's coffee on the porch with her—and held hands while Frankie took Joseph's call.

"He knows where Andy's staying in San Francisco," she told us. "That's good news, my friends."

No. Good news would be: And he has sedated him and is carrying him home on the next plane.

Frankie said good night and made her way back up the path with Undie and Norwich. I felt Emma looking at me. Although we'd been together all day, we still hadn't had a real conversation since Joseph left the first time to look for Andy. I could let go of blaming myself, but that didn't mean everybody else was going to give up blaming me.

"With all this going down with Andy, do I need to keep you from cutting, Petersen?"

It was a minute before I could answer, only because I needed that long to get my jaw back into place.

"No," I said. "I haven't even thought about it. Now, taking one of the trucks and going after him myself, *that* I've thought about."

Emma shook her head. "You wouldn't get out of here without me."

Just when you got your jaw hinged again . . .

"That's not just because you saved my life. It's more what Frankie said: we do this together."

"So . . . you forgive me?"

"No."

"No?"

Emma gave a vintage grunt. "No. I just finally figured out there was nothing to forgive you *for*. Question is: did you give up blaming yourself yet for what your old man did?"

"I'm workin' on it."

She stared uneasily into her coffee cup.

"Spit it out, Velasquez."

"I wasn't trying to get into your business the other day when I went and got Frankie, but the way you were screaming in the bathroom . . . I knew you wouldn't let me go through something like that alone. I mean . . . you *didn't*."

"I *couldn't* have done it alone," I said. "So thank you."

"Yeah, well, you can also thank me for helping Frankie carry your sorry self to the bed and covering you up with ten tons of quilts. How do you sleep under all that stuff?"

I laughed. And then I laughed again. On the third gale, Emma joined me. "Although," she said, "I have no idea what we're laughing about."

———

Frankie didn't hear from Joseph again until the next afternoon. Emma and I were cleaning out the water trough in Bellwether Middle School when she came down with the news, phone in hand, face pure white. Emma shut the pump down and went straight to her.

"What happened?" she said.

"Nothing yet," Frankie said. "Andy is right now sitting in a restaurant on Fisherman's Wharf with several of the DeLucas. Joseph's watching from the other side of the street. He can catch glimpses of them through the window when there isn't someone blocking his view."

"This can't be real," I said.

"No, I'm afraid it's all *too* real." Frankie looked at each of us in turn. "I need your help, ladies. Because I am very, very frightened."

Emma's chin lifted. "You got it. How can we help?"

"We do what she does for us," I said.

———

Emma, of course, made coffee with Hilda cream and I snuggled Frankie into one of the wide chairs in her living room under the perpetually waiting Mary and lit as many candles as I could find. Coffee cups steadying our beyond-nervous hands, we prayed.

We prayed for so long Frankie said it was a vigil. When we stopped to have bread and cheese, the prayers still threaded their way through our conversation.

"God bless our Joseph," Frankie said. She took the wedge of Muenster I handed her, but she couldn't seem to get it to her mouth. "He's out there *again* trying to save Andy from the people my sister took him away from."

"If anybody can do it, Joseph can," Emma said.

Frankie closed her eyes. "Only if Andy wants to be saved. That's what I keep bumping into."

I bumped into it, too, but from a different place. A clear place. Was that why I didn't save Lara's life that night? Because she didn't *want* to be saved?

Just a point of clarification: she's not dead.

But she had no life—not there in that stuffy Missouri bungalow with a mother who kept her there out of guilt. *Was* there another life she could have?

Could I save it this time?

The phone jangled me back to the circle. By the time my mind caught up, Frankie was holding it to her ear. And she was smiling.

"Okay—no questions. We'll talk when you get here."

When she hung up Emma was almost in her lap.

"Well?"

"They're driving the Jeep home. Both of them."

I smiled with Frankie and high-fived with Emma and I was, indeed, glad.

But I knew when Andy came back to the ranch I wasn't going to be there.

———

"He's going to be so angry with me," I told God the next day. I'd intended to wait until I was at the monument to start the talk, but before I'd even left the main road, the quiet question was already being asked.

What are you doing here, Kirsten?

"I'm trying to figure out just how to do this, and I need Your help. That's what I'm doing."

We were both quiet until I leaned against the stone wall I now called mine. I knew what questions to ask because I'd thought them through all night.

What was the point in being there when Andy came back? He'd asked me not to tell and I had. I'd done it for his safety and I would do it again if I had to. But I hadn't heard from him myself, not even a text. In the last text I'd gotten from him, the same night he left, he'd said,

You might not want to wait for me. And then there was the letter with all its past-tense phrases: *what we both tried to see all summer—I got used to sharing everything with you—thank you for the way you were always there for me.* Whatever we were going to have together had already happened.

The question I *didn't* know the answer to was whether I was running away. Now in the silence with the stones pressing their familiar pattern against my back, I heard the *bat kol* answer almost before I asked—in Frankie's words the night we left Bozeman. *"You're not running away. You're running for your life."*

Of course, things were different now. *I* was different. Now I had some power. Not power *over*, I assured God quickly. Power *to.*

I sat up and slanted away from the stones. That didn't seem right somehow. Because something else was different. Not about me. About this place.

I looked around and found the same craggy slopes across the canyon. The same chittering of some cute animal that thought I was there to invade its den. The same endless open space that used to make me want to hide under Crazy Trixie's quilts . . .

I felt the smile almost before I knew. That was it. There was no aloneness—even without Bathsheba and without the hope of Andy and without a plan beyond *Go home to Lara and help her have whatever life is possible.* So I could finally find mine too.

"So it's not just power *to,* is it?" I said. "It's power *with.* Power with You."

The still, small question seemed to sigh.

———

Before I had left for the monument, Frankie had told Emma and me that Joseph was going to call when he and Andy got to Great Falls, probably no sooner than four even though they'd driven all night. That still gave me plenty of time to tell Frankie about my plan and ask Emma to drive me into Conrad so I could catch a bus to Bozeman. If my father hadn't sold that part of my life on Craigslist by now, I could pick up a few things and make arrangements to fly into Kansas City the following day. The clarity of it kept my heart from breaking as I walked down the hill toward the Cloister and saw the chairs rocking with the breeze and heard the bums' bleating voices—

Petey.

My heart *would* break, but I had to say good-bye to her.

I broke into a run and arrived at the bum pen shaky and heaving for air. Several of the bums *baa*ed and scattered, but when I called to Petey, she called back and tried to climb over three who were between her and the gate.

"Over here, baby," I said.

I leaned over to reach for her, but my shaky legs gave way and I was—yet again—on my back in the pen amid a small stampede of lambs whose favorite place to step was on my face. Then suddenly they scattered again, and I was looking up into a dark, handsome grin.

"I've made a decision, Bo," Andy said. "Pulling you out of lamb poop is my new career."

Share this chapter with your friends!
I faced a lifetime of looking the truth
in the face before it had time to burrow
under my skin. #TheMercifulScar

Chapter
TWENTY-ONE

Then could you get on with it?" I said.

Because Andy continued to grin down at me over the side of the bum pen as if *that* were his new career plan.

I sat up amid the lambs and tried to swat away the hand Andy reached down to me but he grabbed both of my wrists and somehow got me by the upper arms and lifted me over the gate, all to the tune of my squealing. The bums, of course, were beside themselves. There was no end to the *baa*ing below as Andy pulled me against him . . . mud, poop, hay, and all.

I felt like *baa*ing myself. From the Things I Want to Say list that scrolled through my head I selected, "You're not mad at me, then?"

Andy pulled his head back to look at me. "Why would I be mad at you? Wait . . . you took over all my chores while I was gone, didn't you? Dang it, Bo, what's the matter with you?"

He tilted his head to kiss me, but I shook mine. "I'm serious, Andy. I told Joseph where you were going. I know you asked me not to—"

"Yeah, I guess I am mad at you for *saving my hide*." The kiss

landed on my forehead. "If you hadn't told them"—on my nose—
"I would be in a world of hurt right now." One on each cheek. "So
thank you. Now, can we continue this conversation someplace that
doesn't smell like poop?" His eyes did a veritable polka. "Of course,
that would be anywhere *you* are . . . but there's always the hose."

"No. No hose." I wriggled away. "I'll go take a shower and then—"

"Unh-uh." Andy pulled me back into his arms. "I don't want to
be away from you that long. I've wasted enough time already."

His voice dropped, and I knew the dance in his eyes had stopped.

"It didn't go well with the DeLucas, did it?" I said.

He shook his head and took me by the hand to a nearby stack of
bales. With an effortless hoist he set me on top and joined me. The
shoulders were still as strong but they were no longer as sure. As he
leaned against me I knew it was more than his body that was jarred.

"I expected them to be thugs but they're classy and polished—all
Armani suits and Rolex watches. And completely charismatic. Direct
eye contact. Witty repartee. 'What can we get you? The tortellini is
excellent.'" Andy squinted. "It would be so easy to be taken in by that.
But that was just it."

"That was just what?"

"They didn't want to take me in. I told them who I was and they
were like, 'Oh, the long-lost nephew. Nice.'"

I shook my head. "So—Joseph was afraid for nothing?"

"I don't know about nothing. There was something dangerous
about these people, but it was more their total lack of real emotion
that scared me."

"I don't understand."

"When I mentioned Joseph's name, they looked at each other like,
'Is this ringing any bells with you?' And I knew I'd be wasting my
breath telling them who Joseph really is, so I told them he'd died of a

heart attack. Just to be on the safe side—which was stupid since they could check that out if they wanted to. But that's the thing: they don't want to. They never cared about avenging my biological father's death, and he didn't really care about me. They just wanted to win." Andy blinked back the angst I'd been waiting for. "I hope you don't think I wimped out. I told them a lie because the truth was wasted on them."

"I don't think you wimped out, I think you wised out. Is that a word?"

"It is now." Andy pressed the sides of his head. "I've got all this stuff to sort out—it's like spaghetti noodles in there. But I know one thing."

"And that is?"

"I'm going to have my last name legally changed to Maxwell-McKee."

"Just to be on the safe side," I said.

"No," he said. "Just to be on the sacred side. I can't get the DeLucas out of my blood, but maybe I can get them out of my soul."

We sat with that for a minute, legs dangling over the hay bales, before he said, "Anyway, after I told them Joseph had died, I left the restaurant and almost had a heart attack myself when I found Joseph sitting in the front seat of my Jeep." Andy's voice grew husky. "I was never so glad to see somebody. I just said, 'Let's go home,' and he said, 'You drive first.'"

I stared. "That was it?"

"Yeah."

"I will never understand men."

Andy shook his head and put one warm hand on my cheek. "You understand *this* man. Maybe better than anyone ever has. I drove double shifts to get back here because I was so afraid you were going to leave before I could tell you." He added the other warm hand to my face. "I love you, Bo."

I knew as Andy kissed me that I had never been kissed in real love before, and that made it my first kiss. My best kiss. And the kiss I had to stop.

"What?" he said. "Are you going to tell me you don't—"

"No," I said. "I do love you. You know I do."

"I hear a but." He put a finger to my lips. "I don't want to hear a but."

"It's not a but. It's a not yet."

"Because . . ."

"Because I have to go to Missouri. There's something I have to do there."

"Then I'll go with you."

The immediate image of Andy trying to get my mother to return his grin almost made it worth agreeing, but I said, "You know how you felt like you had to make things right for Joseph?"

He nodded.

"I have to go back and make things right for my sister if I can." I shook my head at the eyebrows that shot up. "I'll explain it all later. Just tell me you understand."

"Two questions," Andy said.

"Okay."

"One. How long's it going to take?"

"It depends on how cemented my mother is to her guilt," I said.

"Yeah, you really do have some 'splainin' to do. Are you coming back?"

He was already nodding, willing my answer. I pressed my forehead to his to stop it. "Right now, for this moment," I said, "I just want to be here."

———

I didn't leave the Bellwether that night. My talk with Sister Frankie alone took two hours in the garden. I told her that I had to go assess my sister's situation and find out if there was at least an outpatient facility where they might actually be able to help her get back something of what she'd lost.

"I don't know if that's even possible," I told Frankie. "Maybe it's been too long and she wouldn't be able to make any progress, but I have to know."

"That may be the easy part. And it will be even easier if you find a faith community there. It's so much to try it all on your own. I know some people in a wonderful church in that area if you want me to call them."

I couldn't imagine another faith community like the one I was leaving but I nodded.

Frankie's brown eyes were still sad. "Your biggest challenge is probably going to be convincing your mother. We both know how deeply we can be entrenched in guilt."

"It's like standing in cement and letting it set around your feet," I said.

"Good image."

Frankie waited. I was going to miss her waiting.

"I have a plan, though," I said. "I'm going to tell her about my part of the blame for Lara and how I'm dealing with that. Maybe if she doesn't have to carry all the guilt it'll be easier for her to let go."

"That's brave, my friend," Frankie said. "You know she might be extremely angry with you."

I shook my head. "My mother doesn't get extremely anything. In a way I kind of hope she does, though. Then maybe we could start healing."

Frankie's sad eyes shone, as if the sun had just risen in them.

"God has brought you so very, very far. It has been an honor to walk this with you."

I felt my face crumple.

"I love those tears," she said. "And please know you are welcome back here anytime. As my friend and as my fellow lover of the woolies." She squeezed my hand. "I would hire you in a heartbeat."

———

Telling Emma would be harder, I thought, and I dreaded it all the way to the Cloister that night. She didn't make it any easier by being in one of the recliners with a cup of Joseph's blend for both of us. It was Hildegarde's cream that did me in.

"You're leaving, aren't you?" she said.

"How did you know?"

"You mean, besides the look on your face? Because it's time. You're in a good place to get on with your life."

Stiff Upper Lip Alert, Kirsten. This is way too easy.

"What about you?" I said.

Emma hunched her shoulders. "I should probably think about leaving too."

"No," I said.

"No, you don't think I should leave?"

"No, I don't think you should *should*. We don't do *should* here at Bellwether. We work with what God gives us."

Emma blinked at me. "I think you should start your own Cloister."

"I'm serious. What's God giving you?"

In the long pause Emma closed her eyes over the tea steam. Finally she said, "If I rely on the feelings I'm getting, I don't want to leave the ranch. Ever. If I go with the ideas I'm getting, I'm thinking college. A degree in something that would enable me to really help Frankie and Joseph. Maybe have a ranch of my own someday."

"Maybe you'll do both," I said.

"Maybe I will. I still have a lot of healing to do."

"So do I."

"At least you're not cutting yourself anymore. That's big."

I nodded.

"Thanks," she said.

"For what?" I said.

She blinked, though it didn't do much for the gathering tears. "For letting me be there for you. I could finally protect somebody the way I was made to do. Just—thanks."

I couldn't improve on that moment.

———

As I was packing an hour later, something Emma said came back to me as if she were sitting on the bed giving me instructions. *"At least you're not cutting yourself anymore. That's big."*

I knelt on the floor and pulled out the first aid kit and opened it. There were some empty compartments in it now. The one where the gauze had been. The big one for the scissors I'd lost over the side of the mountain almost the first day. But the collection of the as yet unused disposable razors was still there. And the paring knife I'd absconded with from the kitchen to use as a last resort.

I lifted them out, the knife and the razors, and I pulled up the legs of my sweats and looked at the scars that had faded on my thighs. I didn't want to add to them. Ever. But somehow I knew I might feel that pain pulsing under my skin again someday . . . maybe even soon when I saw Lara again.

Might and maybe? What about Let us pray? *Or do you need to sign up for another thirty days?*

I folded my arms. "Who *are* you anyway, Nudnik?" I said out loud.

Seven years and you just now got around to asking me that.

I thought I was just crazy.

I tried to drive *you crazy. It made a nice alternative to the pain.*

"But who *are* you? Really?"

I'm you, Brain Child. The snarky, get-real, don't-go-wacko-on-me side of you . . . the side that's really starting to like the rest of you.

"Oh," I said. And then I laughed. "Welcome to me."

A light rap on the front door made me jump.

And just so you know: that *isn't me.*

Still giggling, I let myself out the front door to meet Andy on the porch.

"Did I interrupt something?" he said.

"No," I said. "I was just talking to myself."

Andy and I sat on the front steps and watched the last tendrils of sun go down on my fifty-fifth and last day. We talked some. After I explained all about Lara, I told him I would stay in Missouri until I was sure I'd done all I could there. After that, I didn't know, except that I was definitely not going to become an architect.

"I think I can trust God'll take me where I need to go," I said. "I guess I better major in faith first, huh?"

Andy said he wasn't going back to MIT either. He'd work at the ranch for a while and, like me, pray his way to the next thing.

"I know it's going to take me a long time to absorb all this stuff I just found out and figure out if it makes a difference in who I am, and I have to do that before I do go on to the next thing." He brushed a strand of hair from my face. "But whatever it is, Bo—I want you in it."

"Well," I said. "Since it's faith and prayer we're talking about—I think we're already in it."

I kissed him first this time.

———

Andy fell asleep on the porch floor with his head in my lap. I stroked his dark waves for a while, and then I slid carefully out from under him and walked in the moonlight to the back of the Cloister.

I could see the sheep, still as statues in their pen, just like the first night I was there. They didn't make a sound. Even Avila was quiet. But I could hear Frankie's voice, echoing like *bat kol*.

"Their needs are met and they have no fear."

I hugged my arms around me and closed my eyes and felt the peace, because I no longer had to envy them.

"Thank You, Good Shepherd," I whispered. "Thank You."

> Share this chapter with your friends!
> *Being entrenched in your guilt is like standing in cement and letting it set around your feet.* #TheMercifulScar

Reflection Questions and Resources for *The Merciful Scar*

Although we want girls and women who have experience with self-injury to find hope in Kirsten's story, we don't think you have to have been there personally to relate to her and find a door to healing for whatever it is you *are* dealing with (and everybody is dealing with something, right?) As you consider our reflection questions, just apply them to your own situation and see what happens. We've got your back in prayer.

Blessings,

Rebecca and Nancy

Questions to ponder:

1. Just to get you focused on you, what part of Kirsten's story did you relate to the most? What made you go, "Oh, I hear *that*!"?
2. Right now in your life, are you "settling" in any way, like Kirsten was settling for Wes and a career she didn't really care about?
3. How are you at expressing your deepest feelings? Do you feel

like you have a true voice? Are there places where it can be heard without judgment?

4. Can you identify certain experiences in your life that have led you to coping behaviors that aren't healthy for you? That keep you from getting to the real issue? For Kirsten that included her sister's accident, her father's Disneyland Dad approach, her mother's denial, and her own guilt. What are yours?

5. Along with damaging experiences, Kirsten had a way-faulty understanding of her self-worth that led her to cutting. What beliefs about yourself might be wounding you in some way?

6. What did you learn from Kirsten's journey that you could possibly apply to your own? (Things you wouldn't have to go to a sheep ranch to do!)

7. What practices that Frankie gave Kirsten (listening, doing art, taking communion, taking care of something weaker than herself, etc.) could help you be more aware of God's presence and voice?

8. Do you have a mentor like Frankie? If not, can you think of someone you respect who could offer you wisdom and help you find your way?

9. Picture a free, secure, whole life for yourself, the kind God intends for each of us. Write it down, maybe in a journal. Now consider: what keeps you from living in that place?

10. Find your own Shepherd's Monument, a place to get quiet and listen, deeply, for that still, small voice—away from the fires and the winds and the earthquakes of your life. What is He whispering to you?

Resources for those who self-injure or want to help someone who does:

- FAQs About Self Injury. FocusOntheFamily.com. There are actually six different articles here that give great information in a loving, understanding way. http://www.focusonthefamily .com/parenting/parenting_challenges/cutting_and_selfinjury/ faqs_about_selfinjury.aspx
- S.A.F.E. (Self Abuse Finally Ends) website. Here you'll find an online community that's moderated to provide a trigger-free environment. www.selfinjury.com
- Cornell Research Program on Self-Injurious Behavior website. That sounds kind of academic but it actually provides a slideshow with additional links at the end for those who are visual learners. http://breeze.cce.cornell.edu/recovery
- SIOS (Self-Injury Outreach and Support) website. This is a Canadian site that offers information on coping with the urge to cut, personal stories, and lots of resources. http://www .sioutreach.org/

And just so you know: if you Google "self-injury" you'll find some sites that offer advice on how to continue self-injury without people finding out and support for maintaining your "right to cut." If you accidentally come upon one of those, please get out of it as fast as you can. That is not the *bat kol* of God's still, small voice.

Acknowledgments

Even though two of us created Kirsten's story, a whole flock of other people (pardon the pun . . .) were involved in bringing it to life. If you're one of those who likes to know that kind of thing, here's our list.

Rebecca would like to thank:

- **Nancy Rue**—what a wonderful partner you are, sweet sister! Thank you, thank you.
- **Andrea Heinecke** at Alive Communications for your belief in me as a writer.
- My father, **David Smallbone,** for giving his all to our ministry for nearly two decades! Love you, Dad.
- My husband, **Cubbie Fink,** for being my best friend, soul-mate, and number one supporter! I love you beyond words.
- **Our Lord Jesus**—for inspiration and the privilege of serving You with the written word. It is because of Your love and our love for You that we write!

Nancy would like to thank:

- **Brenda Anderson-Baker** and **Larry Baker** for showing me Bozeman and introducing me to the beauty of Montana. And for knocking the sheep poo off my boots before sending them home to me.

- **Lisa Schmidt** and **Steve Hutton**—and young **Abby** too— for an awesome five days at the Graham Ranch in Conrad, Montana. They took me through every sheep-related, cow-related, dog-related task Kirsten would do and shared their passion for caring for the land and feeding the world. Thanks to Lisa and Steve, I am not the same person I was when I drove through their gates.

- The **eight brave women,** ranging in age from fourteen to fifty, who shared with me their stories of self-injury, including their recovery and their continuing struggle. I am still in awe of their faith.

- **John Painter,** RNC, MSN, FNP (which means nurse practitioner extraordinaire), who took me through the emergency room scene so it didn't come out sounding like I obtained it from an episode of *Scrubs*. His compassion for the people he has treated who self-injure helped me create the character Roman.

- **Connie Young,** my sister in Christ from the Academy for Spiritual Formation, who led me through the sheep symbolism in Scripture and opened my eyes to nuances I'd never experienced before.

- My way wonderful husband, **Jim Rue,** who showed me how to handle a gun—something I hope never to have to do again. My aversion to firearms surpasses Kirsten's.

- **Lee Hough,** my literary agent, who brought this opportunity to my door, and literary agent **Andrea Heinecke,** who carried it through, and **Amanda Bostic** and **Jamie Chavez,** our editors, who caught my mistakes. If you find any, they're all mine.
- Authors **Carol Nadelson, MD, Patricia McCormick, Caroline Kettlewell, Rachel Eagen,** and **Patricia and Peter Adler,** whose work in the world of self-injury provided the factual foundation for Kirsten's story.
- And of course to my kindred spirit **Rebecca St. James,** whose love for God and young women was the mustard seed for this project, and whose commitment to it is . . . awesome.

Sarah is on the fast track to success.
Until one discovery threatens all
she has accomplished.

Based on the film starring
Rebecca St. James,

Sarah's Choice:

a novel, written by Rebecca
St. James and Nancy Rue,
will be available June 2014.

9781401689223-A

About the Authors

Author photo by Allister Ann

Rebecca St. James is both a Grammy and multiple Dove Award recipient as well as a best-selling author whose books include *Wait for Me* and *What Is He Thinking??* Her leading role in the pro-life film *Sarah's Choice* won critical acclaim. A passionate spokesperson for Compassion International, more than 30,000 children have found sponsorship through Rebecca's worldwide concerts.

Author photo by Hatcher and Fell Photography

Nancy Rue is the best-selling author of more than 100 books for teens, tweens, and adults, two of which have won Christy Awards. Nancy is also a popular speaker and radio guest due to her expertise in tween and teen issues. She and her husband, Jim, have raised a daughter of their own and now share their Tennessee lake home with two yellow labs.